IMAGES
of America

EMANUEL COUNTY GEORGIA

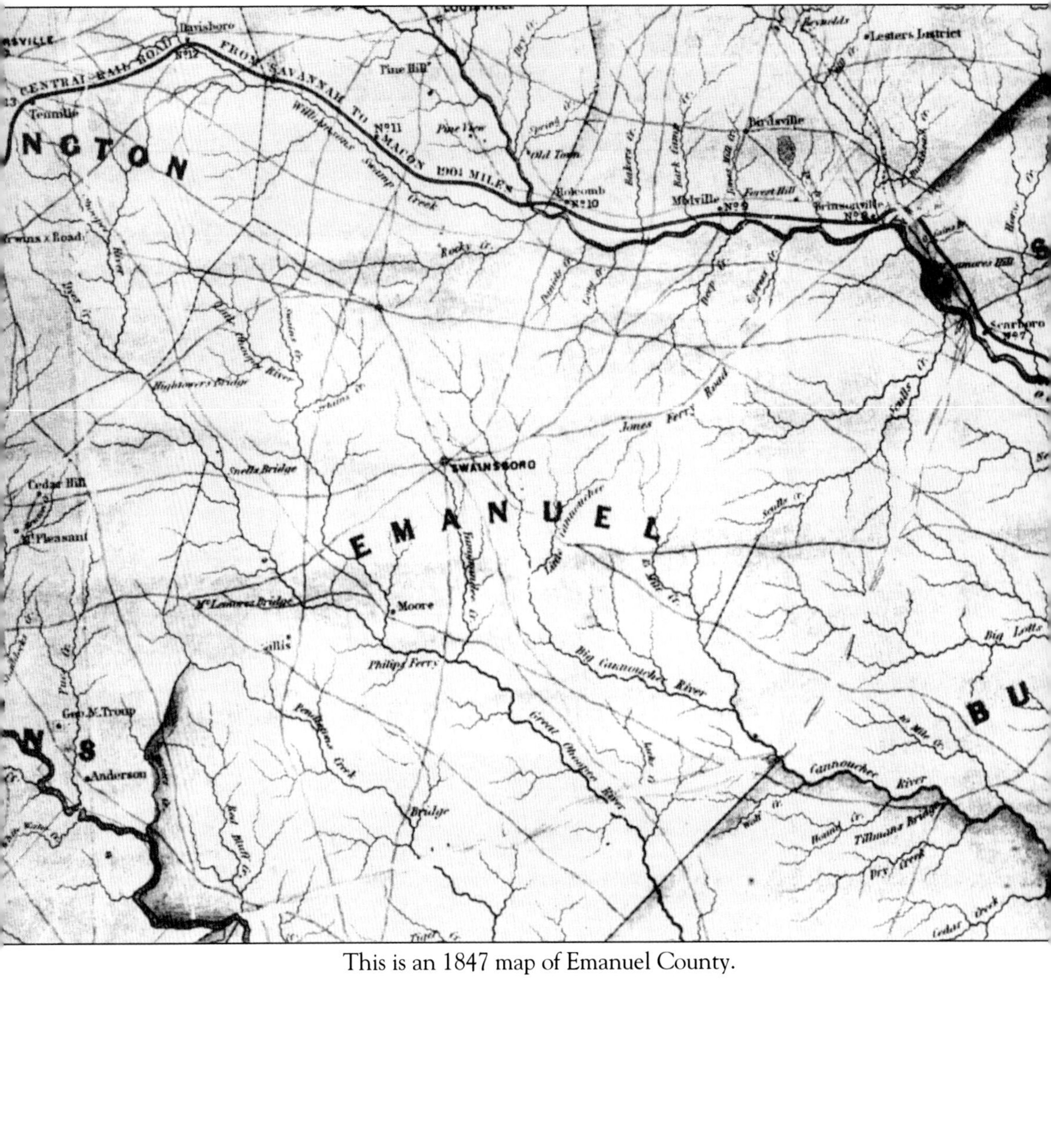

This is an 1847 map of Emanuel County.

IMAGES
of America

EMANUEL COUNTY
GEORGIA

The Emanuel County
Historic Preservation Society

ARCADIA
PUBLISHING

ISBN 978-0-7385-6896-6

Published by Arcadia Publishing
Charleston, South Carolina

Printed in the United States of America

Library of Congress Catalog Card Number: 98-88251

For all general information contact Arcadia Publishing at:
Telephone 843-853-2070
Fax 843-853-0044
E-Mail sales@arcadiapublishing.com
For customer service and orders:
Toll-Free 1-888-313-2665

Visit us on the Internet at www.arcadiapublishing.com

Contents

Acknowledgments

No work such as this could be undertaken and finished without the support and assistance of many people and a number of institutions. First, we would like to give our heartfelt thanks to the many citizens who were willing to share with us their valued photographs as well as those who were so helpful in identifying persons and locations within them. Many of the photographs within are reproduced here for the first time and, therefore, will be preserved in this form for future reference. Among the donors and collectors were Ann Farrar, Jimmy Morgan, Sam Smith, Sarah Underwood, Ida Pearl Lawson, Farris Cadle, Peggy Sammons, Mary Ann Smith, Nina and Frank Herrington, Linda Carmichael, Connie Thurman, Dr. Willie D. Gunn, Helen Bishop, David Morgan, and Dr. W.H. Black. The Emanuel County Historic Preservation Society sponsored this effort and encouraged the editors in their endeavor. East Georgia College was generous in offering its extensive local history photographic archive.

During the final weeks, as the project moved beyond the planning and collecting stage to the final pre-publication stage, Jimmy Morgan's office in Swainsboro was cluttered with photographs, labels, and boxes. We deeply appreciate Mr. Morgan's patience and willingness to provide the space while we completed our work. Historical sources that helped to provide context and understanding for the visuals included *Emanuel Memories, 1776–1976* (The Swainsboro Forest-Blade Publishing Company, 1976), edited by Bill Rogers Sr., and *Footprints along the Hoopee: A History of Emanuel County, 1812–1900* (The Reprint Company, Publishers, 1978) by James Dorsey. In 1976, the bicentennial year, James Dorsey and John Derden edited *Heritage '76: A Visual Salute to Emanuel County* (Swainsboro Exchange Club, 1976), a collection of historical photographs. In addition, all students of Emanuel County's past are indebted to the first generation of local historians, Jessie Coleman Black (1883–1965) and Hattie Daniel (Humphrey) Fountain (1877–1963), who authored the first brief accounts of the history of Emanuel County.

Every effort was made to identify the people in the photographs. We hope that this publication will encourage people to assist us in identifying those whom we were unable to, as well as to make us aware of historical photographs that did not surface in time for inclusion in this book. We further trust that this book will stimulate interest in the past and the need to preserve its visual record.

INTRODUCTION

The Emanuel County Historic Preservation Society is pleased to present this collection of historical photographs and documents. The items in this book were selected to illustrate the history of Emanuel County and the lives of the people who have lived there. Obviously, this photographic record reflects the vagaries of history, deriving from what the record included, what survived, and what is available. Nonetheless, the editors have taken care to solicit, gather, select, and try to present a representative sample of what illustrative material remains.

Emanuel County is located in the southeastern portion of the state of Georgia. It lies almost in the middle of an imaginary triangle whose apexes are Macon, Savannah, and Augusta, and it continues to retain an essentially rural character. Visitors find themselves enveloped in a gently rolling landscape of fields and woods and sandy soil. Under the ubiquitous canopy of piney woods, the forest floor is carpeted with wiregrass, and the flora and fauna are profuse. The native deer, rabbits, raccoons, opossums, alligators, fish, bobcats, quail, foxes, snakes, turtles, and other wildlife compete with recent immigrants such as coyotes and armadillos. The Ohoopee, Ogeechee, and Canoochee rivers flow through the county, and the smaller streams and innumerable ponds make the region an excellent recreation and fishing area. Along the waterways and low-lying areas are stands of hardwoods.

In the cultivated fields, common crops include cotton, corn, tobacco, soybeans, peanuts, and wheat. The lumber and pulpwood industry continues to be important. Hogs, goats, and cattle represent the major varieties of livestock. However, Emanuel County has a mixed economy. Besides agriculture, banking, metalworking, manufacturing, and public sector employment make for a more balanced economy.

Whatever Emanuel County has become, the pictures in this book represent the area's past—a past that has shaped the present. The original inhabitants were, of course, Native Americans. In historical times, Creek Indians lived in the area and, although little material evidence remains to document them here, the names of rivers, historical accounts, and archeological artifacts testify to their presence. The Indian cessions of 1773 and 1783 conveyed the land that now comprises Emanuel County to the state of Georgia. The county was established by legislative action in 1812, and was named for David Emanuel, who served briefly as the state's chief executive in 1801. Swainsboro has been its seat since 1814, except for a brief period in the 1850s when its name was changed to Paris. In addition to Swainsboro, several smaller towns and communities developed over the years and continue to dot the landscape, including Adrian, Twin City (once the separate towns of Graymont and Summit), Stillmore, Summertown, Oak Park, Nunez,

Covena, Lexsy, Modoc, Canoochee, Coleman Lake, and Blundale, to name a few.

The pioneer settlers of Emanuel County began to move into the area in the late 1700s in the aftermath of the Indian cessions. Noting the characteristic massive, open pine forests of the region, they called their new home the "pine barrens" or "wiregrass Georgia." Early migrants acquired property by land lottery and the headright system and also by means of land granted for military service in the Revolutionary War. Several veterans of that conflict lie buried in the county. The fact that many of the names left by the pioneers—Thigpen, Sumner, Lane, Durden, Brinson, Overstreet, Thompson, Moore, Rountree, Edenfield, Tapley, Key, Coleman, among many others—survive among today's inhabitants lends a strong sense of familial continuity to the region. These settlers engaged in subsistence farming. They raised a few crops and livestock; they hunted and fished; and they set about the task of carving out of the forests the communities that were to characterize the county. Progress was slow and as late as the Civil War, Emanuel County was lightly populated and wild lands predominated over cultivated areas.

But, as the 19th century progressed, Emanuel countians underwent significant transformations as they found themselves caught up in larger political and economic events. As the sectional crisis erupted into secession and led to the Civil War, a large percentage of the county's young men volunteered to serve in the Confederate cause and left home, some never to return. Those who remained at home, although seemingly far removed from the major venues of the conflict, found themselves inundated by Federal troops in late November and early December of 1864 as Union General Sherman's forces marched through on their way to Savannah and the sea. For those who witnessed it, the March to the Sea was traumatic, and it left a scar that continues to be felt over 130 years later. The war lives on in the stories passed down by local families and in the cemeteries where can be commonly found the graves of soldiers who fought in the conflict.

Remarkably, however, the devastation of defeat was followed within a few decades by an economic shift that led to revitalization. Recognition of the potential of the great pine forests and the advent of the railroads into the county resulted in industries that centered on timber and other forest products. In addition, more land was brought under cultivation, and commercial agriculture became commonplace. Small communities flourished and featured churches, stores, railroad-loading platforms, turpentine stills, lumber mills, and schools. Sharecropping and tenant farming were commonplace, and the countryside was full of families who worked the land. This social and economic scenario remained typical of Emanuel County until after WW II. It is this era, from the late 19th century through the Depression, from which most of the photographs derive. They portray what might be termed the "classic" era of Emanuel County. This is the period that most of the older people talk about when they tell of the "good ole days" or the "way things used to be."

In many ways, as is true throughout the South, these times are gone. Economic changes have brought additional transformations. Although old families continue to play vital roles in the community, many newcomers have moved into the county. The opening of new businesses, government agencies, and schools have added to the mix. In recent years, the influx of Hispanic workers has added a new element to the population. The countryside is no longer full of families trying to make a living on small farms, and sharecropping has disappeared. Farming remains important but often as only one source of a family's income. The forestry tradition remains strong, but turpentining has been almost wiped out by the introduction of synthetic substitutes. Today, the bulk of the population lives in Swainsboro or in one of the smaller towns and engages in non-agricultural vocations. The "classic" era remains in the memories of those who lived in that time, in the material evidence that remains, and in the photographs included here.

One

We Lived in the Country

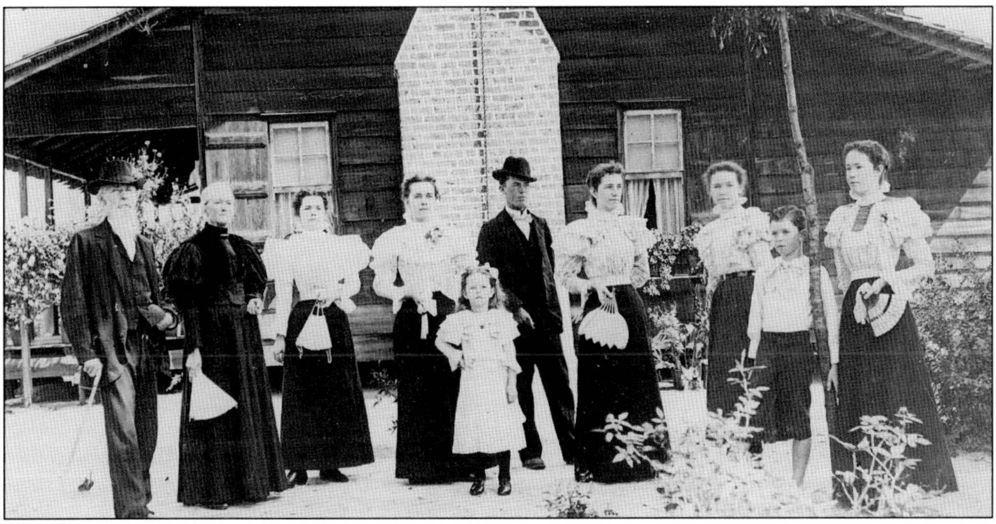

Pictured is James Emmett Coleman (1838–1912), son of Rev. Elisha and Mary Scott Coleman, and his wife, Sarah Missouri Brinson Coleman (1845–1923), daughter of Benjamin E. and Mary Lewis Brinson, at their home near Canoochee. They are shown at left with their children Sallie Evelina, Sudie Alice, Emett Caleb, Mary Lucretia, Jessie Madelaine, and Hattie Arabella, with Annie Brinson and Edwin Loran in front. In November 1864, Emmett was with Company E, 5th Ga. Cavalry fighting a delaying action in front of Sherman's army. His unit came to Canoochee, where Sarah Brinson was serving as postmistress, in time to warn her that a Yankee Cavalry unit was just behind them. Arriving soon after, the Yankee unit began loading pigs, hogs, and taking everything they could find including butter out of a butter dish. Sarah gave a masonic distress signal she had learned from her father. A young lieutenant ordered his men to unload everything and posted a guard to protect her. Sarah and Emmett were married shortly after the war.

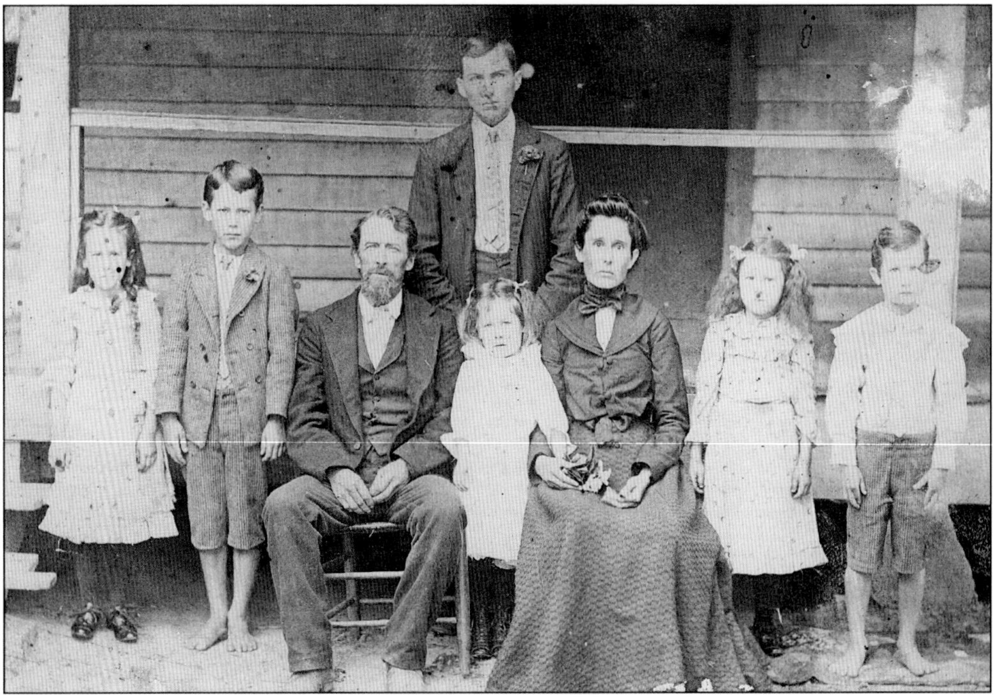

J.H. Sparks, Summit, Georgia, 1990s, is the only readable name on the back of this picture.

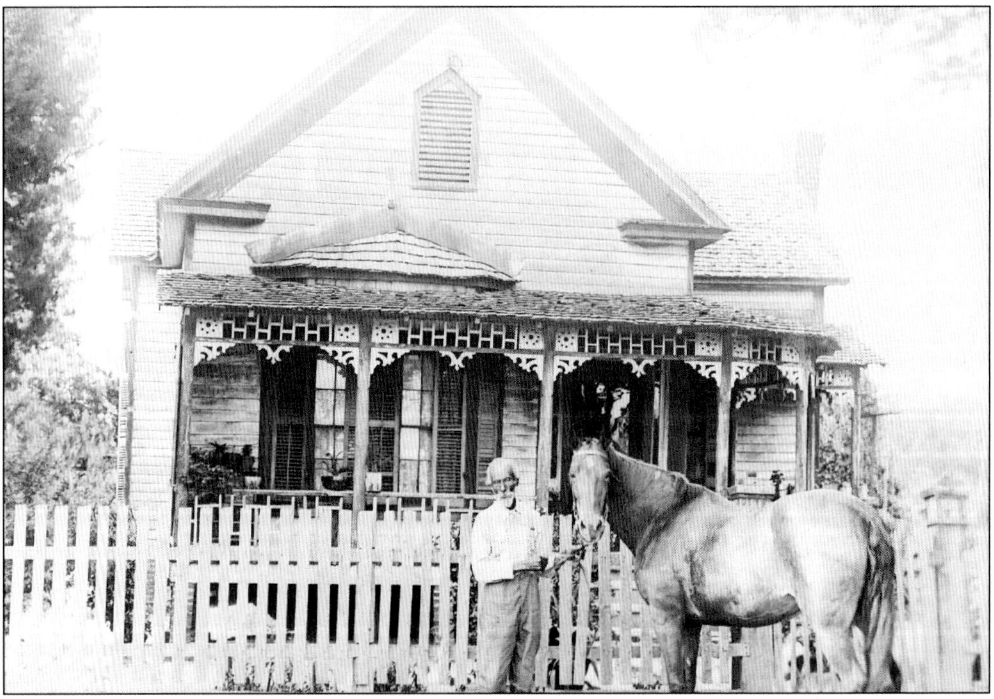

This is Peter Brinson and his horse Belle in front of his house, which he designed, located just off what is now Sam Overstreet Road. Born in 1845, Peter Brinson became a successful landowner and businessman. When he died in 1923, Belle pulled his coffin to the nearby cemetery, became sick, and died days later.

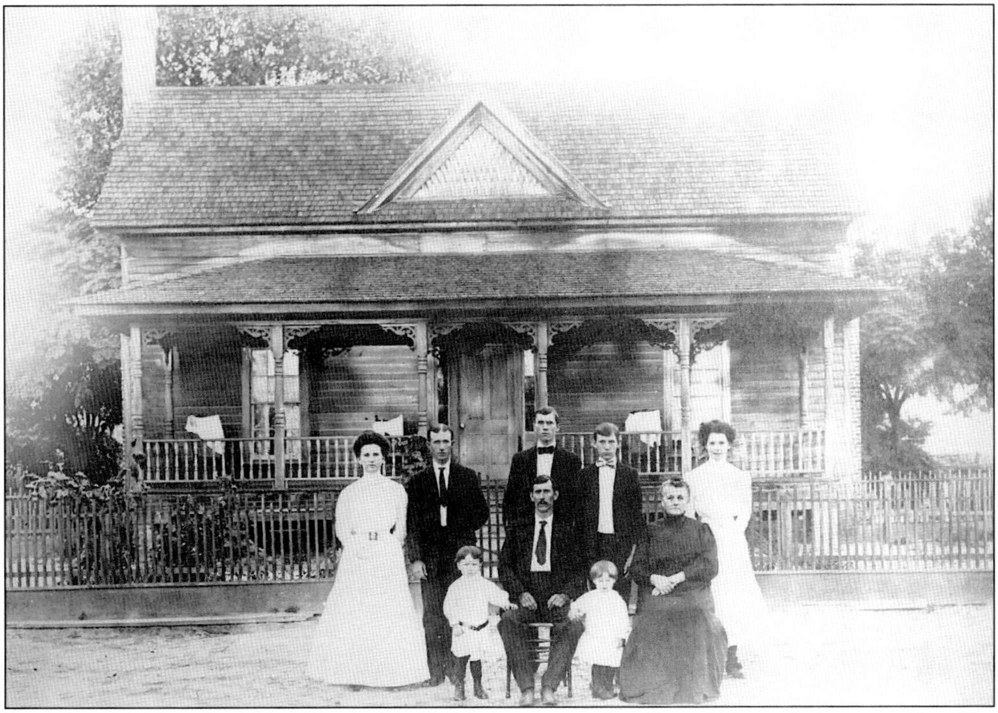

The David Oscar Fordham Home was built in 1905, and still stands in what is now Candler County. This picture was taken in 1909.

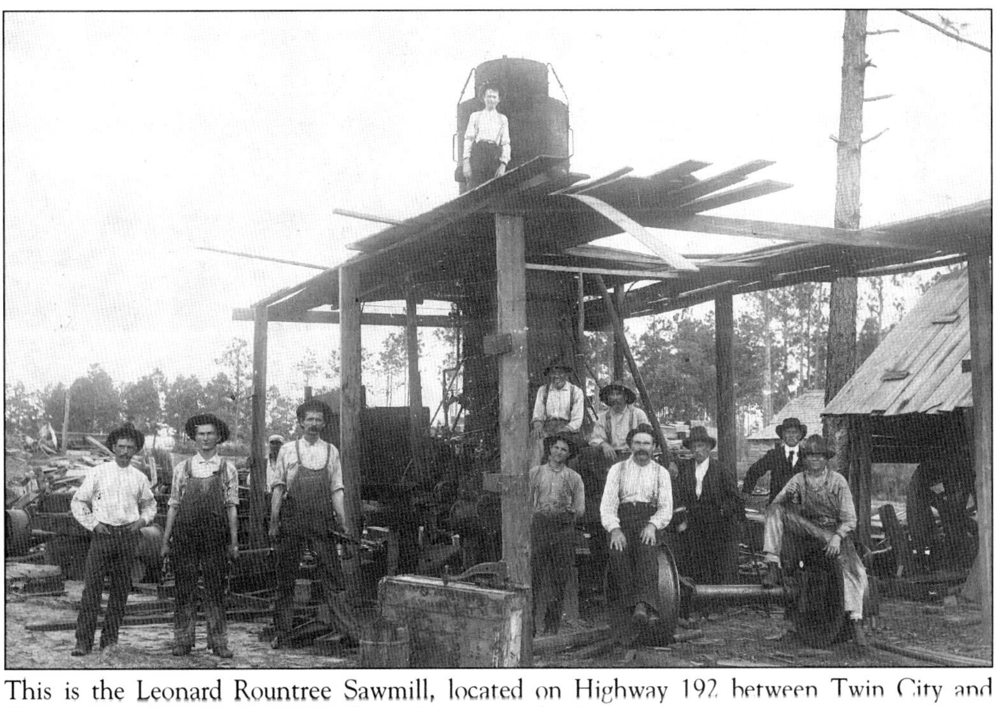

This is the Leonard Rountree Sawmill, located on Highway 192 between Twin City and Canoochee. Wade Carley is fifth from the left, on the front row.

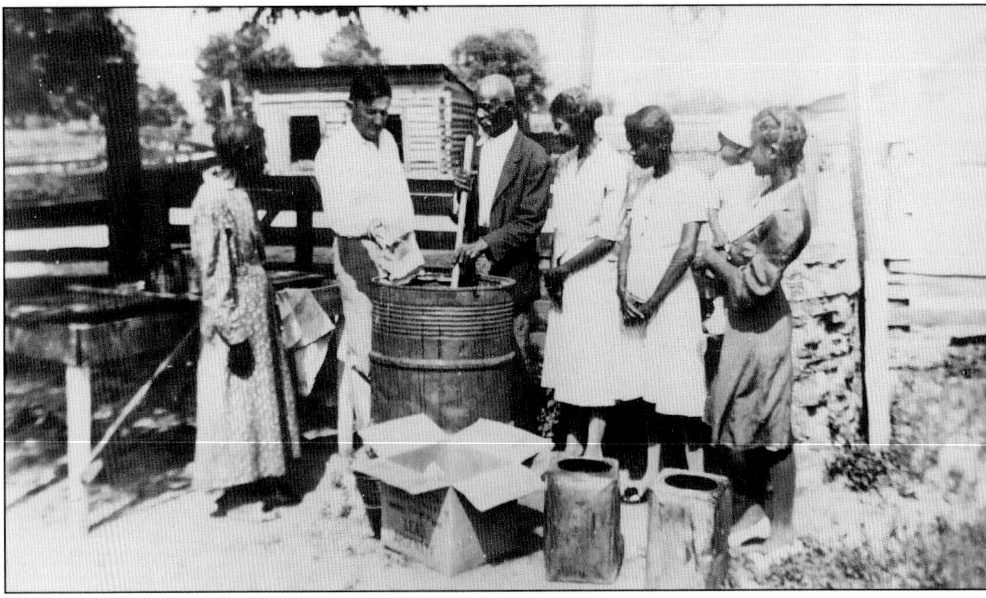

This *c.* 1946 photo shows sweet potatoes being treated.

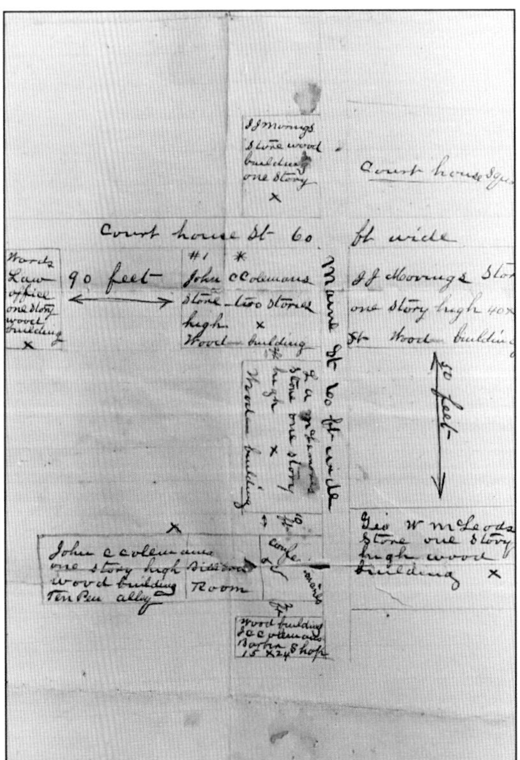

The north and east sides of the courthouse square in downtown Swainsboro, can be seen in this 1870 drawing by John C. Coleman. East and West Main Streets were named CourtHouse Street. All buildings were wood frame construction and the streets were unpaved.

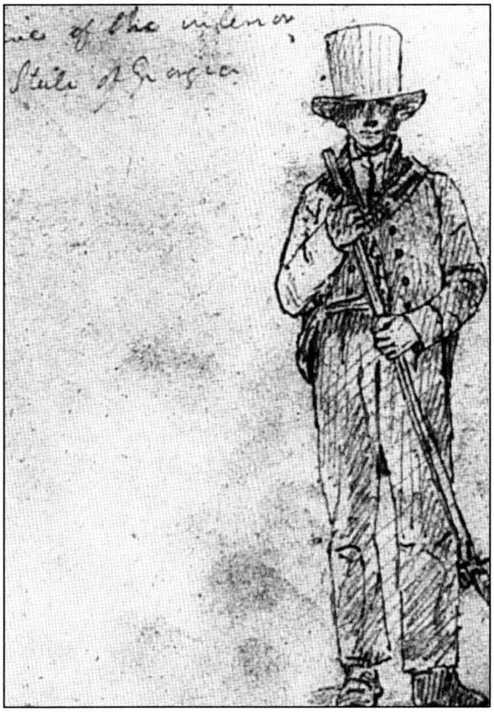

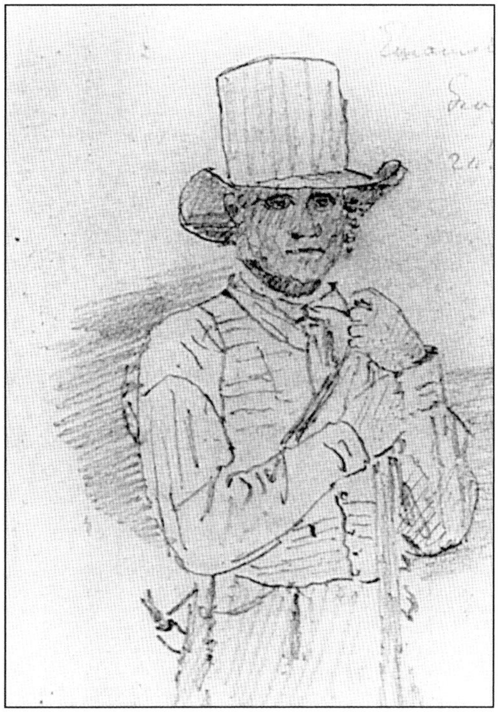

In the spring of 1828, Basil Hall, an Englishman, passed through Emanuel County on his way from Savannah to Macon. He kept a diary and drew sketches of the sights he saw. These represent the earliest views of the area. The scene at bottom portrays the house of a Mr. Ricks on March 24, 1828. The log house is fenced with oxen standing near the front gate. Resting against a stump are Mr. Rick's hunting accouterments, including a rifle, shot bag, powder horn, and knife. (Courtesy of Farris Cadle, Manuscripts Department of the Lilly Library, Indiana University, Bloomington, Indiana.)

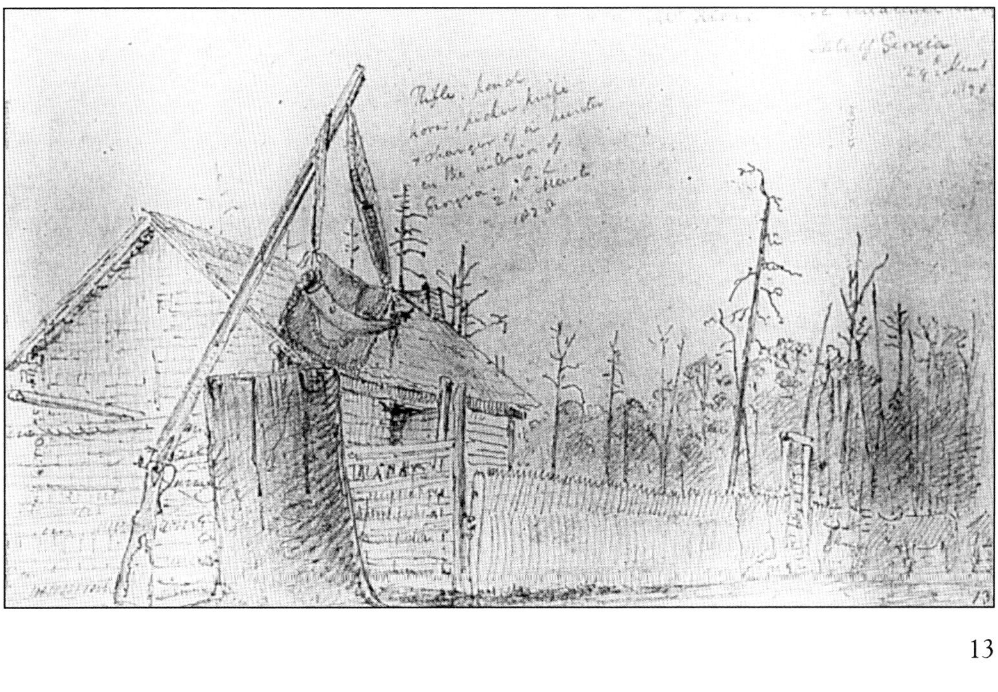

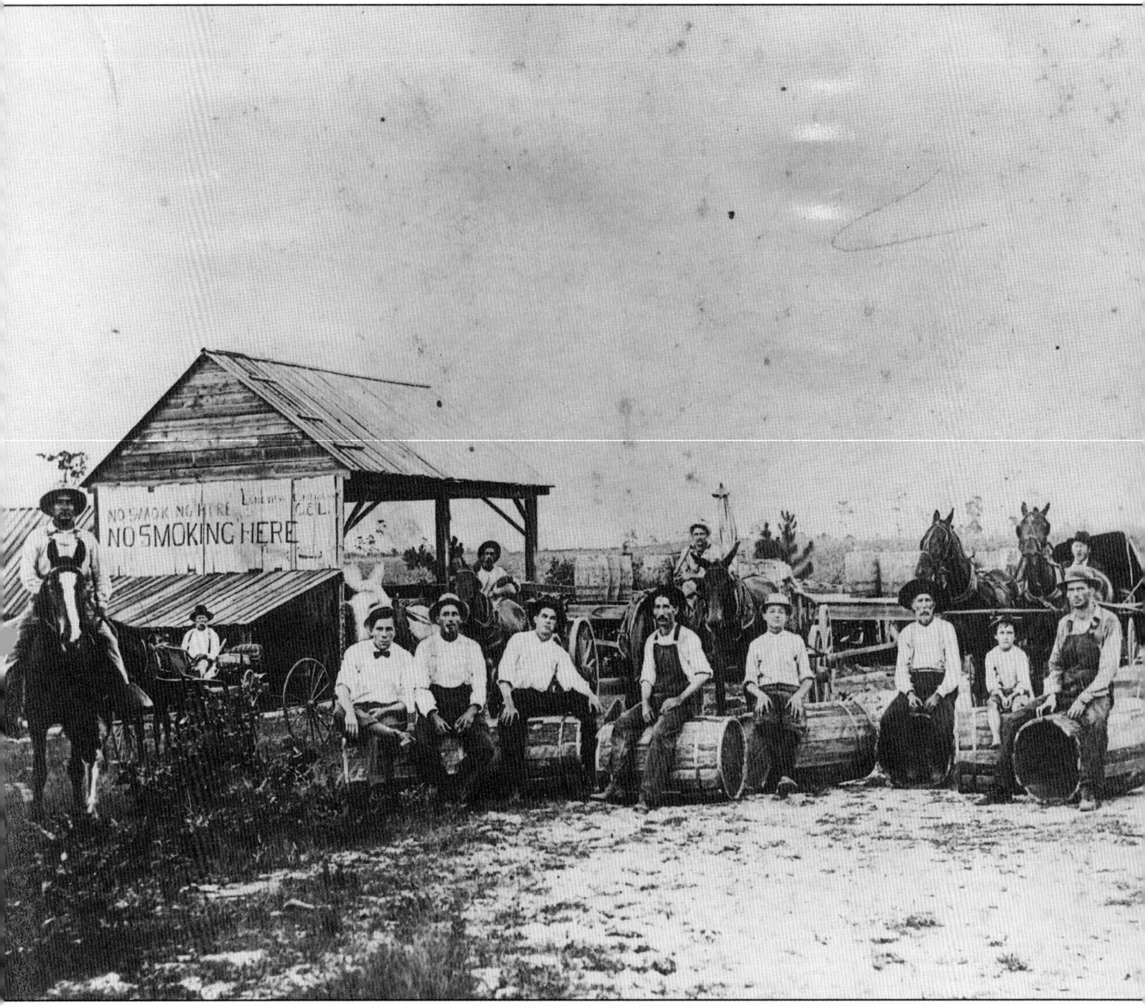

The Longview Establishment, an early turpentine still, was located northeast of Swainsboro on what is still Longview Road. Longview was apparently a thriving settlement, as evidenced by a 1901 *Forest Blade* article that reported, "All the news of the County as told by our wide-awake quill drivers." Residents of the time included George Battle, Uncle Henry Vales, E.P. Rentz, and Miss Pearl White. The article, signed by Grace, further stated, "All girls in Longview have a pleasant smile for Fred Layton when he is about."

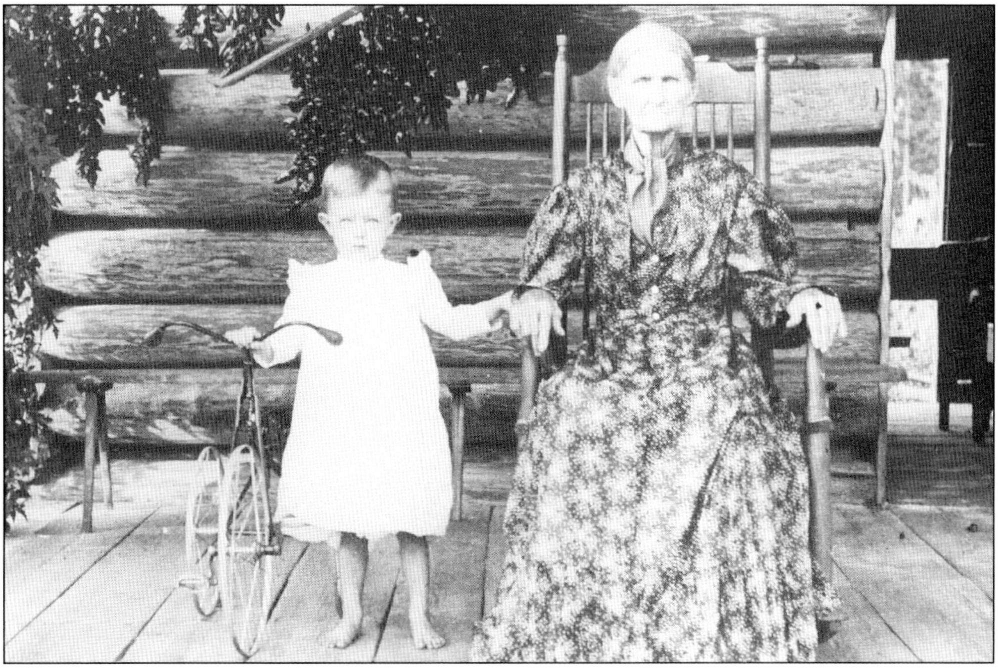

Elizabeth Barwick, with her grandson Verdie Hicks, was married to William Durden (8/15/1817–7/2/1864). She was one of three Barwick sisters, Mary (Polly), Elizabeth, and Susannah, who married three Durden brothers, Eleaser, William, and Simeon. She was born in this cabin in 1817 and was living there at the time of her death in 1909, 92 years later. She was survived by 11 children, 65 grandchildren, 132 great-grandchildren, and ten great-great grandchildren. The cabin, still located near Norristown, is one of the oldest surviving structures in Emanuel County.

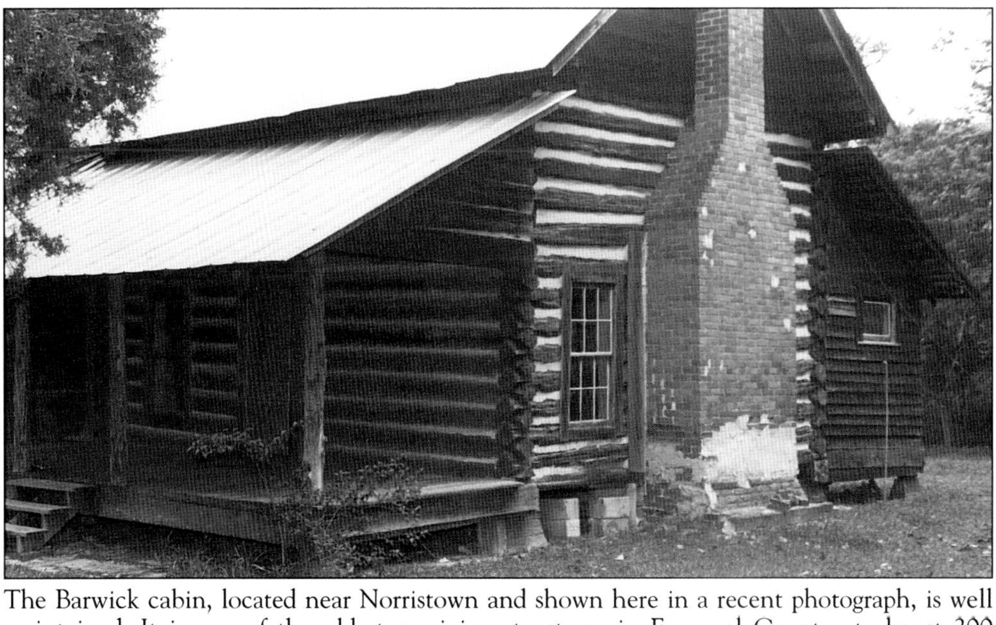

The Barwick cabin, located near Norristown and shown here in a recent photograph, is well maintained. It is one of the oldest surviving structures in Emanuel County at almost 200 years old.

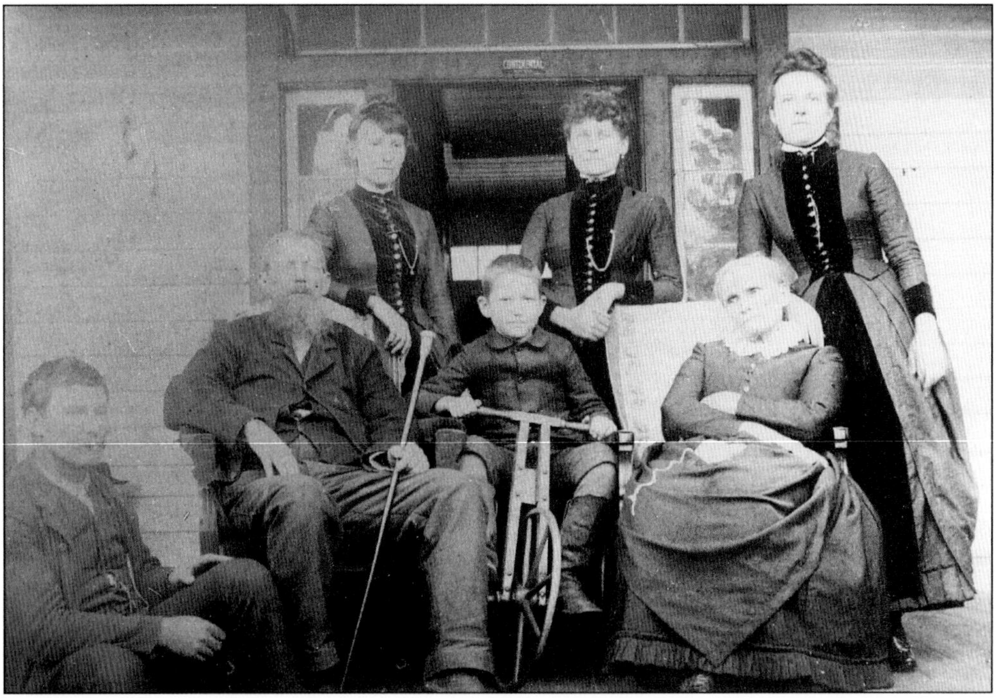

Dr.Edward Wood Lane and his wife, Caroline Lanier Lane, are pictured with three of their daughters, Susie, Fannie, and Mollie, a son, Dr. Remer Young Lane, and their first grandchild, Horace Lane. Dr. Lane was a Georgia State Senator from Emanuel County in the 1890s. The picture was made *c.* 1891.

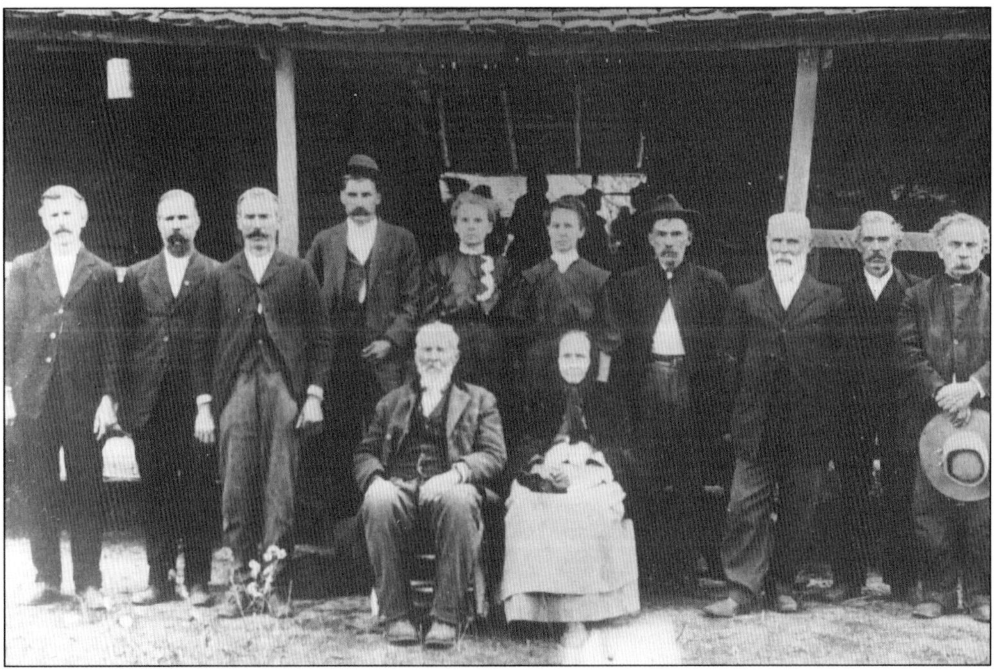

This is the John Peebles family in 1906. In front are John and Rebecca Peebles, age 85, followed by Jerden, Tom, Cal, Burk, Lizzie, Della, Chris, Cicero, Samps, and L.H.

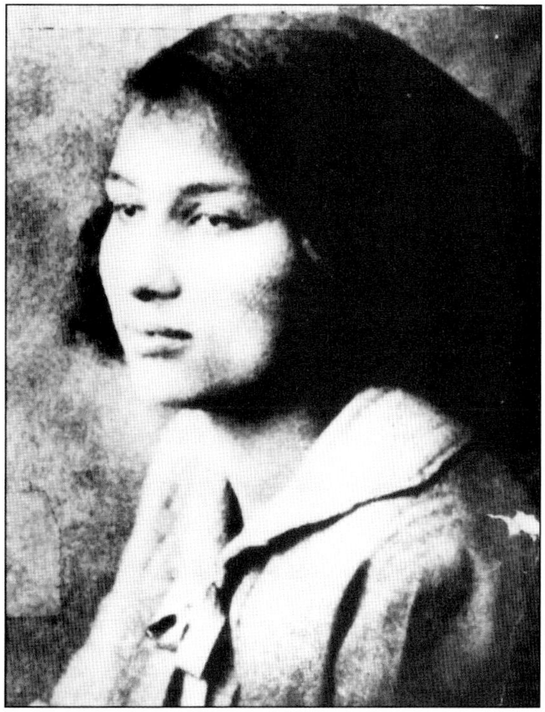

Irene Chance Greene, widow of Joseph Greene and daughter of Pherabe Chance, is pictured below with six of her children, including Jessie "Doll" (pictured at right). Jessie "Doll" lived in the "Promised Land" near Summertown and had been married to Joe Bynes for 70 years at the time of her death in 1996.

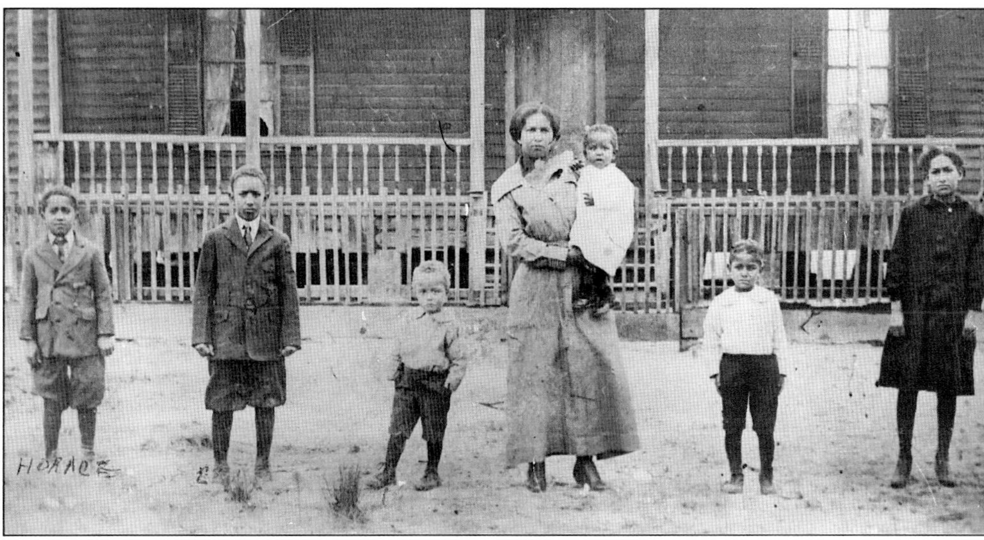

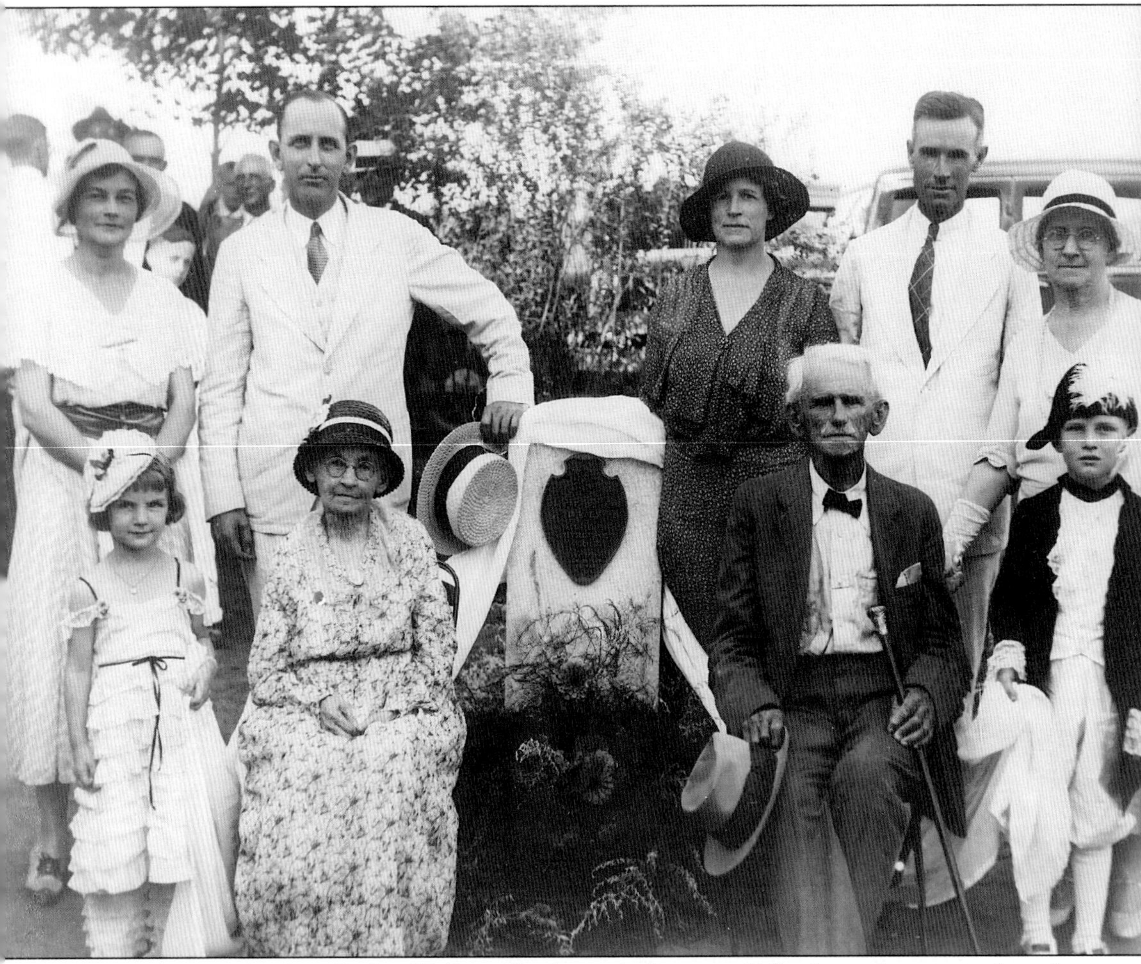

On July 10, 1932, Gov. Richard B. Russell, whose mother was a Dillard, was the principal speaker at the unveiling of a bronze marker honoring Phoebe Dillard Durden (2/26/1807–4/26/1874) by the Adam Brinson Chapter of the Daughters of the American Revolution. Phoebe Dillard, who married Dennis Durden, was the daughter of Sampson Dillard, a Revolutionary War veteran. From left to right are: (front row) Jane Schneider, Millicent Moore Durden, Allie T. Durden (Phoebe Dillard's only surviving son), and Bill Gray; (back row) Maude McLemore, Gov. Russell, Mrs. I.A. Brannen, Homer Durden Sr., and unidentified. Also present was Tena Durden Rountree, Phoebe Durden's personal maid, originally bought from the slave market in New Orleans in 1847. The cemetery is located off of Old Reidsville Road.

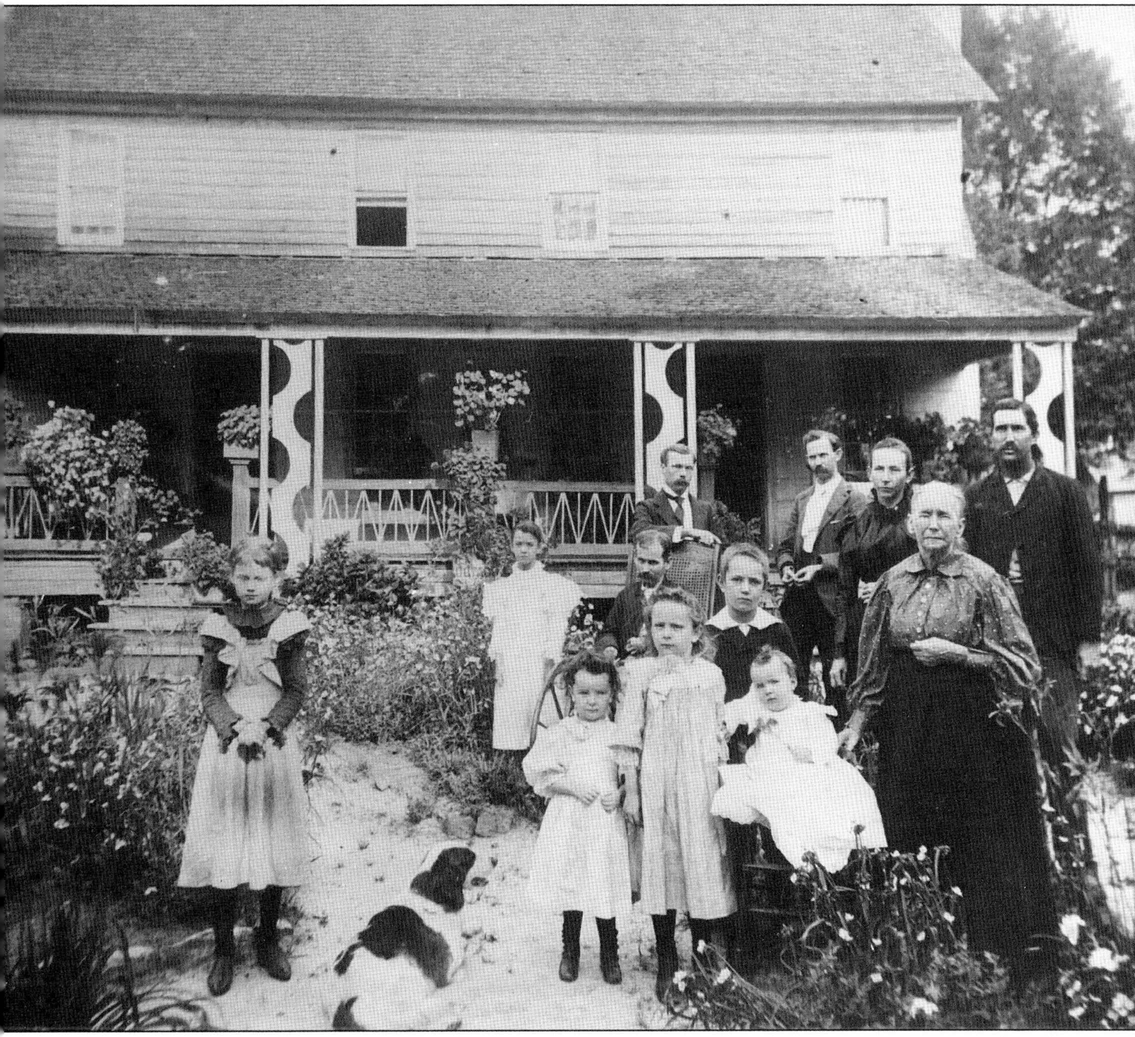

Elizabeth Durden Brinson, widow of Noah Brinson, is pictured at the Brinson home. Behind Mrs. Brinson is her daughter Mary Phoebe (Doll) and her husband, Simeon Turner. On Doll's right is her brother, Dr. Fair Brinson, a dentist in Swainsboro. The house has been bricked up but is still located on Old Reidsville Road.

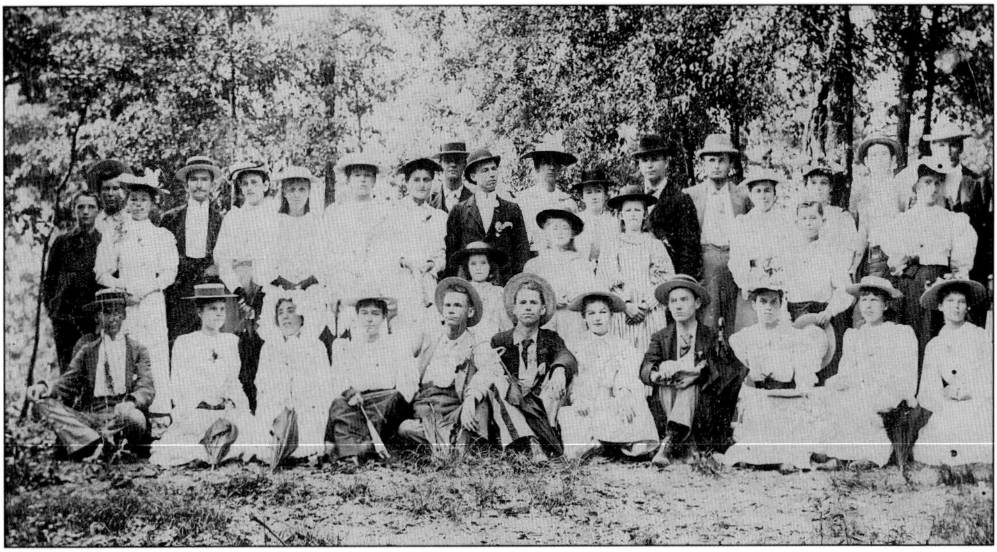

Pictured in this group photograph taken August 1898, from left to right are: (front row) Dora Coleman Burton, ? Byrd, Fred Coleman, Lewis Coleman, Nannie Thompson Boatright, unidentified, Maxie Durden, and Carilee Coleman Walsh; (middle row) Jewell Durden, Ruby Durden, and Pearl Durden; (back row) eight unidentified children, Robert Coleman, Wallace Coleman, unidentified, unidentified, George Rountree, Ben Rountree, Mollie Durden, unidentified, unidentified, and Mary and Dr. Virgil Franklin.

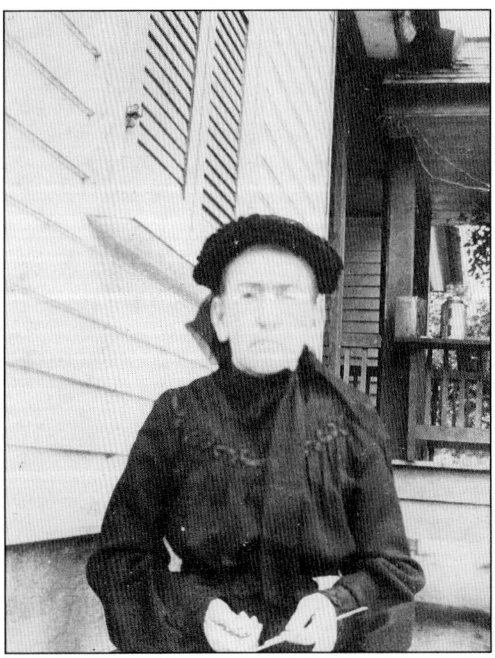

Eliza Brinson Durden (4/8/1833–10/6/1911) was the wife of Albert Neal Durden (3/2/1828–3/28/1904). In November 1864, while she and her oldest son, Math, age 11, were at home near Canoochee, a detachment of Sherman's army came through pillaging and burning. She put Math in bed with all of the family silver and valuables and told the soldiers that he had Scarlett Fever, a dread disease of the time. The soldiers were afraid to go into his room and the valuables were saved.

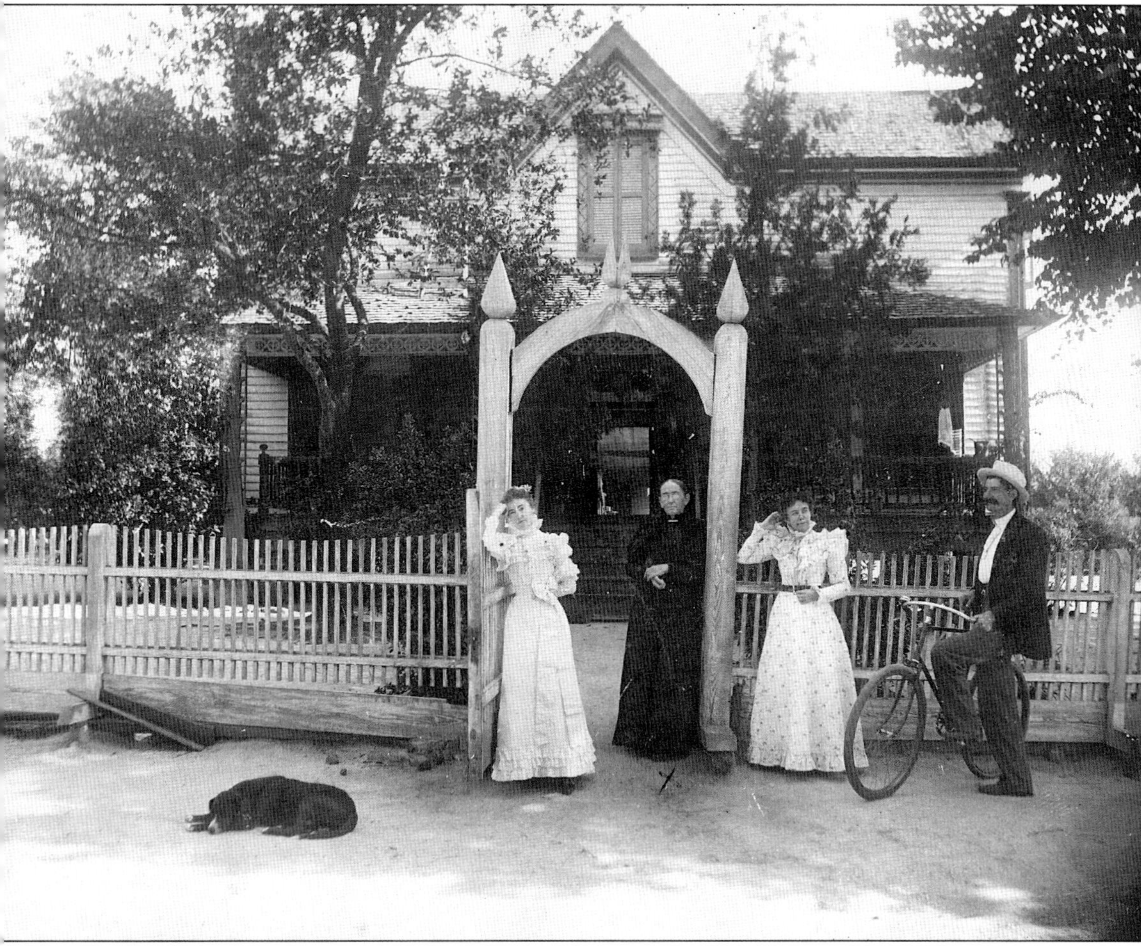

The Albert Neal Durden home, at Math (later called Kilburn), was constructed in 1850 and 1870. Pictured from left to right are: Fannie Durden Farmer, Eliza Brinson Durden (widow of Albert Durden), Mary "Mollie" Durden, and Matthew S. Farmer, on bicycle. The Kilburn Post Office was located on the back porch. The house, located on Fannie Brewer Road, still looks much as it did when this picture was taken in the 1890s.

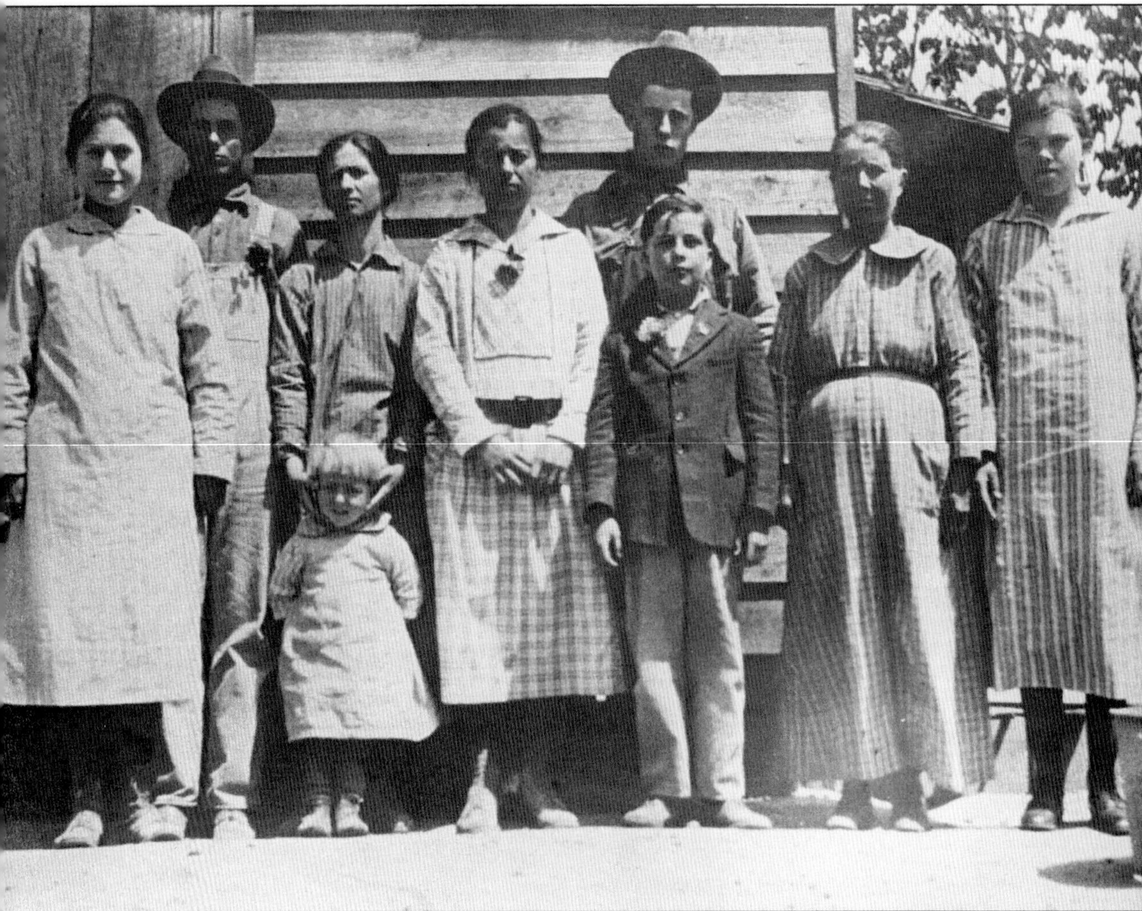

This is the Scott family *c.* 1922. Pictured from left to right are: Lula Scott Sherrod, Luther, Clifford, Arrie Scott Martin, Macie, J.D., Ernest, Dorcus Coleman Scott (mother), and Ermie Mae Scott Moxley. The father, John H. Scott, born in 1869, had passed away in 1918.

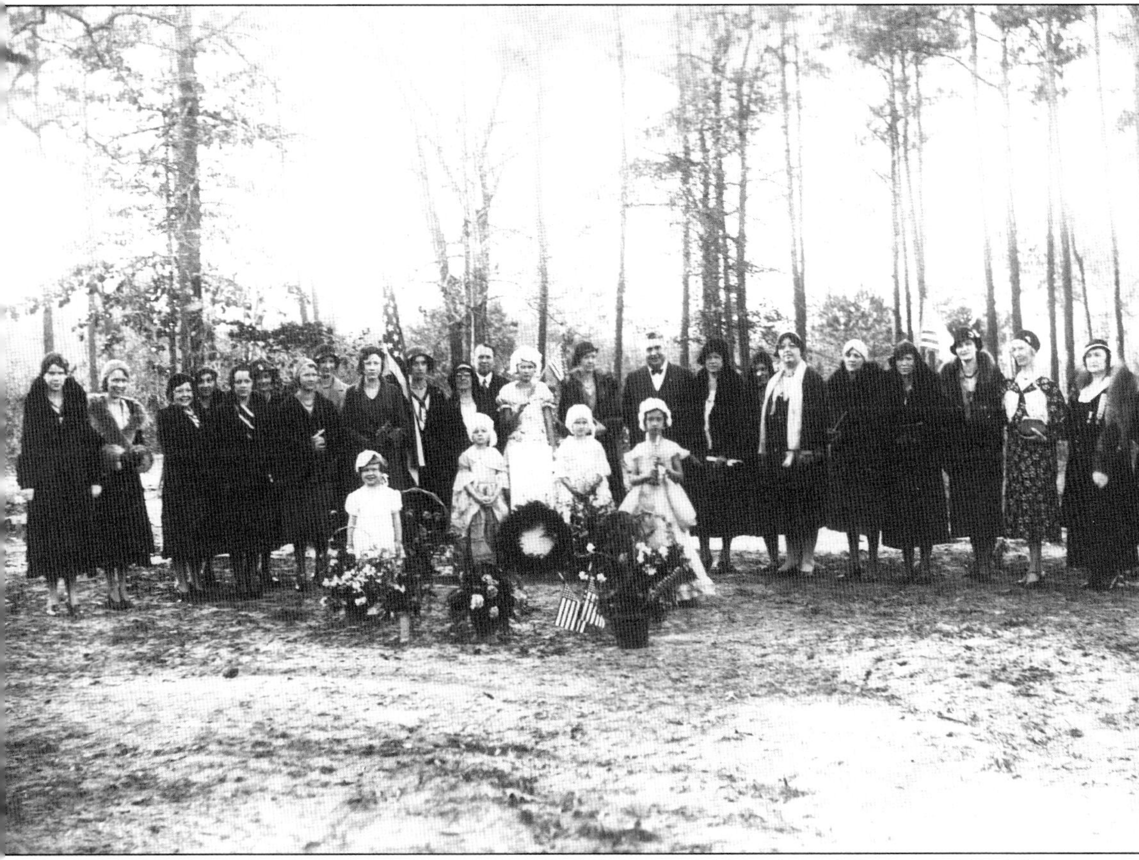

The Adam Brinson Chapter of the DAR marked the grave of Jonathan Coleman (10/9/1750–12/30/1838), located at Bark Camp Church in Burke County, on September 29, 1931. Mrs. I.A. Brannen, regent, presided over the program, which included a speech by Col. Ivey W. Rountree and a solo by Allen Rountree. The four young ladies in front, from left to right are: Dorothy Coleman Griffen, Mary Alice Hodges, Evelyn Snellgrove, and Annette Coleman. Also pictured, from left to right are: Clarabelle Durden, Carolyn Walsh Lamb, Nettie Snellgrove, unidentified, unidentified, unidentified, Bertha Coleman (Rocker), unidentified, Sarah Flanders (Underwood), Louise Black (Phillips), Ada Brown Smith, Rev. Rufus Hodges, Annie B. Coleman Hodges, Col. Rountree, Mrs. Brannen, unidentified, Daisy Lee Smith, Rosa Mae Brown, Annie Belle Brinson (Overstreet), Nettie Edenfield Black, Jessie Coleman Black, Ruby Durden Buttrill, and Fannie Brewer.

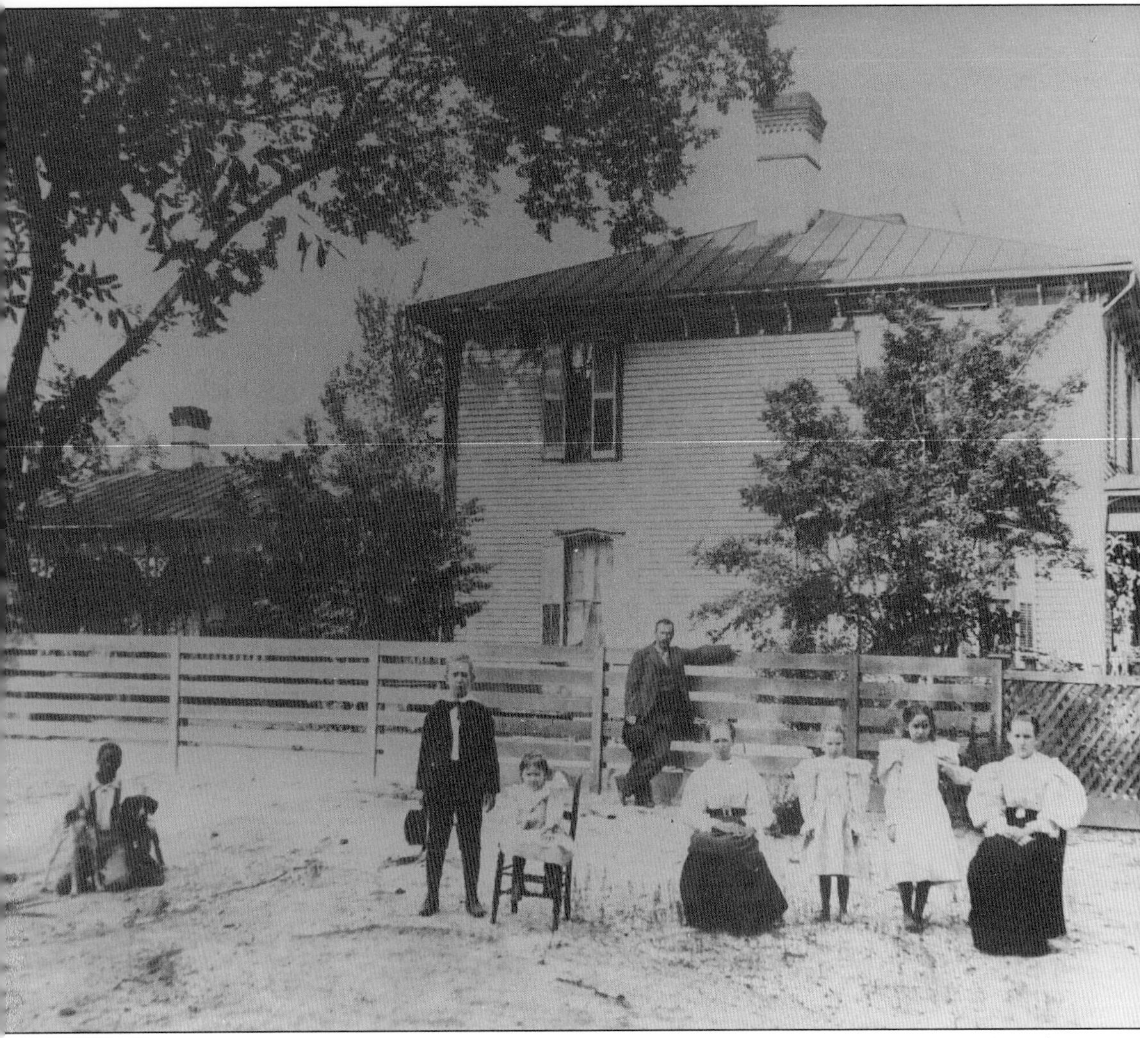

Dr. Ben Lane, his wife, Kate Brinson Lane (center), and their children are pictured at their home, built in the 1880s and located south of the Ogeechee River, near Bennett's Landing in what is now Jenkins County. The house is still standing.

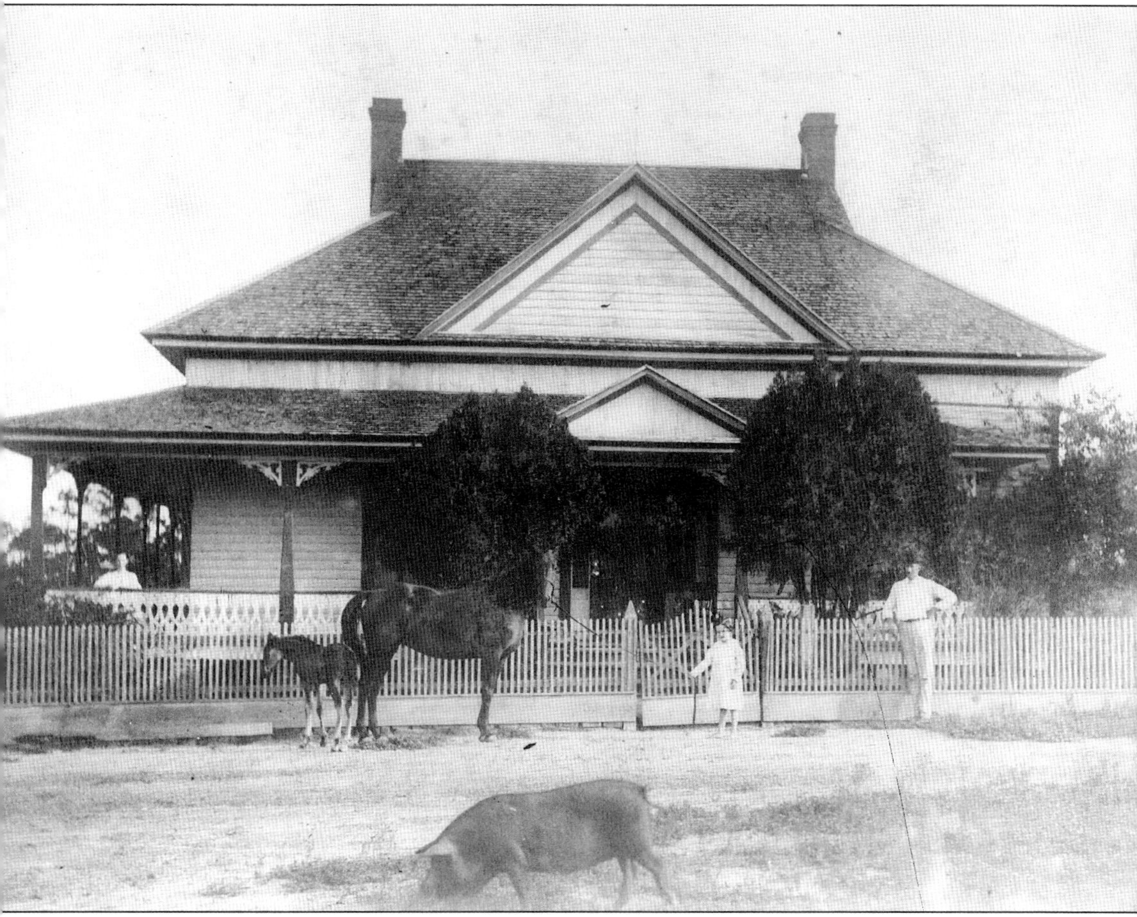

"Monte," *c.* 1885, was home of William Matthew and Emma Kennedy Durden until 1906 when they moved to Graymont. Thomas L. Black then occupied the house. Black, standing next to the fence, was a veterinarian and also trained fine racehorses. On the porch is his wife, Jessie Black, a teacher, genealogist, and historian of note. The young girl is Louise Phillips holding her pet hog. The house burned in the mid-1980s.

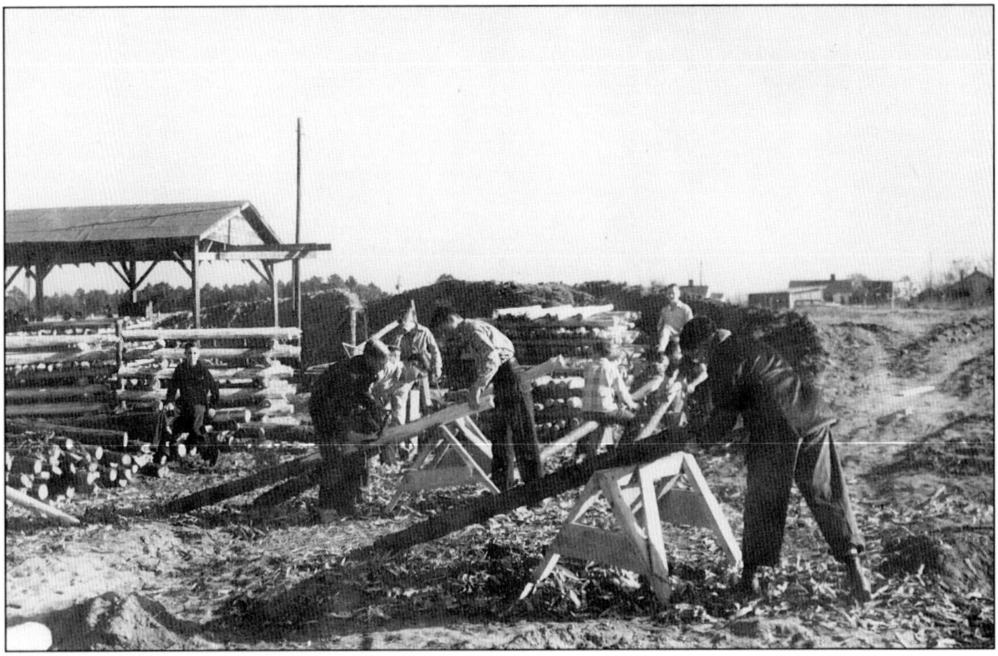

The men shown here are cutting and debarking logs.

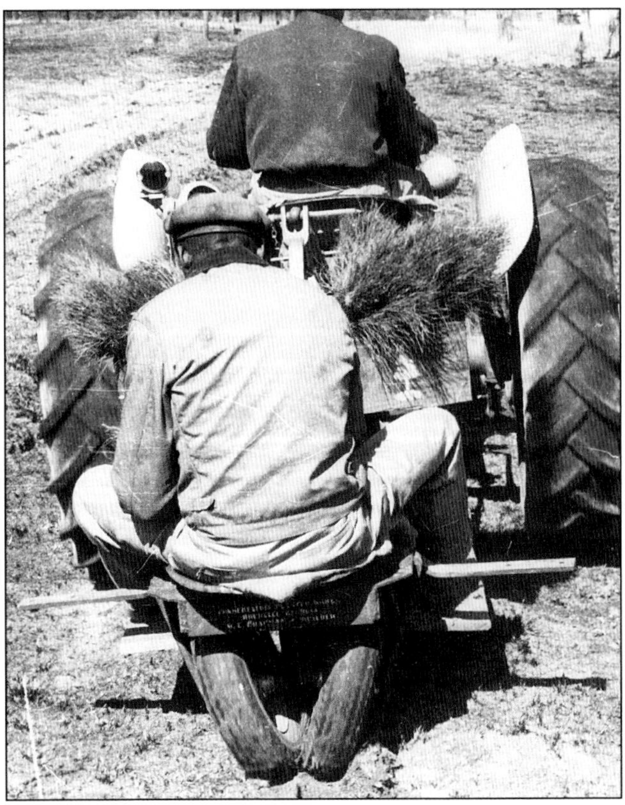

This man is planting pine trees.

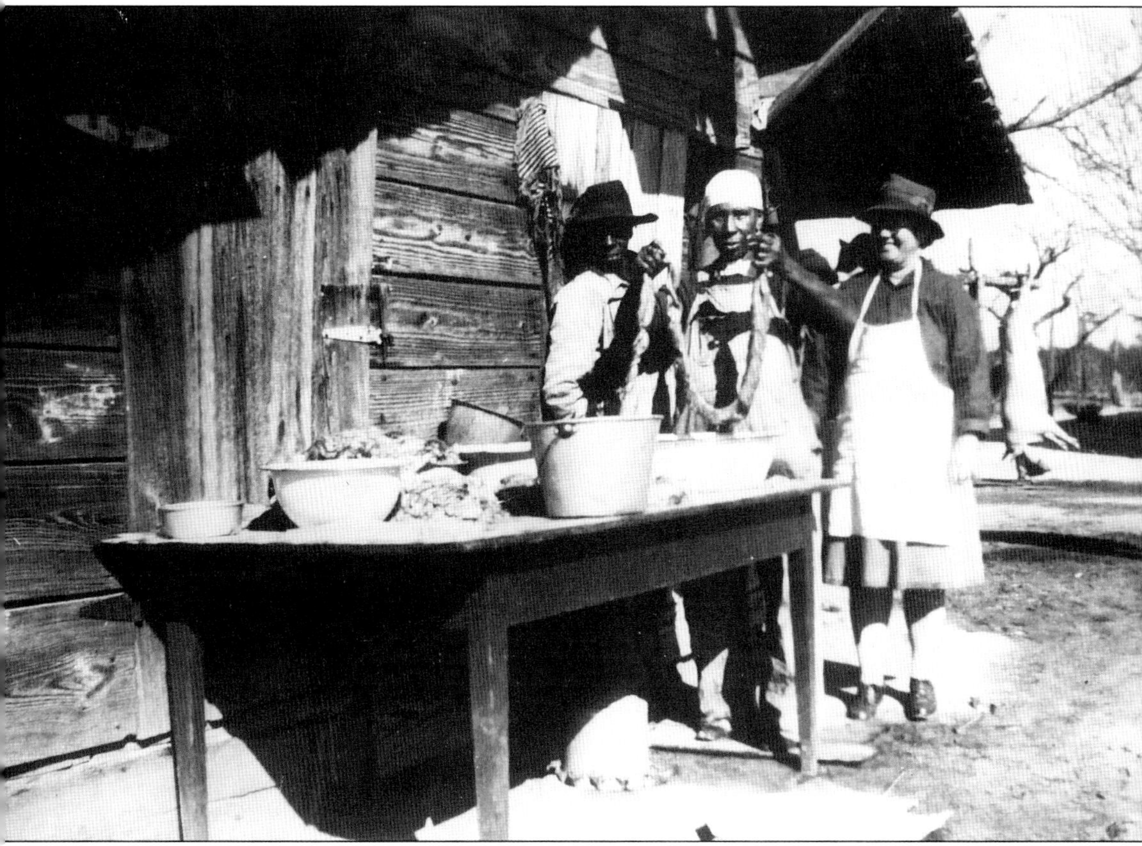

These women are washing chitterlings at the home of I.E. Fordham Sr., which is now located in Candler County.

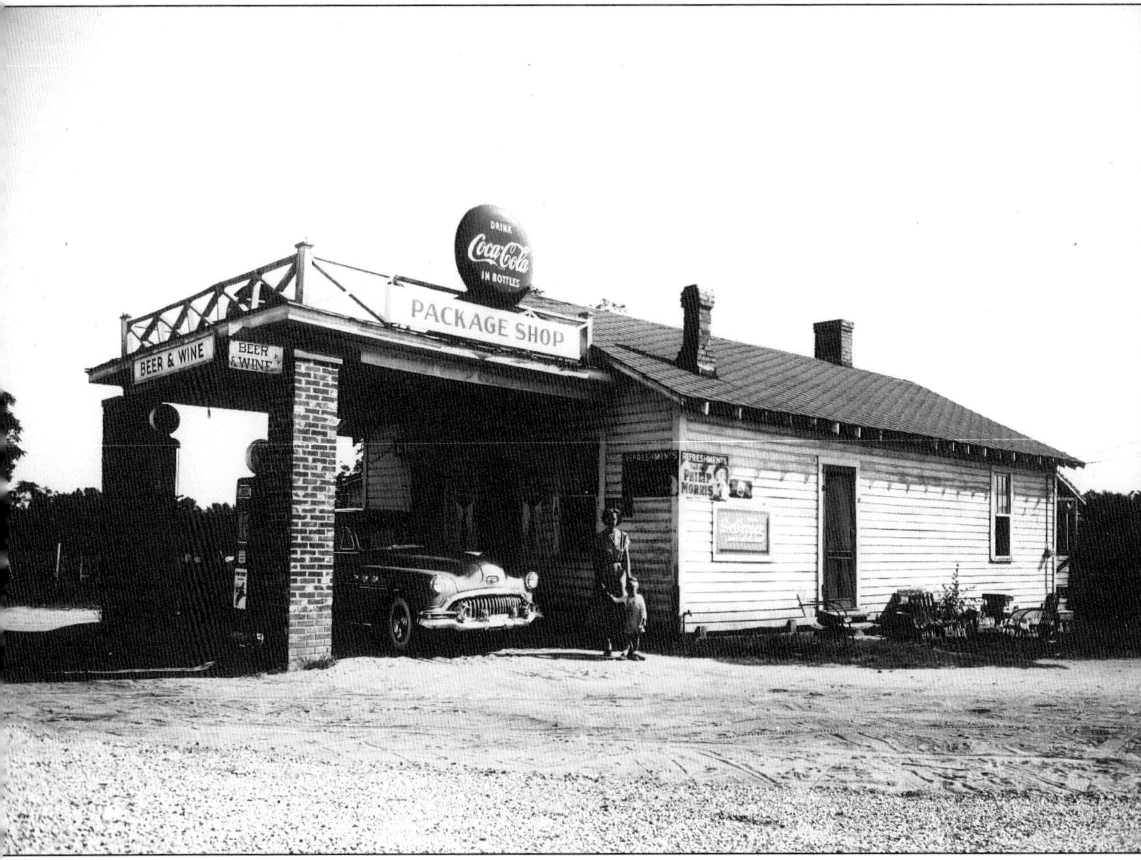

This is the Package Shop, located at the intersection of Highway 56 and McKinney's Pond Road, as it appeared in 1952.

Two

We Lived in Town

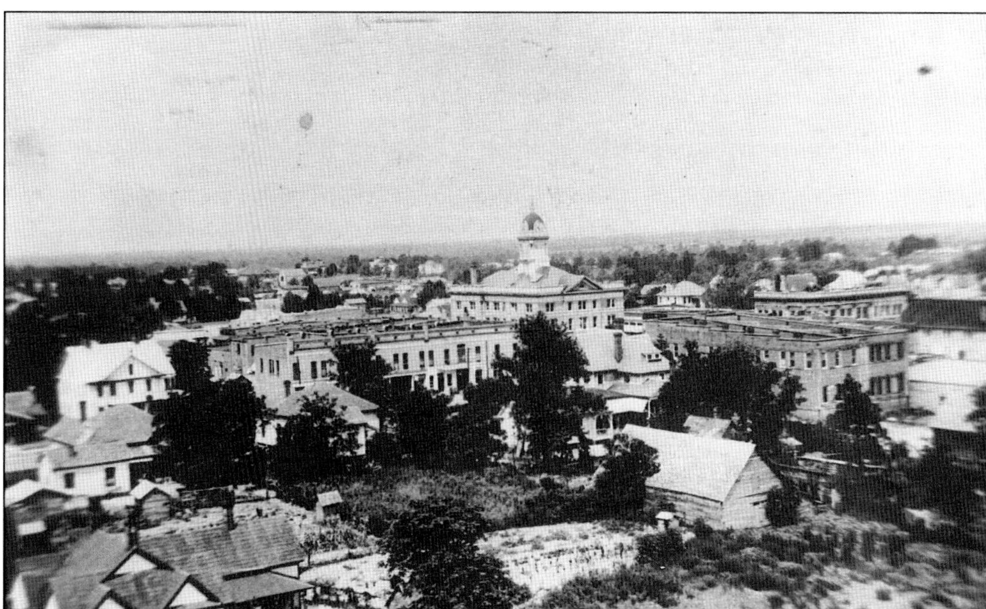

This is a panoramic view of Swainsboro, taken between 1920 and 1936. The picture was probably taken from the top of the Coleman Street water tank.

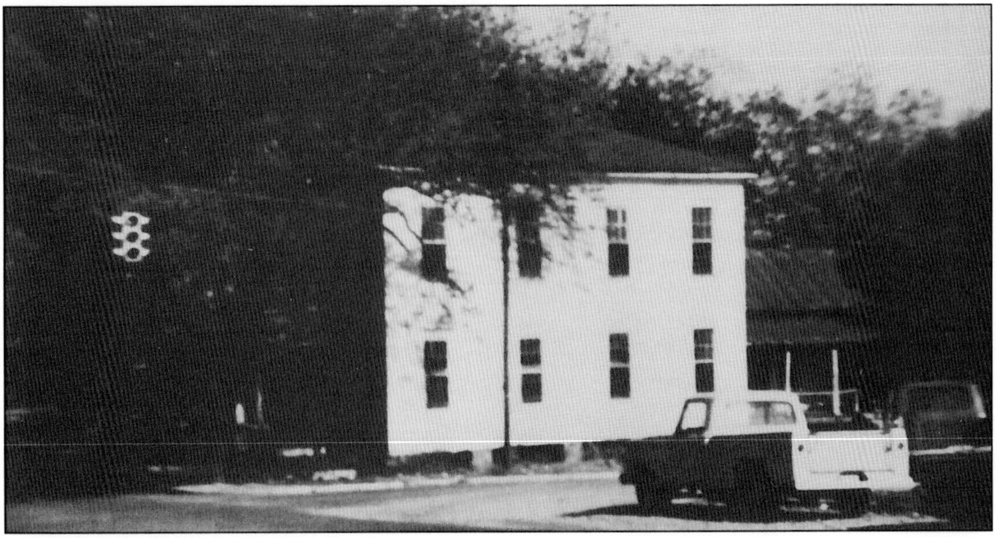

In 1895 the fourth courthouse, the Daniel's house, was moved to the southeast corner of Moring and S. Green Streets to make room for the fifth courthouse. It was torn down in 1960 to make room for the parking lot where Harvey's supermarket is now located. Prior to this, Emanuel County had three courthouses. The first, a clay-chinked, hand-hewn log cabin built about 1814, burned in 1822. The second, also a log cabin, was constructed by Henry Durden in 1822. He was later charged with burning this courthouse in 1841, but was found "not guilty." Some accounts list another courthouse, the third, built in 1875, which burned two years later.

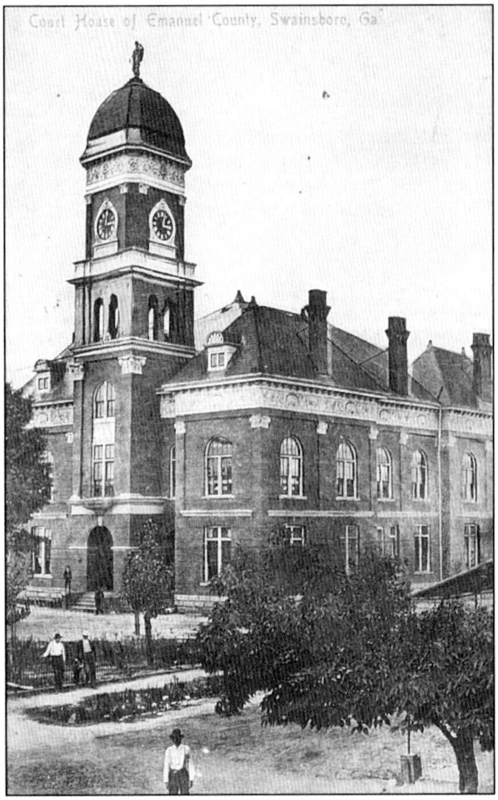

Emanuel County's fifth courthouse, an imposing structure, cost all of $25,000 when it was constructed in 1895. It burned in May 1919.

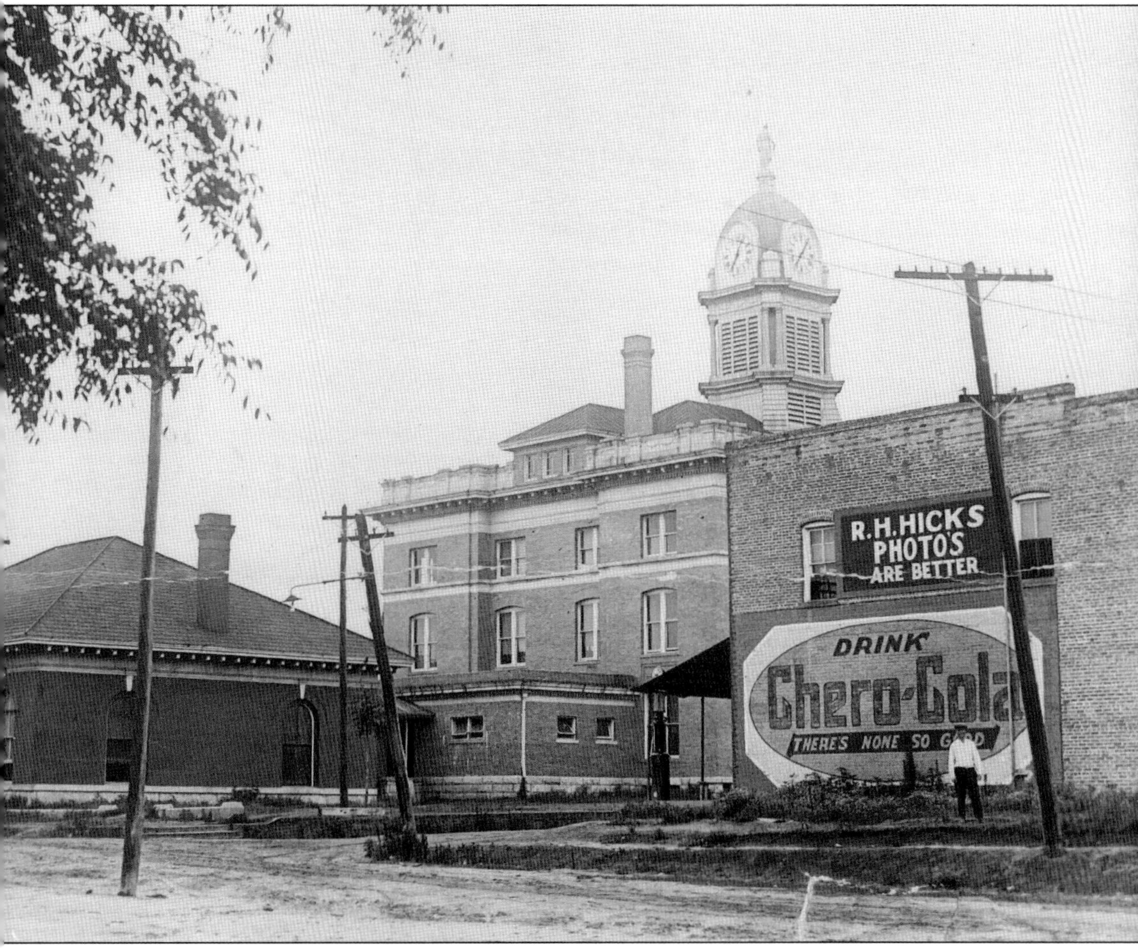

The sixth Emanuel County Courthouse, constructed in 1920 at a cost of $140,000, was destroyed by fire in 1938. On the window at the right of the door, a sign reads, "R.H. Humphrey, Attorney At Law," above that, "G.C. Powell, Attorney At Law," and above the door, "Alfred Herringron Jr., Attorney At Law."

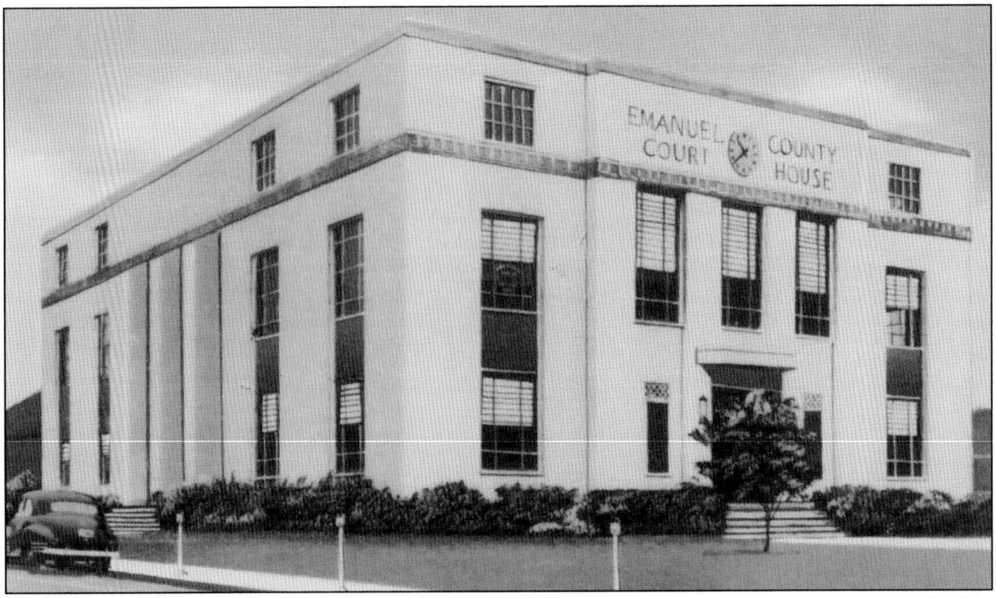

The seventh and present Emanuel County Court House was built in 1940 at a cost of $85,000.

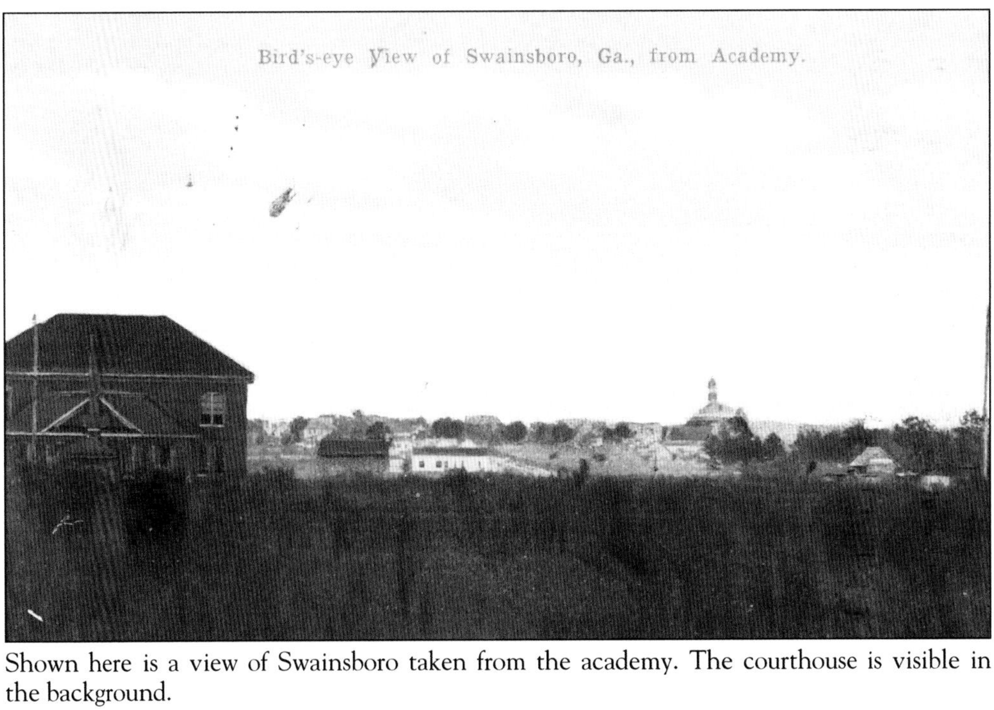

Shown here is a view of Swainsboro taken from the academy. The courthouse is visible in the background.

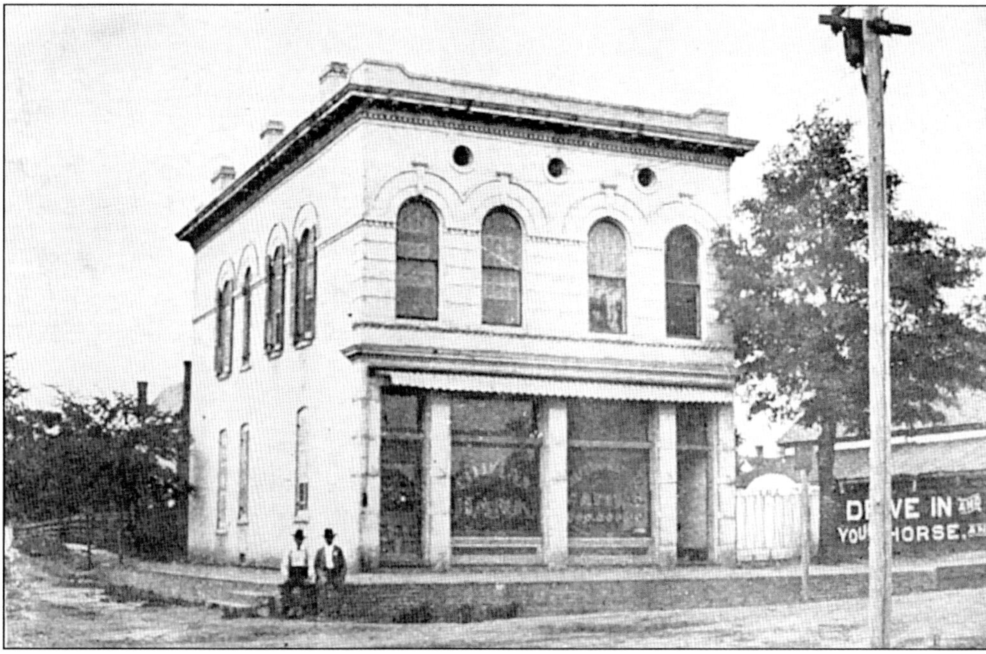

Pictured is the Citizens Bank Building, constructed about 1900, located on the corner of N. Green Street and West Main. The bank was incorporated on November 10, 1900 by George Rentz, E.P. Rentz, and C.E. Westbrook, and was moved to the present city hall building in 1925 and to its present location in 1970. Bangles now occupies this building.

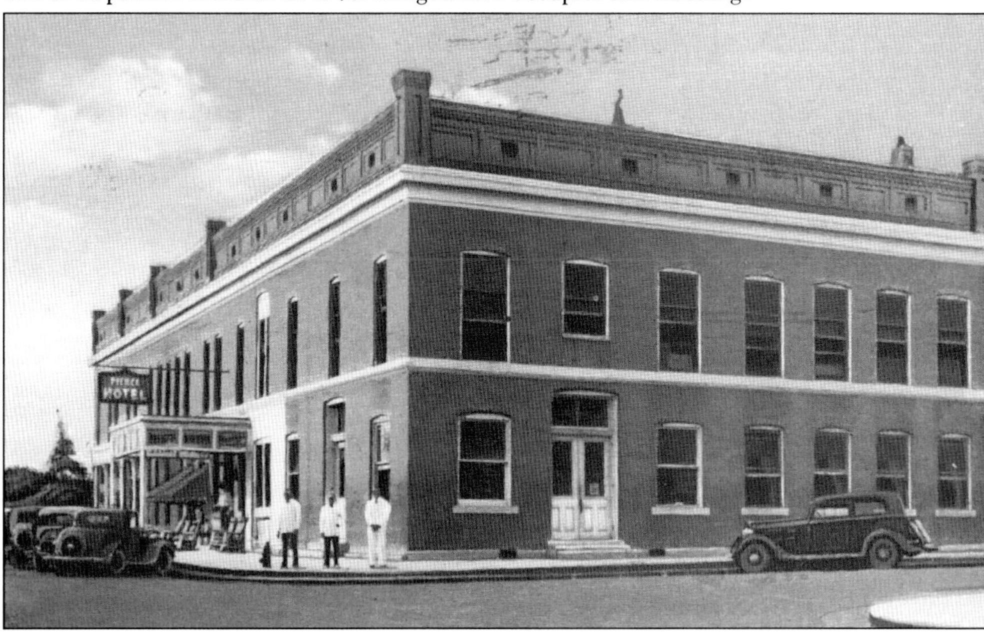

The Pierce Hotel, originally named the Marguerite Hotel by Mrs. M.M. McLeod in order to honor her eight-year-old daughter Madge and her sister-in-law Margaret McLeod Smith, was completed in 1898 on the site of the McLeod House, a private residence and guest home. Later it became the Pierce Hotel, for Mrs. Pierce who rented the property, and finally the Durden Hotel, after the owner, Madge Mcleod Durden. The building partially burned in 1994.

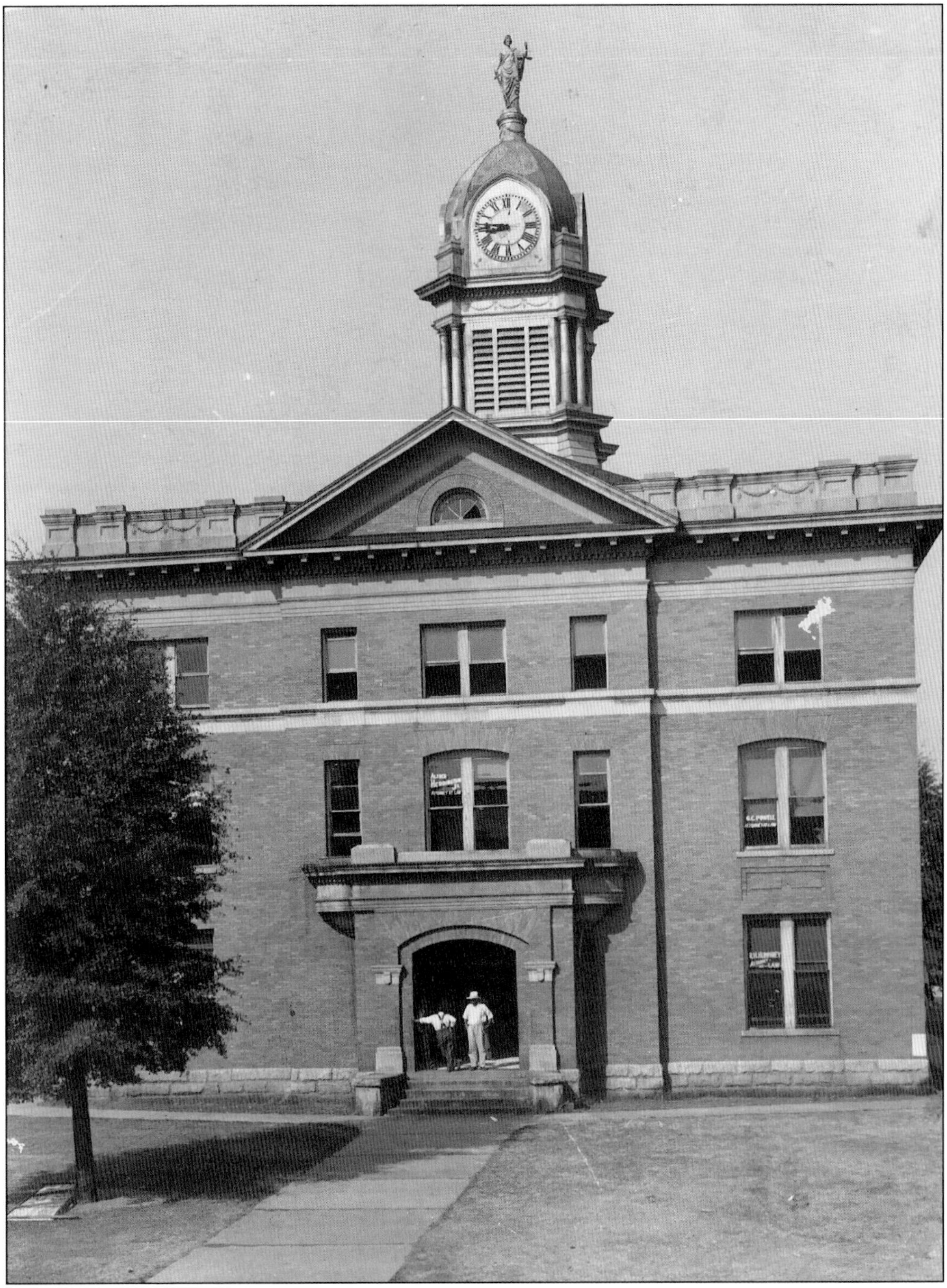

This is another view of the Emanuel County Courthouse. (See page 31.)

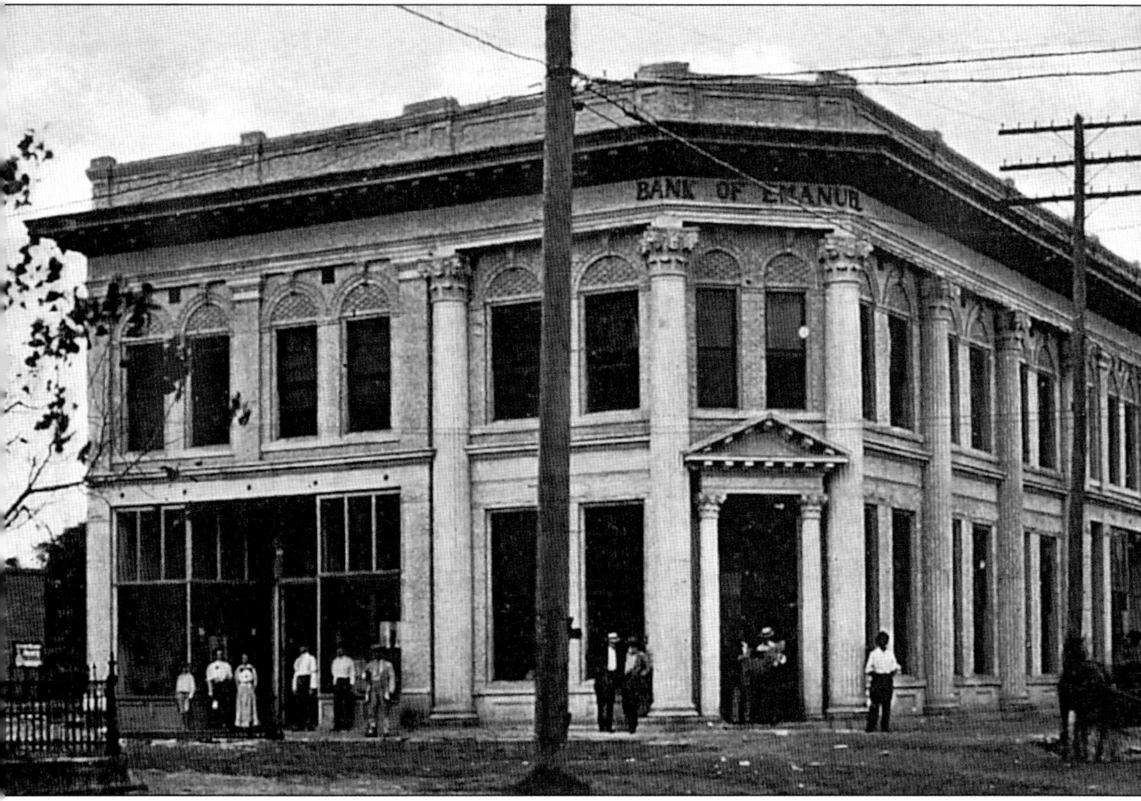

The Bank of Emanuel was incorporated on March 22, 1905 by Dr. Green Bell, J.L.Carmichael, W.G. Wood, Joe Ehrlich, George M. Heath, Arthur Thompson, W.W. Larsen, and F.H. Saffold. Later occupied by the Citizens Bank, it presently houses Swainsboro City Hall. Note that the streets are still unpaved in this view.

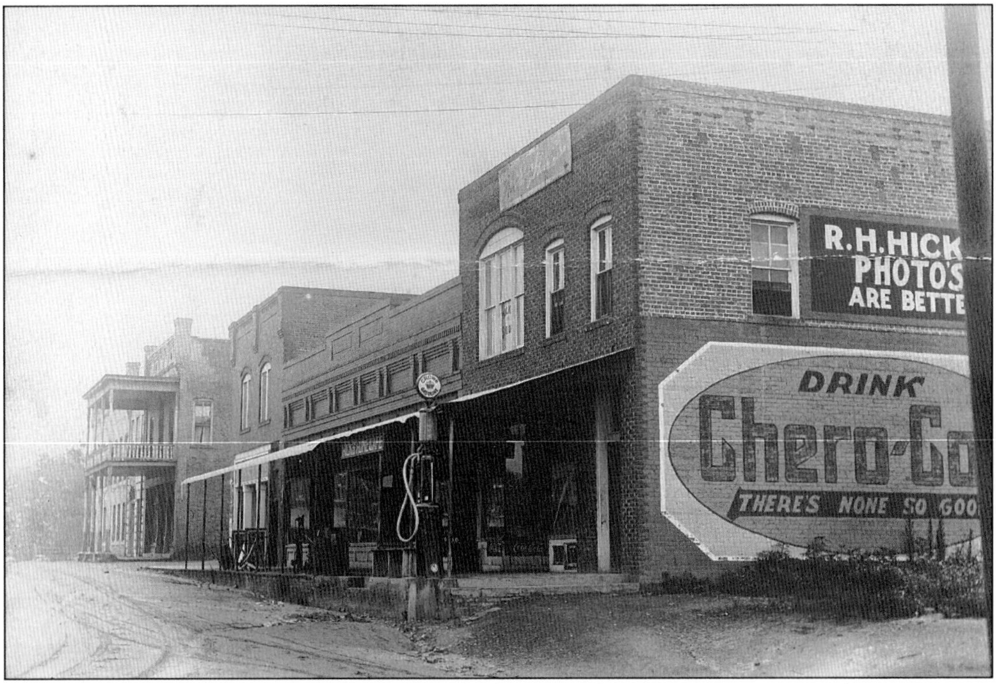

Pictured above is Court Street, Swainsboro, looking east from Green Street. On the near corner is Hicks Home Cafe on the first floor and R.H. Hooks Studio on the second. Farther down the street with the porch was, for many years, Swainsboro Hardware, and on the far corner, Durden Hotel.

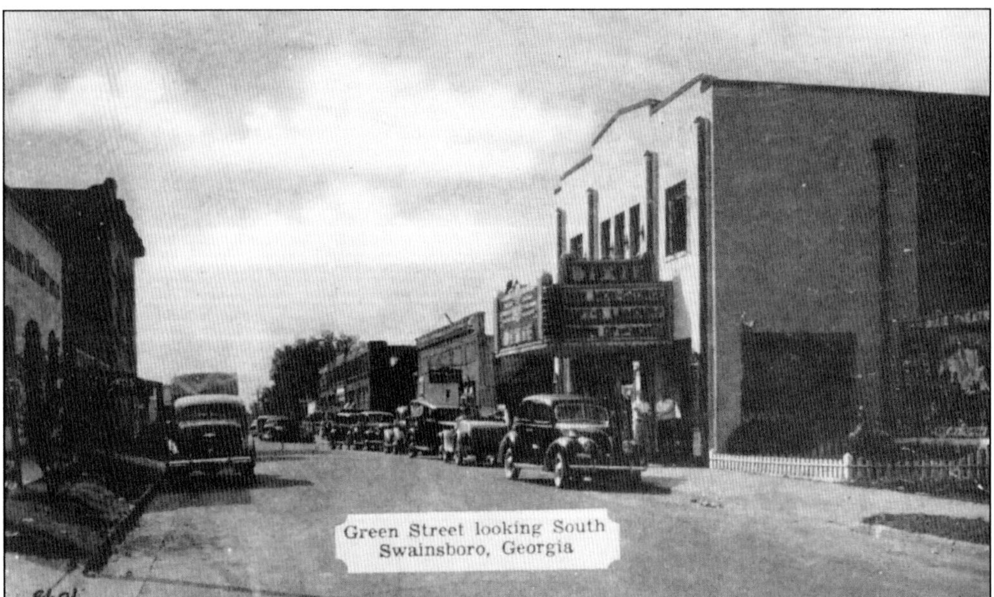

Shown here is downtown Swainsboro, looking south on Green Street. The Dixie Theater, owned by Bill Karrh, opened November 19, 1934, and closed in the 1960s. *Spawn of the North*, starring George Raft and Dorothy Lamour, was showing at the time of this picture.

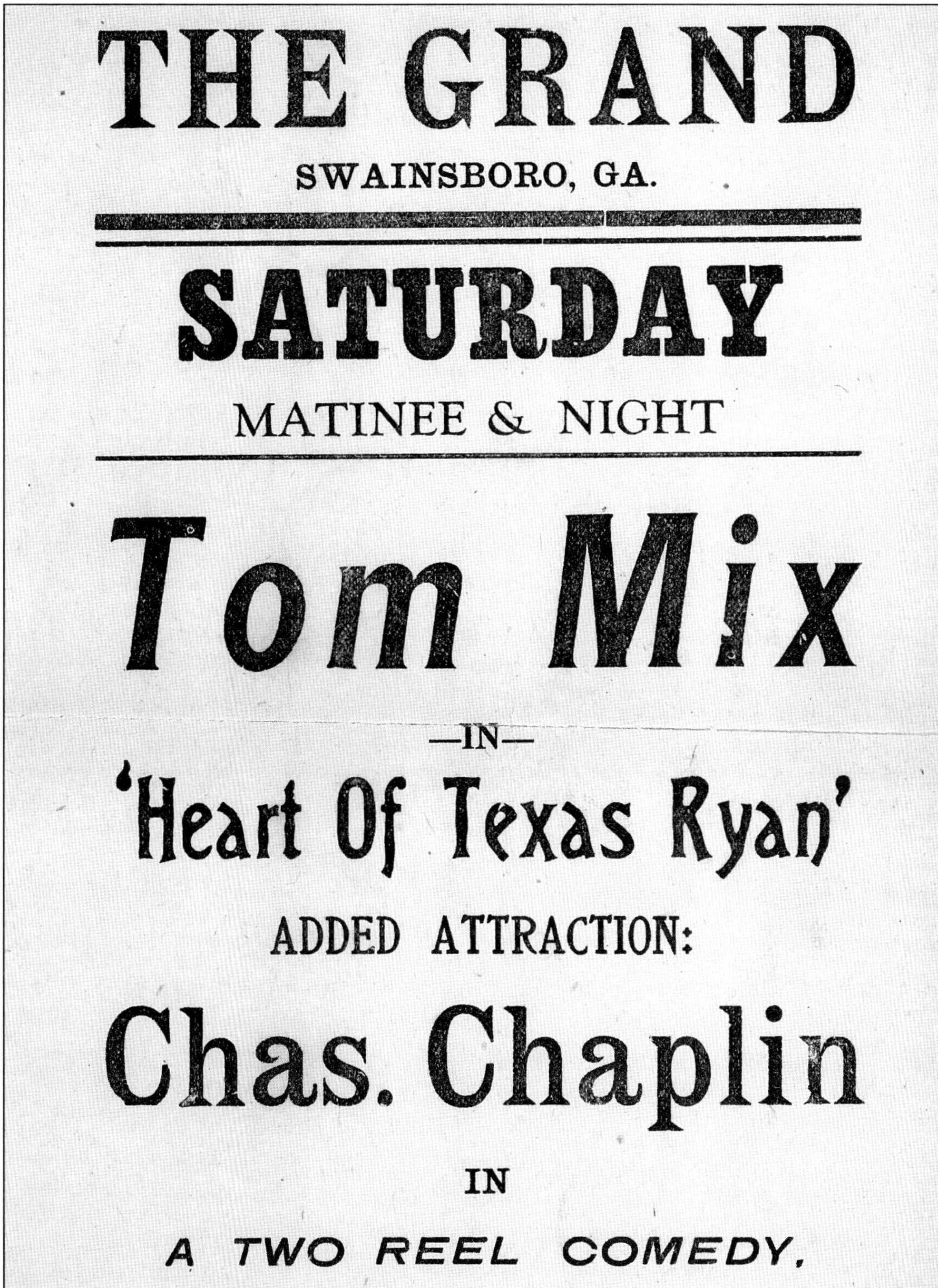

This is a playbill for the Grand Theater, which had established prior to 1919 as the American Theater by Louis Proctor and W.H. Odom. The theater was sold in 1920 to Pierce and Griner and the name changed to the Grand.

Later it became the Swainsboro Theatre, then the City Theatre, and finally the Princess Theatre, under the management of Daisy Smith. The building was located in the middle of the block on the south side of Court Street, and burned in 1931.

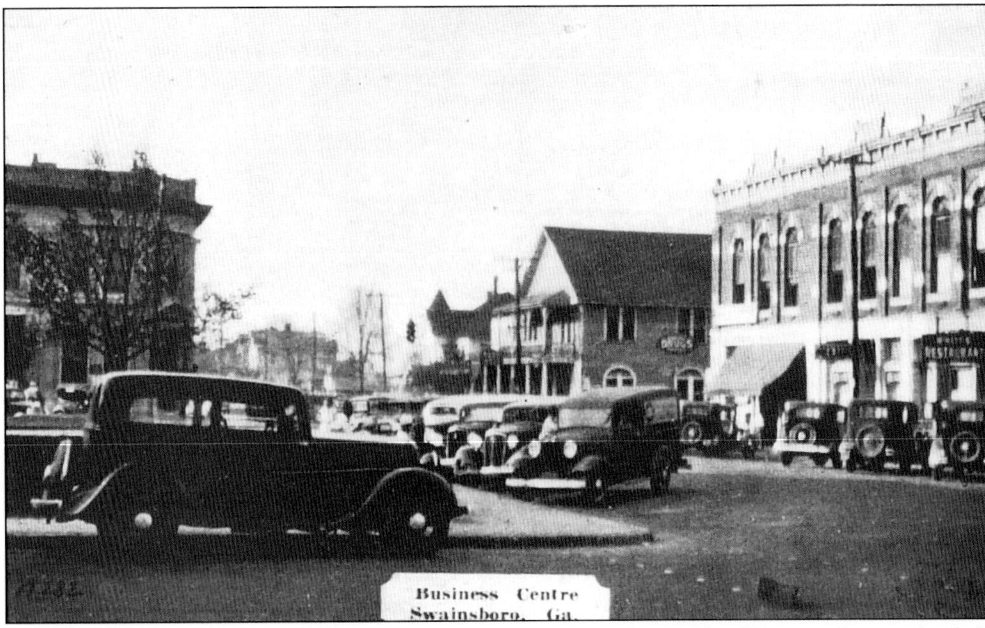

In this view of downtown Swainsboro, taken about 1930, the Bank of Emanuel is on the left, the White House Cafe and Barber shop, formerly John C. Coleman's general store, is in the center where the Coleman Hotel building now stands, and the Mitchell building is on the right, with W.H. Brannan Drug Store on the corner.

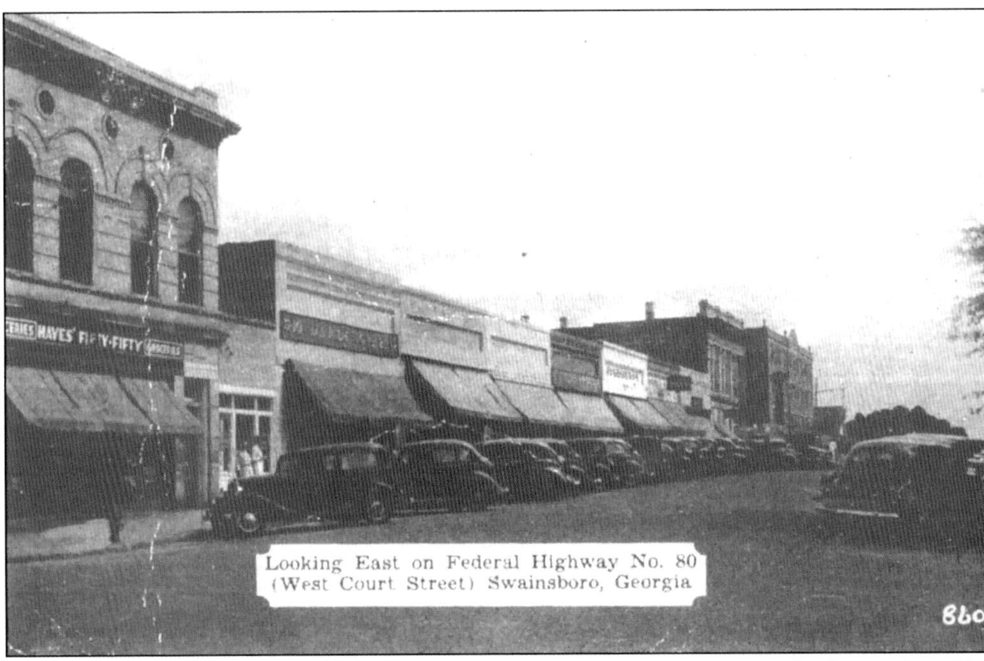

This is a view of downtown Swainsboro, looking east on Main Street in the late 1930s. The store on the corner is W.L. Hayes's Fifty-Fifty grocery. Among the other stores were Ehrlich's Dry Goods store and Mason's Pharmacy. The Bank of Emanuel is at the far corner.

Shown here is Moring Street in Swainsboro, looking west. The old houses were located on the present site of the Womack Furniture and Sanitary Market parking lot.

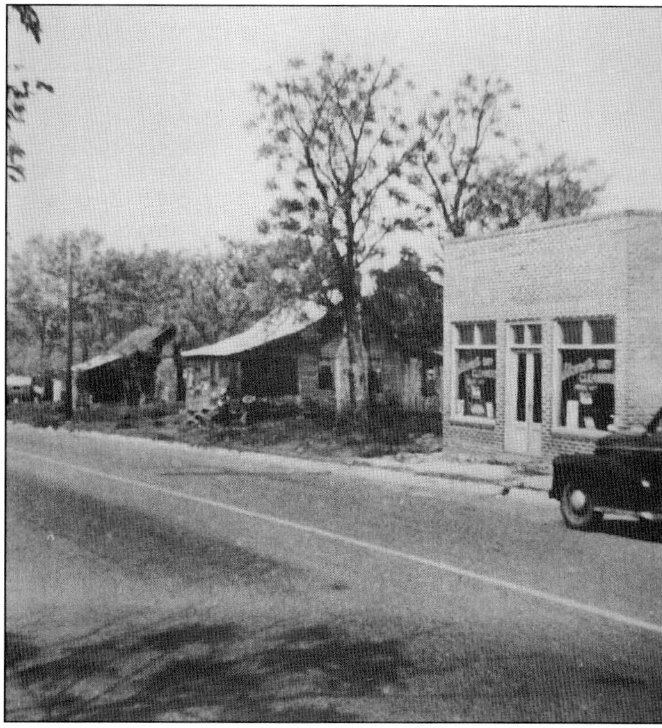

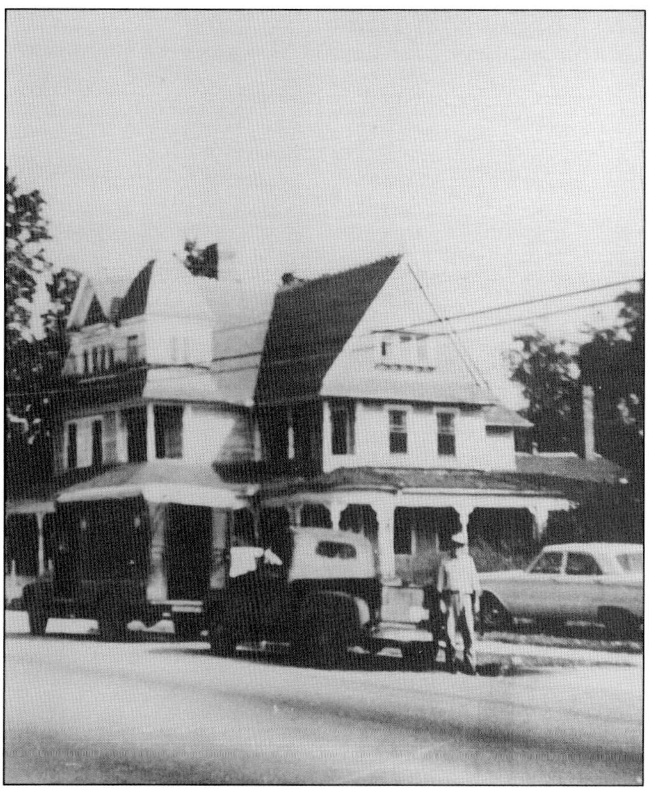

The John C. Coleman home was located on South Main Street, where the law offices of John Thompson now stand.

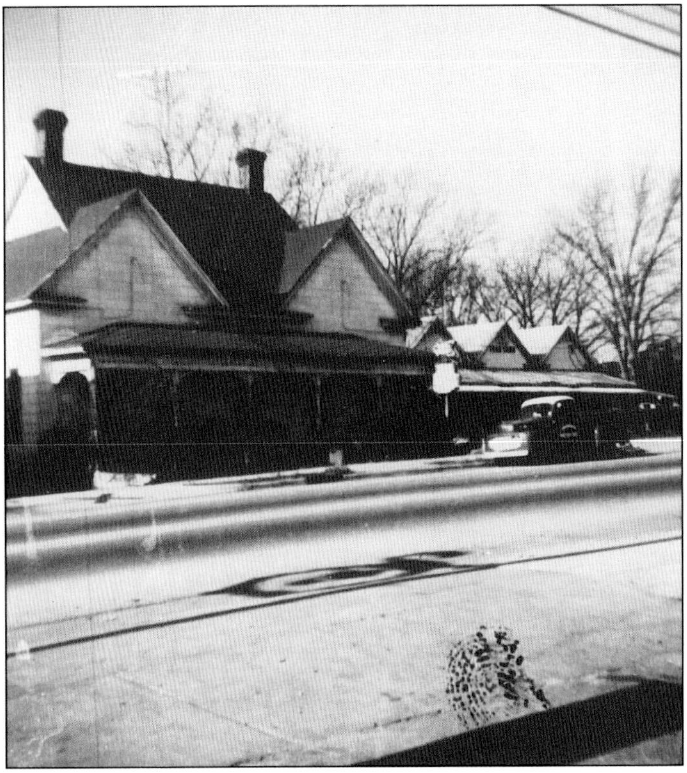

Dr. Youman's home was located on South Main Street, where Plaza Drug Store is now.

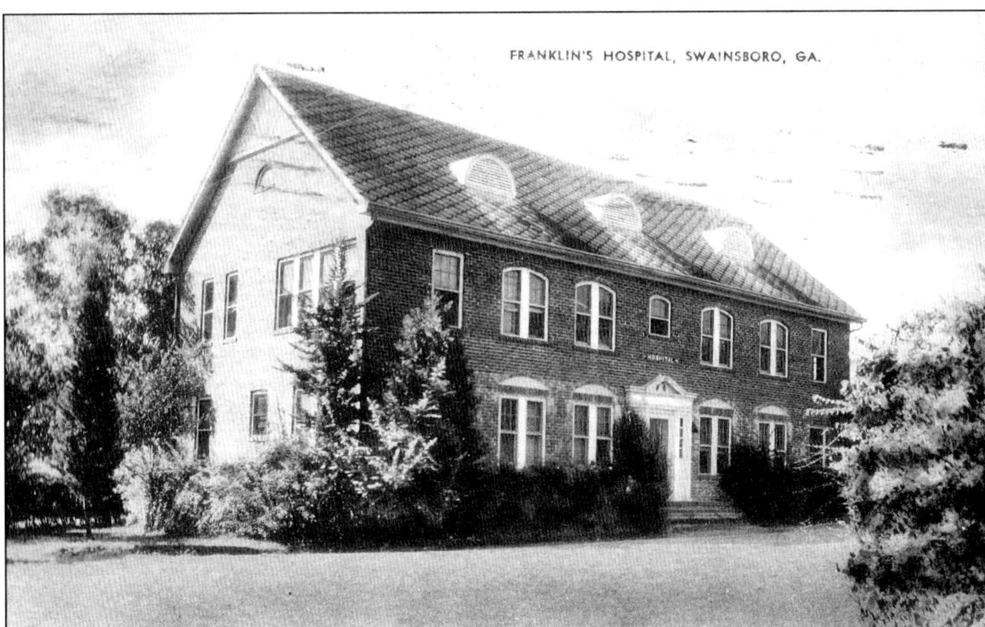

Franklin's Hospital was constructed in 1929 by Dr. Rufus Cecil Franklin. It was later occupied by Dr. Wilder Smith and Dr. James Ray. The building was being demolished in July 1998.

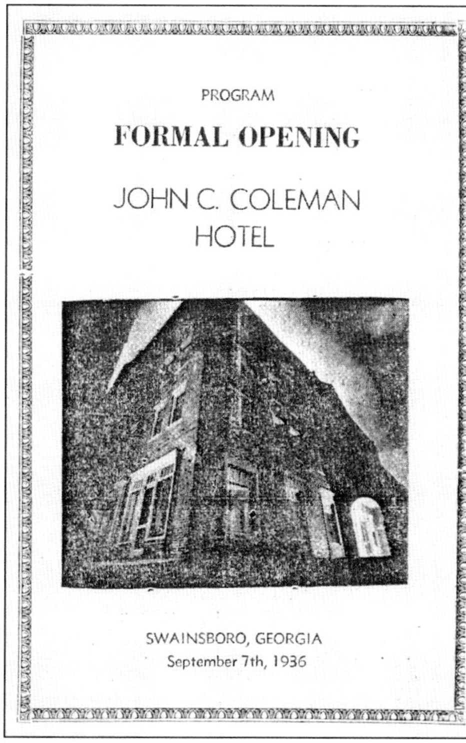

PROGRAM

FORMAL OPENING

JOHN C. COLEMAN
HOTEL

SWAINSBORO, GEORGIA
September 7th, 1936

The John C. Coleman Hotel, owned by Judge and Mrs. Frank Mitchell, was completed in 1936. The formal opening was held on September 7, 1936, with a receiving line of Judge and Mrs. Mitchell, Mr. and Mrs. W.H. Flanders, Dr. and Mrs. George L. Smith, and Mr. and Mrs. Collins Byrd. Other activities involved Frank and Luck Coleman Flanders placing flowers, a dedication by Felix C. Williams, a barbecue in the parking lot by Will McMillan, and dancing in the Rathskeller to the music of Graham Jackson.

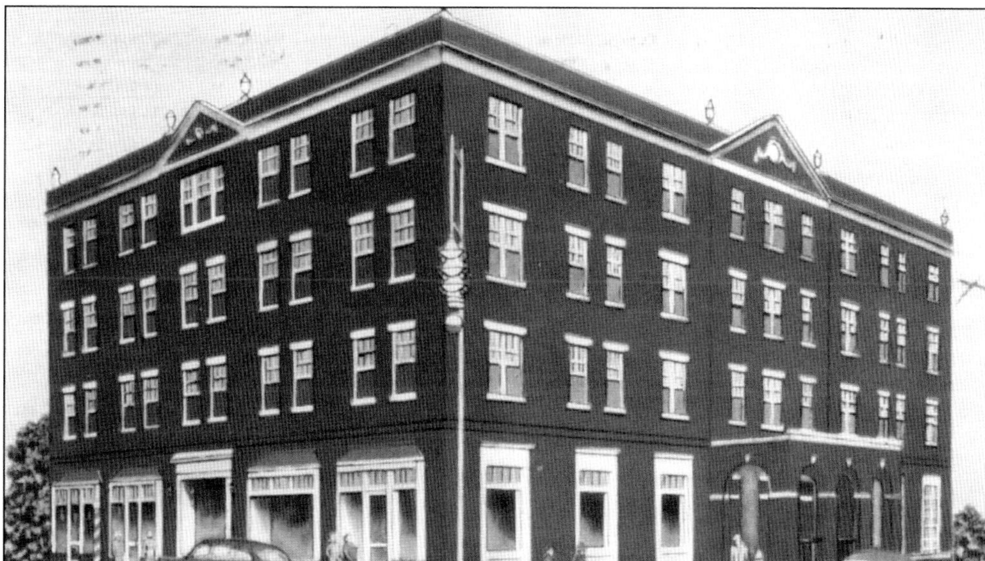

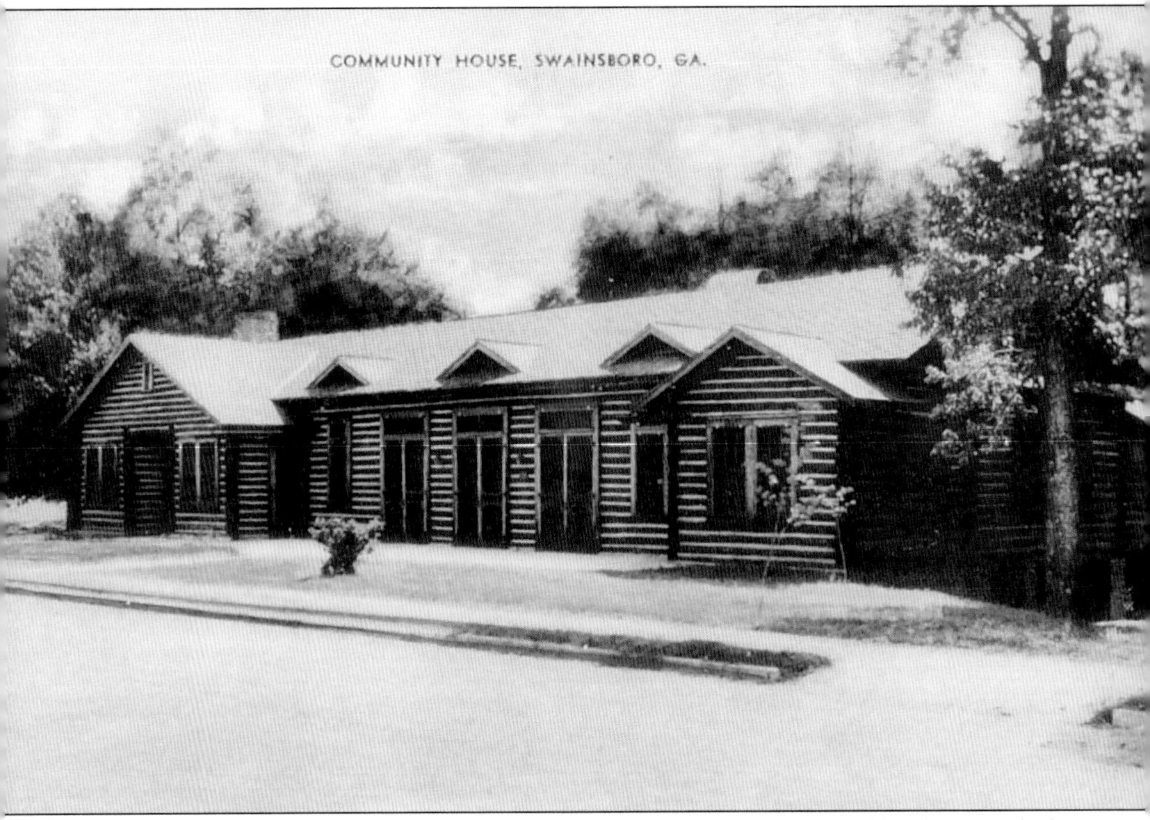

The Community House in Swainsboro was built in 1936 by the WPA, and has been used often for receptions, parties, reunions, and political rallies. Margaret Mitchell was present when the Georgia Press Association met here in June 1938. Eugene Talmadge and other political leaders have attended meetings here. It was restored in 1997.

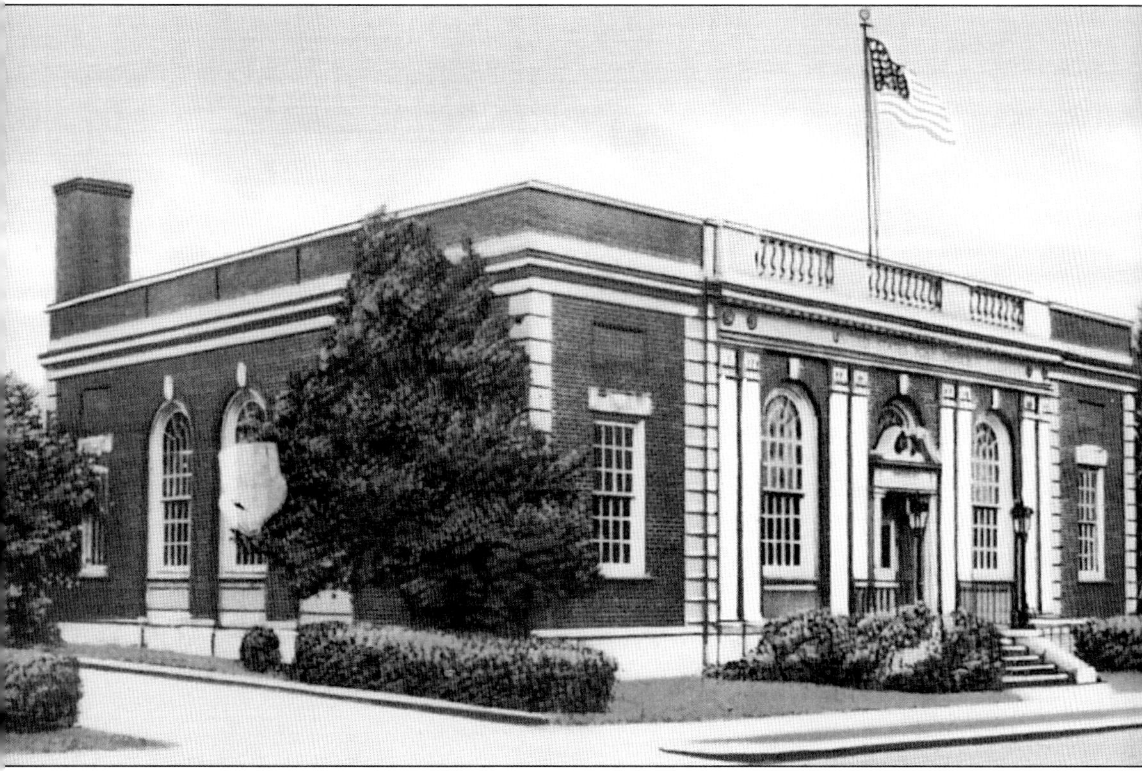

The U.S. Post Office in Swainsboro was completed in 1936. Postmaster General Jim Farley attended the dedication. A fine mural completed by the WPA is located in the lobby.

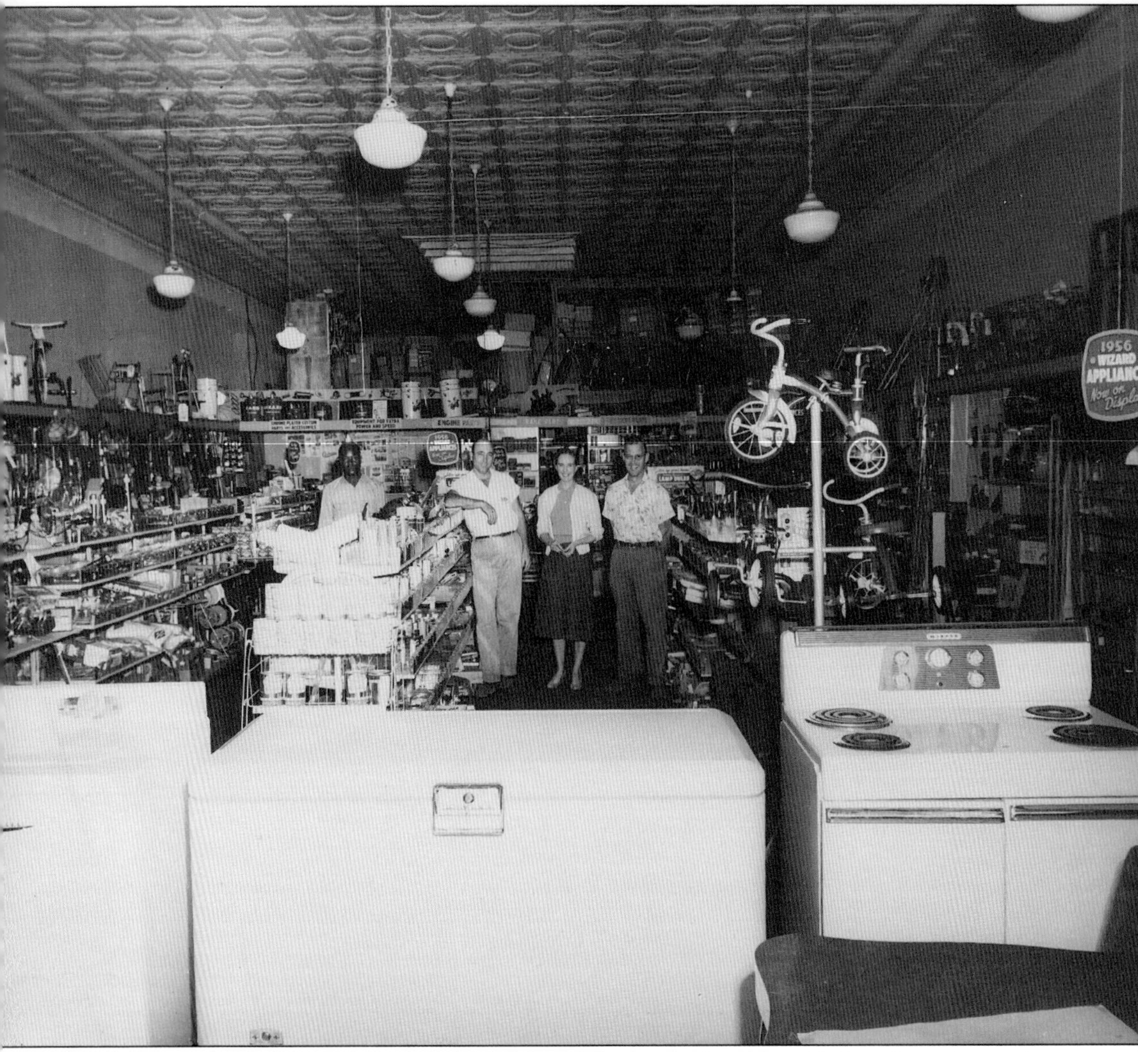

The Western Auto Store, operated by F.H. Cadle, opened in May 1948 and was located next door to the present city hall. Shown are Jake ?, Paul Farmer, Emily Coleman Bazemore, and F.H. Cadle Jr. This picture was taken in 1956.

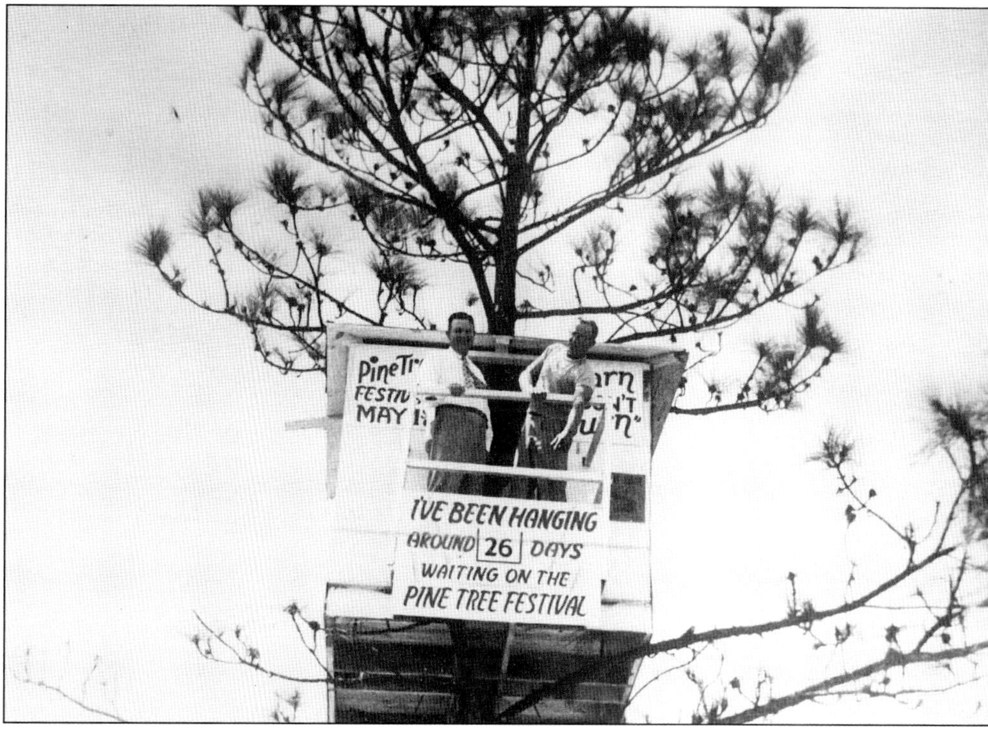

Here, pine tree sitter Ray Brinson is visited by Foots Mathis.

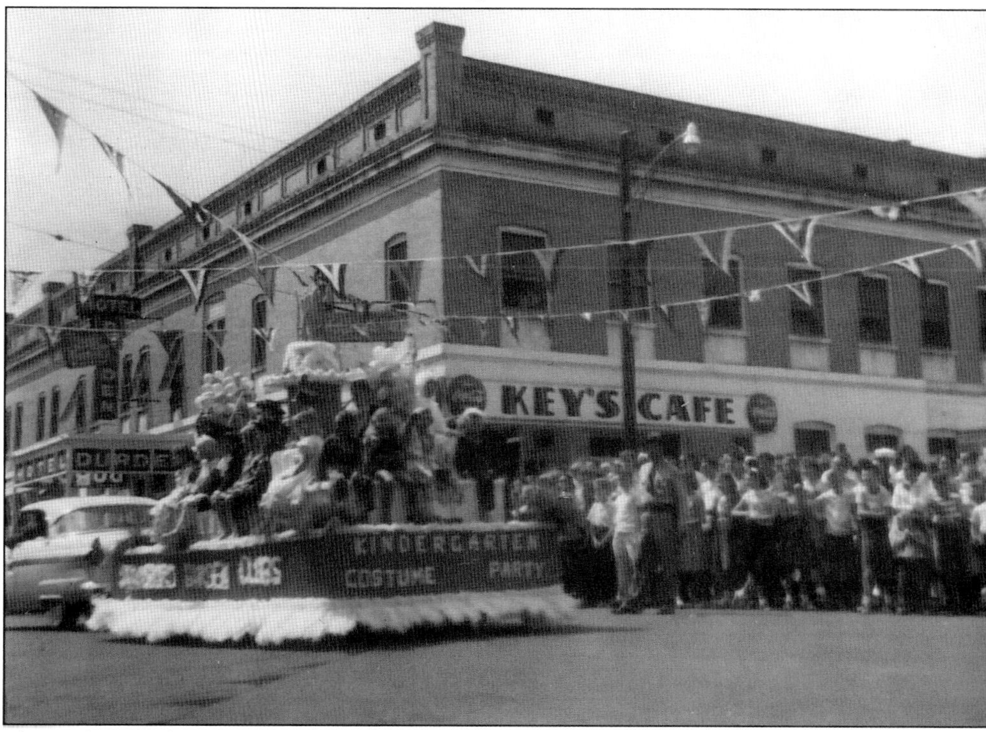

Shown here is the Pine Tree Festival in 1958. Note Key's Café in the Durden Hotel building, a popular eating and meeting place.

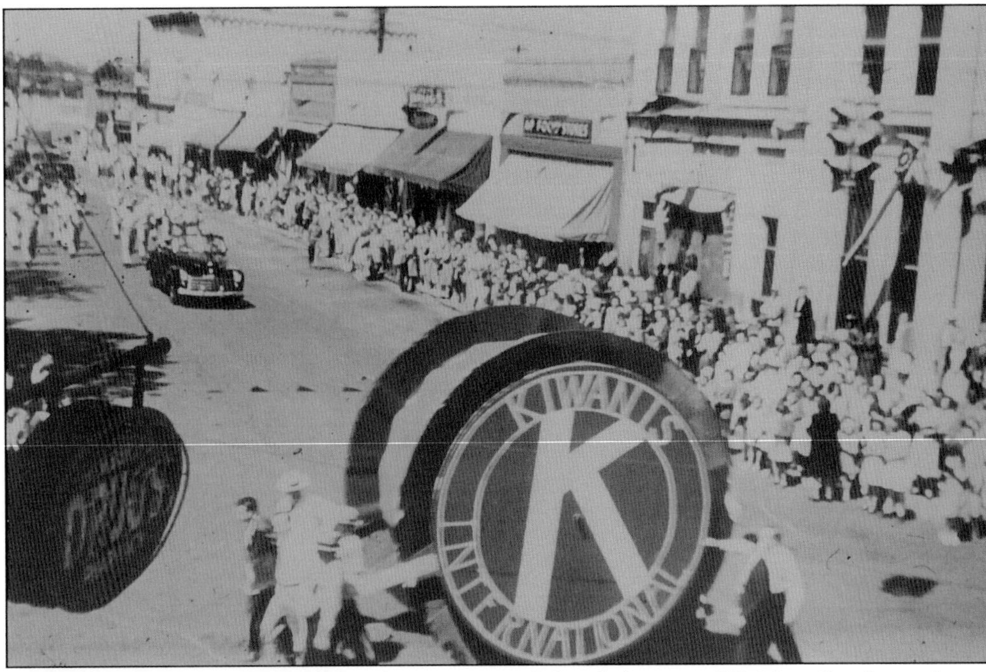

The second Pine Tree Festival Parade, May 9, 1947, headed east on W. Main St., Swainsboro.

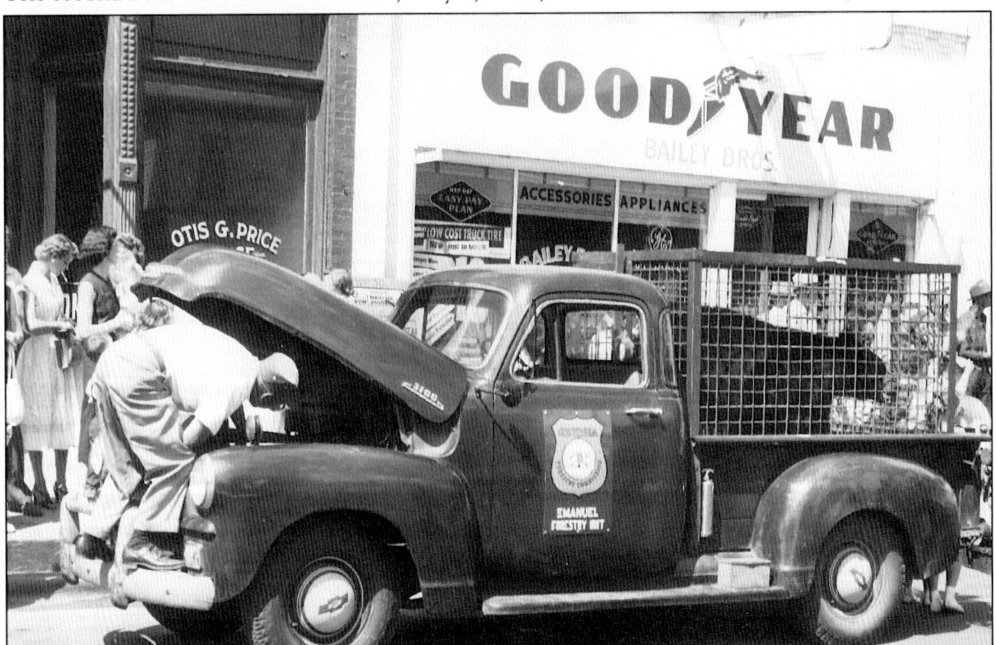

Taken in the 1950 Pinetree Festival parade, this picture shows a parade unit from the Emanuel Forestry Unit of the Georgia Forestry Commission. Apparently the truck has some mechanical problem, but the bear in the back, perhaps a south Georgia version of "Smokey," seems unconcerned.

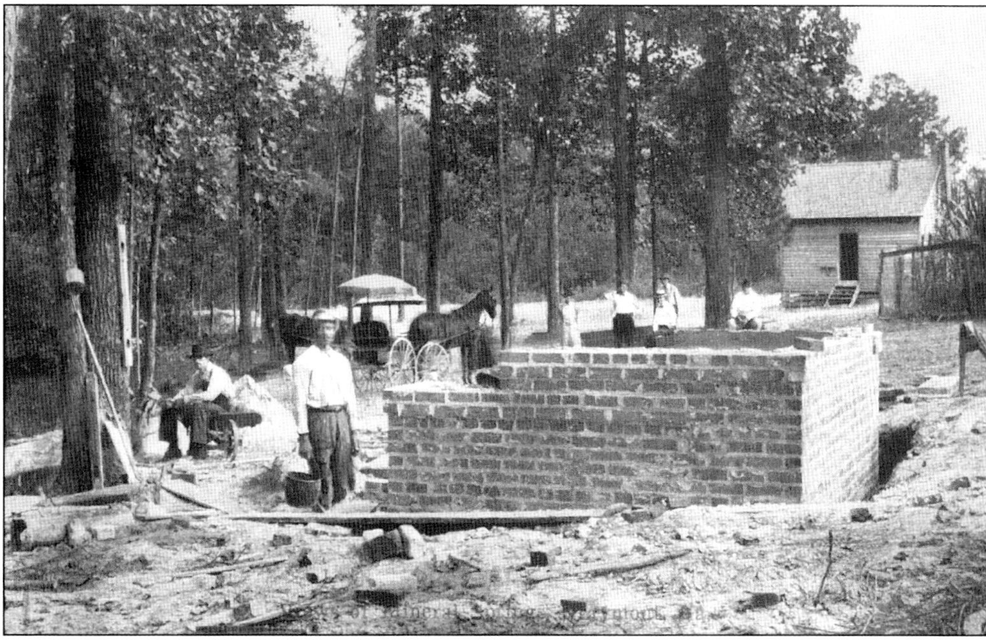

Pictured is Belton Springs, Graymont. Named after owner Belton Sutton, the springs were a popular watering spot in the early 1900s. The springs still exist but are covered by underbrush.

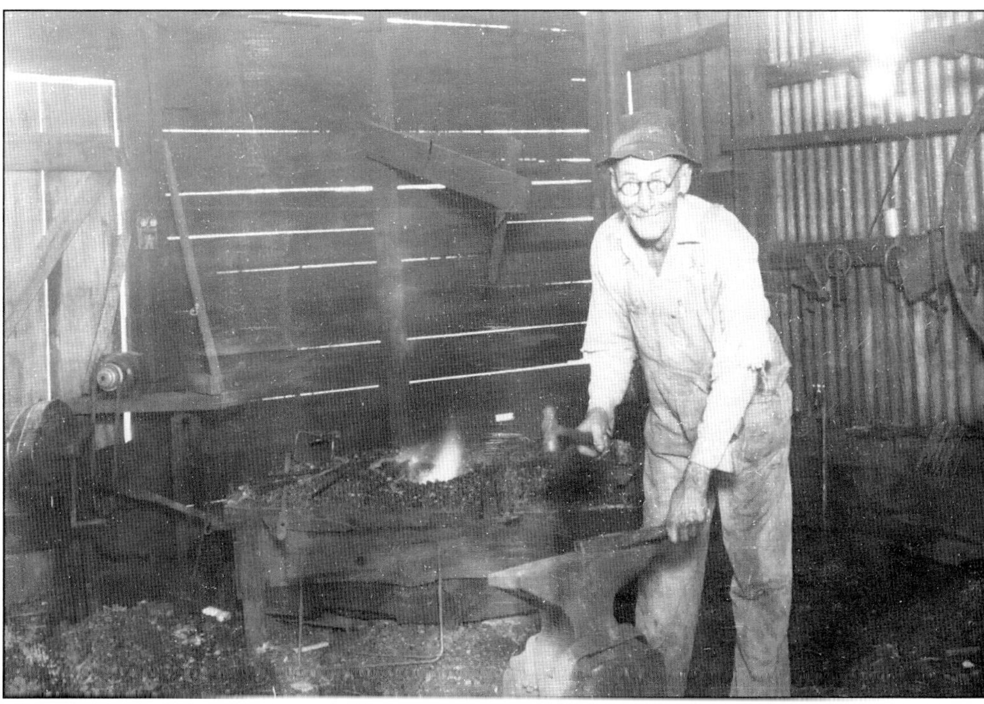

This is Josh Woods's Blacksmith Shop, located in Summit, as it appeared in the early 1900s.

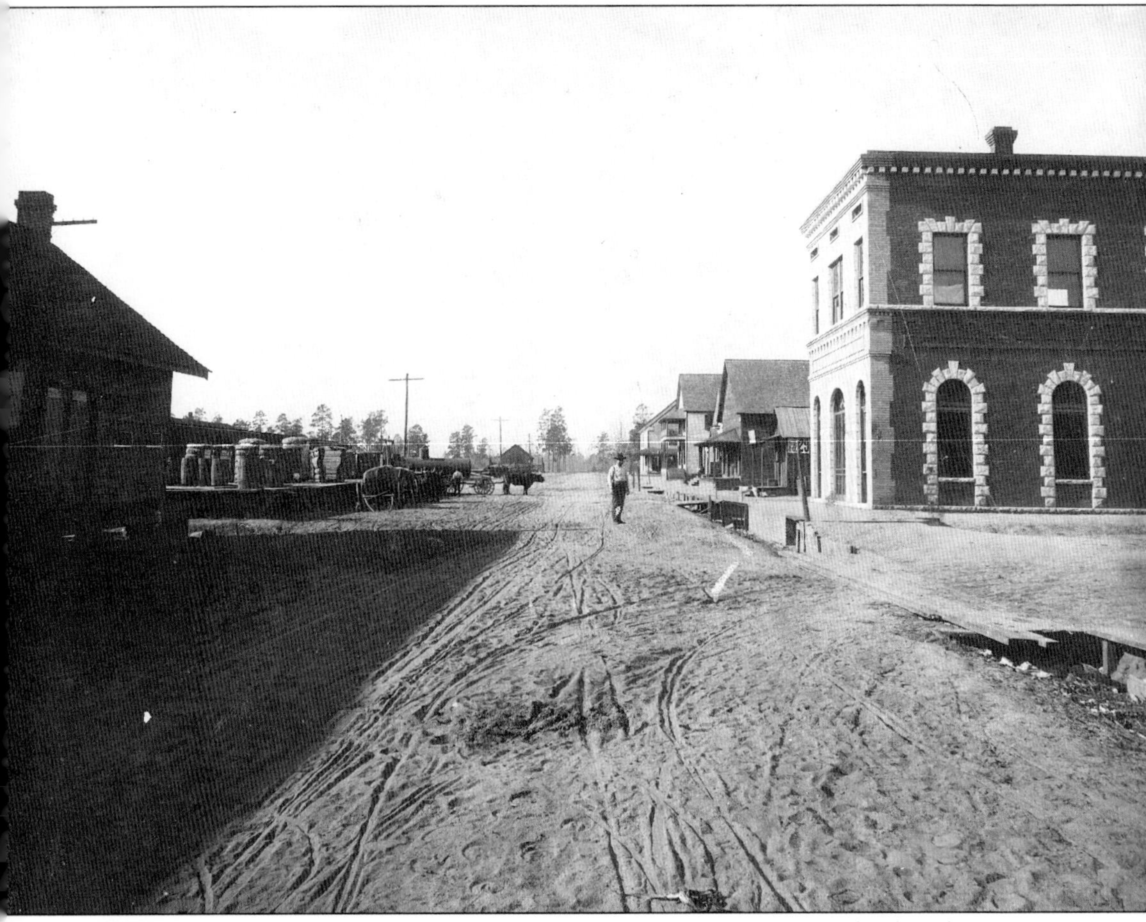

Shown here is downtown Summit as it appeared in the early 1900s. Jott Flanders, former county ordinary, is standing in the middle of the street in front of the Peoples Bank where he worked. At the railroad depot on the left a steam boiler is being loaded on a wagon drawn by a brace of oxen. The bank building is still there.

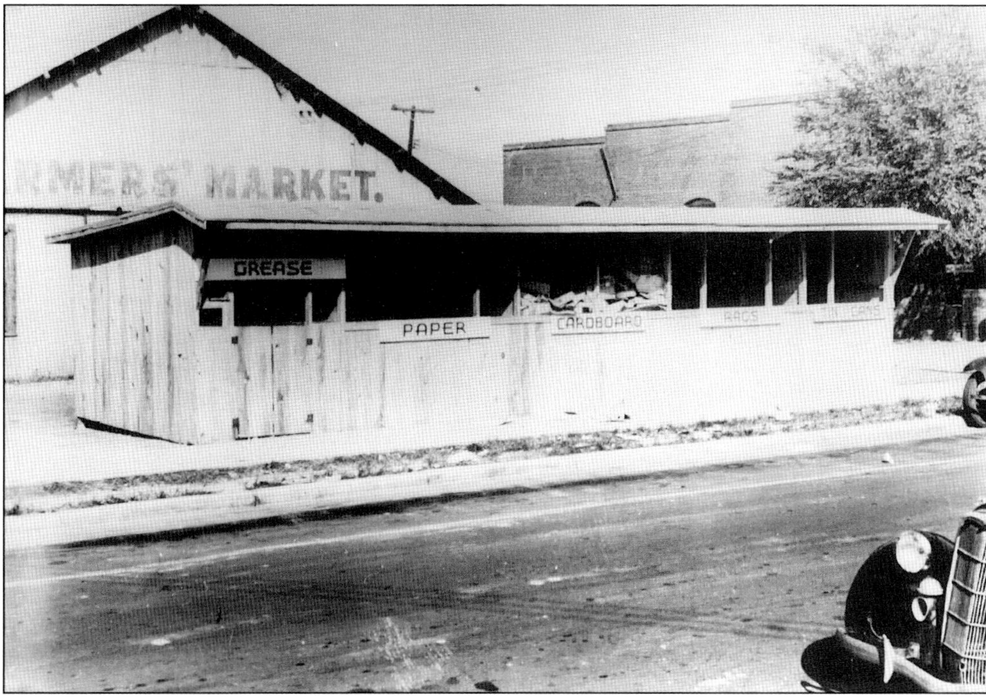

Recycling is not just a recent phenomenon. During WW II, scrap drives were organized for the war effort. Pictured is the collection center on the Boneyard facing South Green Street.

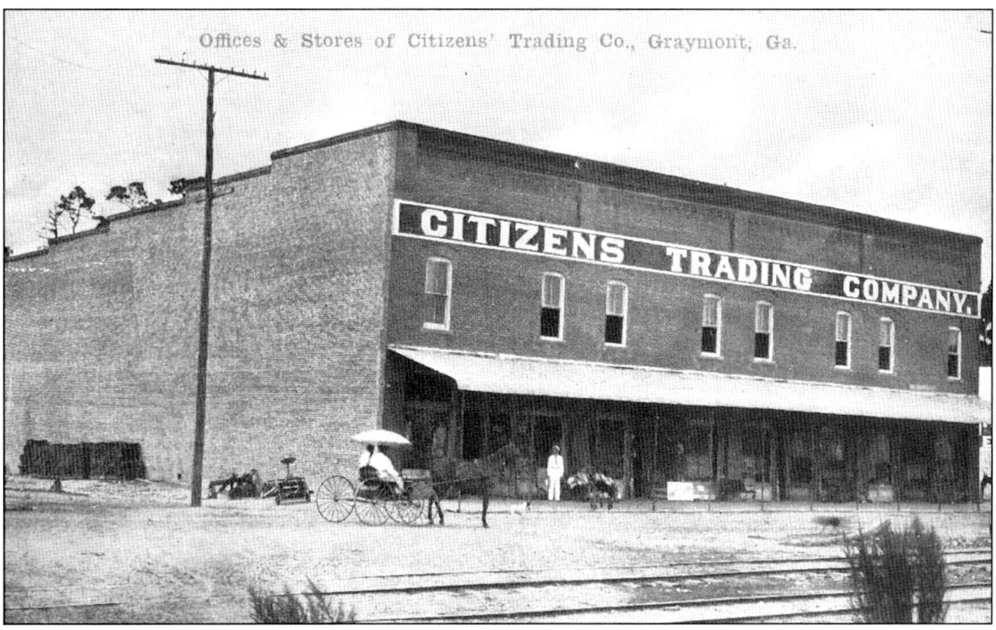

Citizen's Trading Company in Graymont, constructed in 1904, was a large general merchandise store handling everything from "cribs to caskets." It was owned by the Durden Brothers, Math, Dennis, and Frank. It is now occupied by the Twin City Manufacturing Company.

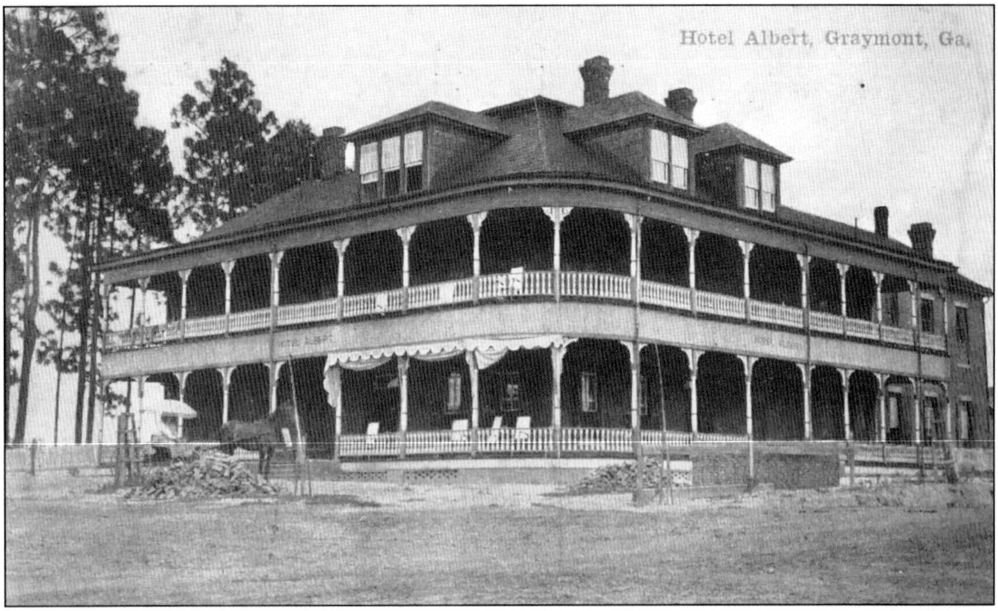

Hotel Albert in Graymont, named after Albert Neal Durden, was constructed about 1900 by his sons Dennis and Math Durden. Located on what is now the southeast corner of Fifth and Elm Streets in Twin City, the building burned in 1937.

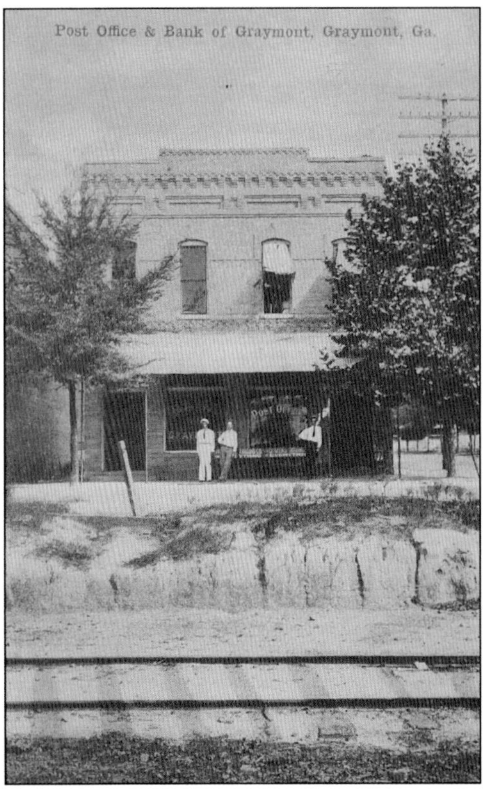

The post office and bank of Graymont was incorporated on April 27, 1901, by W.M. Durden, D.B. Durden, Joe A. Durden, Allen Jones, and J.A. Jones. Note the Millen & Southwestern Railroad tracks in the foreground.

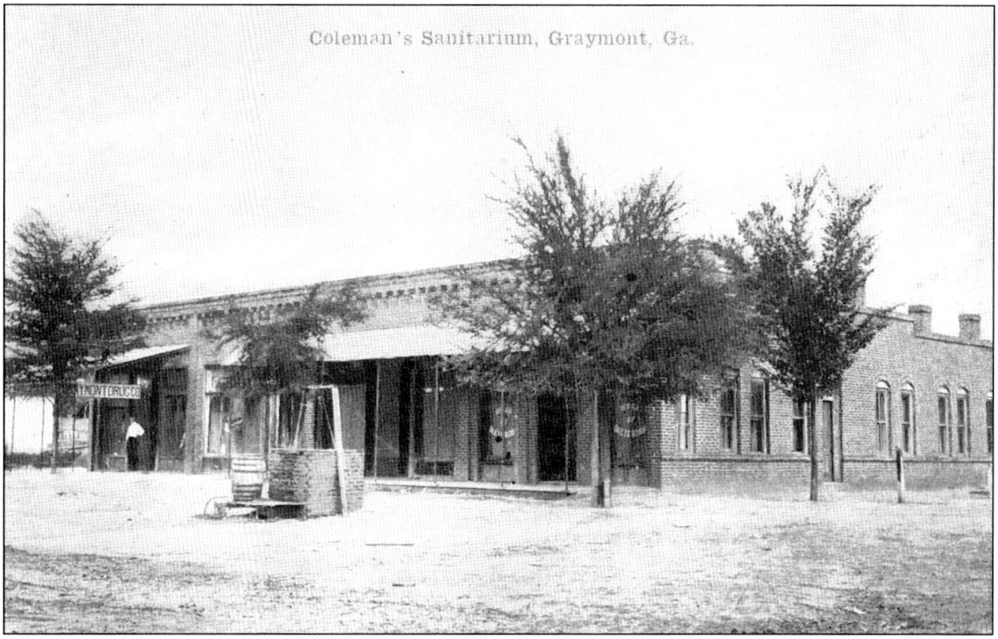

Coleman's Sanitarium and Graymont Drug Company in Graymont was opened in 1904 by Dr. Edward T. Coleman (1/20/1863–9/18/1929). It was said to be the first clinic in the area.

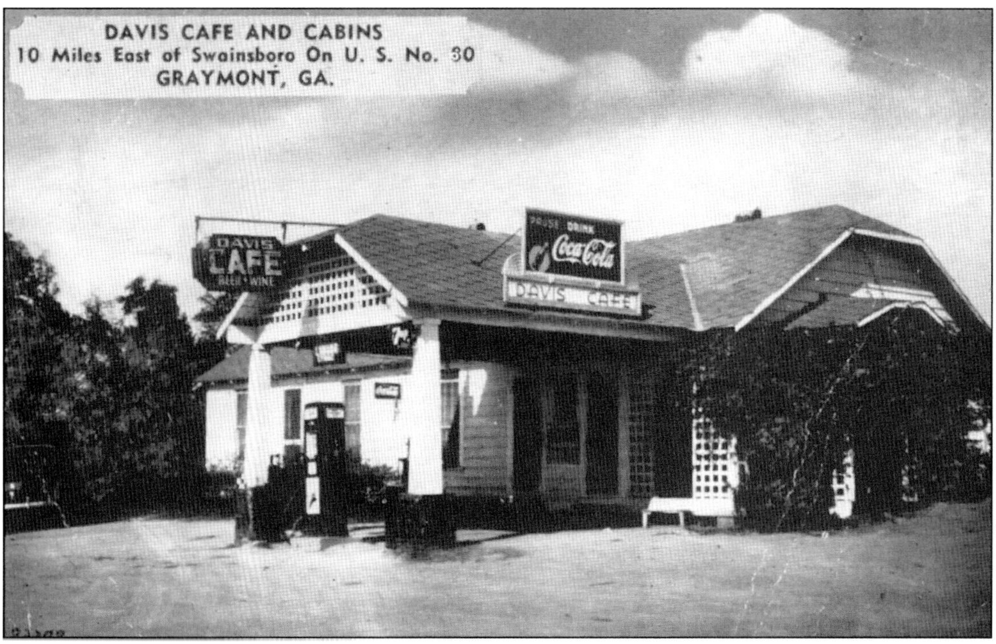

Davis Cafe and Cabins, in Graymont, was operated by Mr. and Mrs. Ray Davis. The building is still located at the northwest corner of U.S. 80 and Georgia 192 in Twin City.

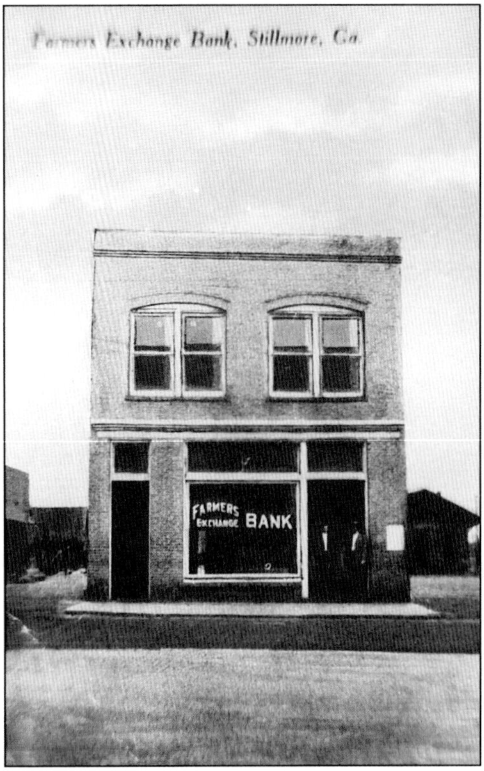

The Farmers' Exchange Bank, in Stillmore, was incorporated on May 26, 1910 by John D. Walker, J.C. Trafmell, Dr. R.E. Graham, E.H. Heath, J.I. Warren, W.D. Bell, and John Durden.

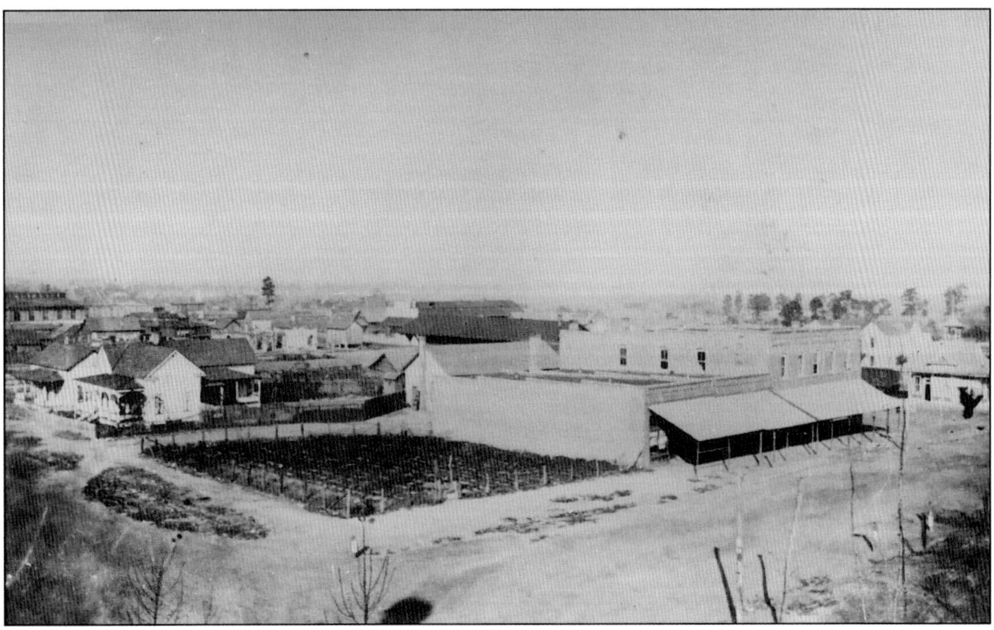

This is Stillmore as shown from above, about 1910.

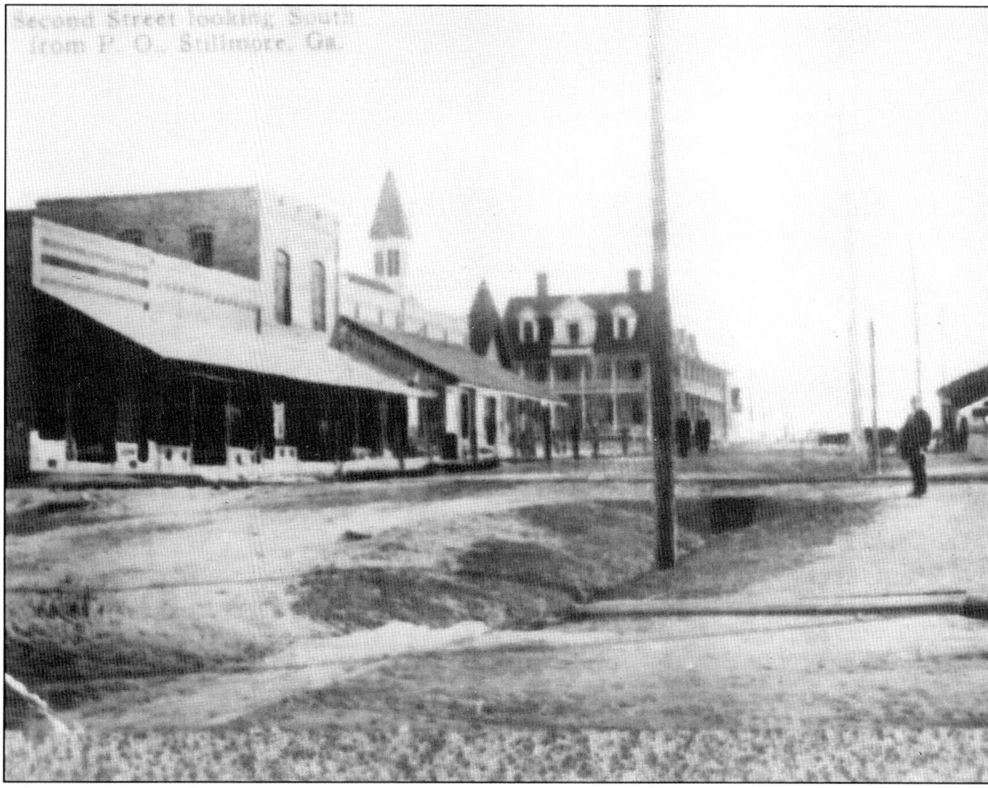

This is a view of Second Street in Stillmore, looking south from the post office, with the Canoochee Hotel at the far end of the block.

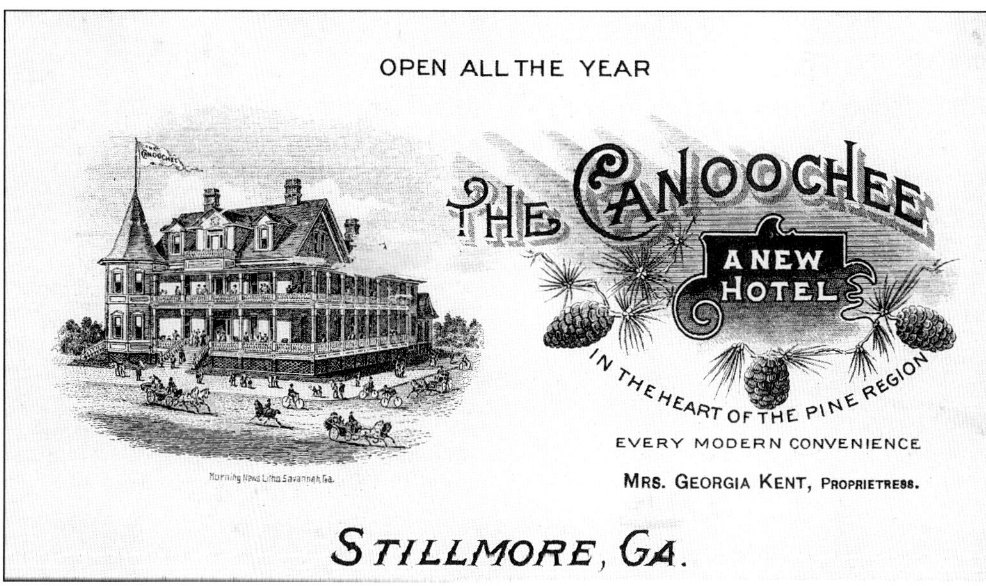

Shown here is a visitor's card advertising the Canoochee Hotel in Stillmore.

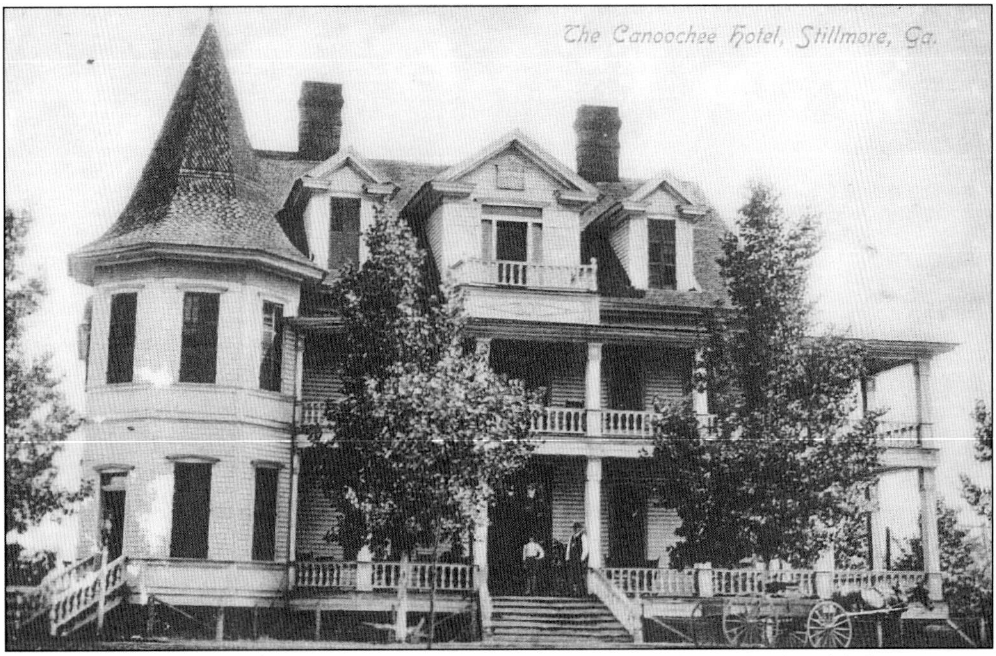

The Canoochee Hotel, Stillmore, was famous over a large area for its food and lodging. It was reported that guests would come by train from as far as 50 miles away for a one-day trip to enjoy a meal.

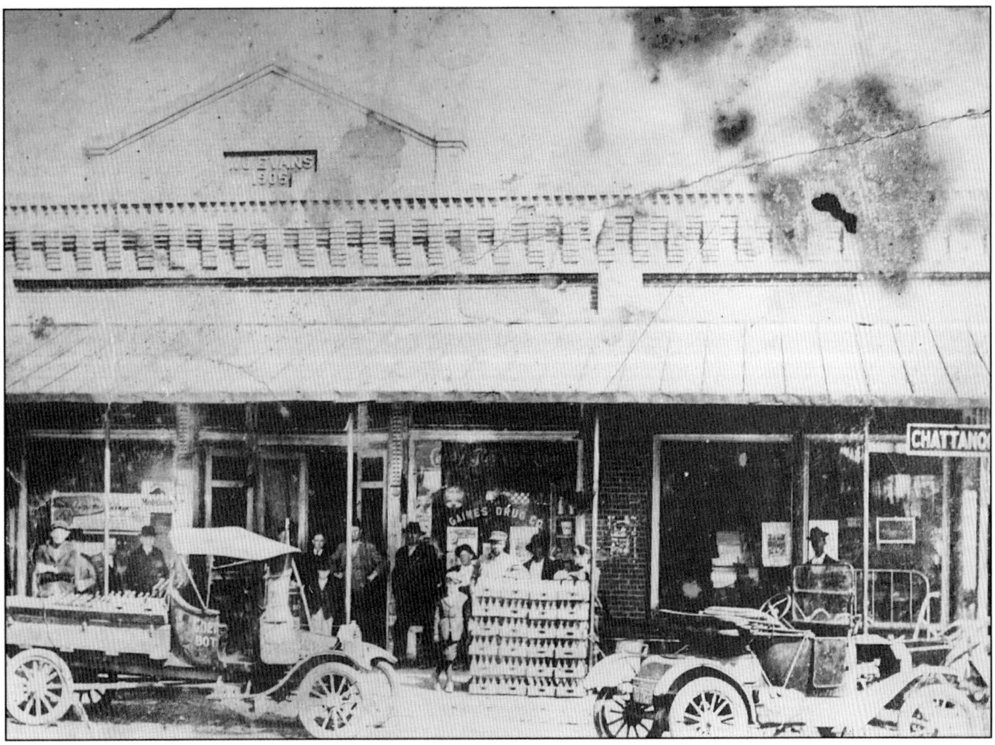

A Stillmore Street Scene, taken about 1915, shows a Cheericola Truck making a delivery to Gaines Drug Company.

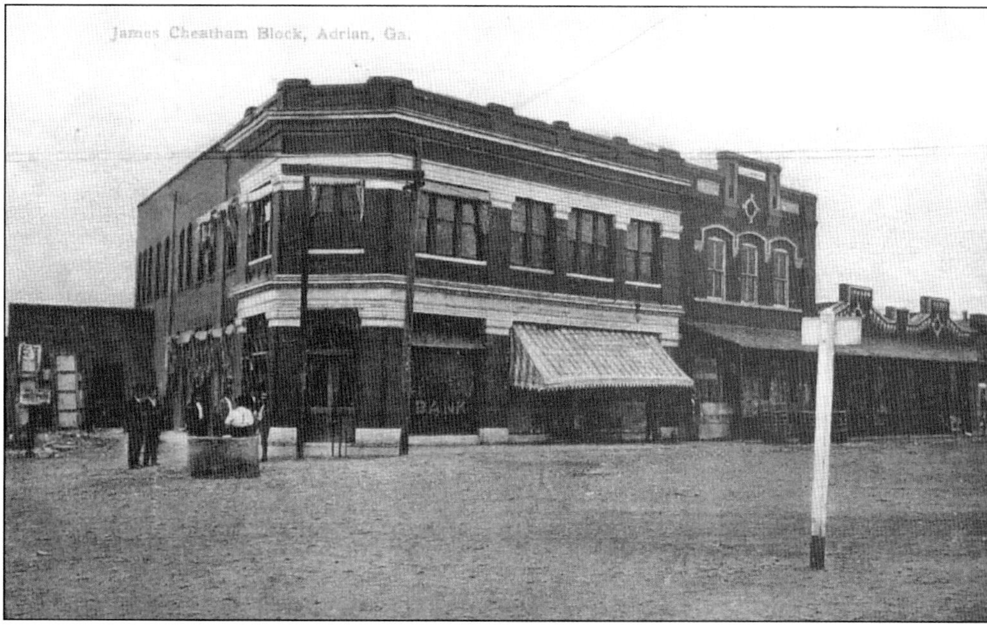

The James Cheatham Block, in Adrian, named for Capt. T.J. James and Tom Cheatham, was constructed in 1902 and 1904. It housed the Farmers' Bank, incorporated December 21, 1902, on the corner, and at one time, Yarbrough Furniture, T.J. James Drugs, and a general store.

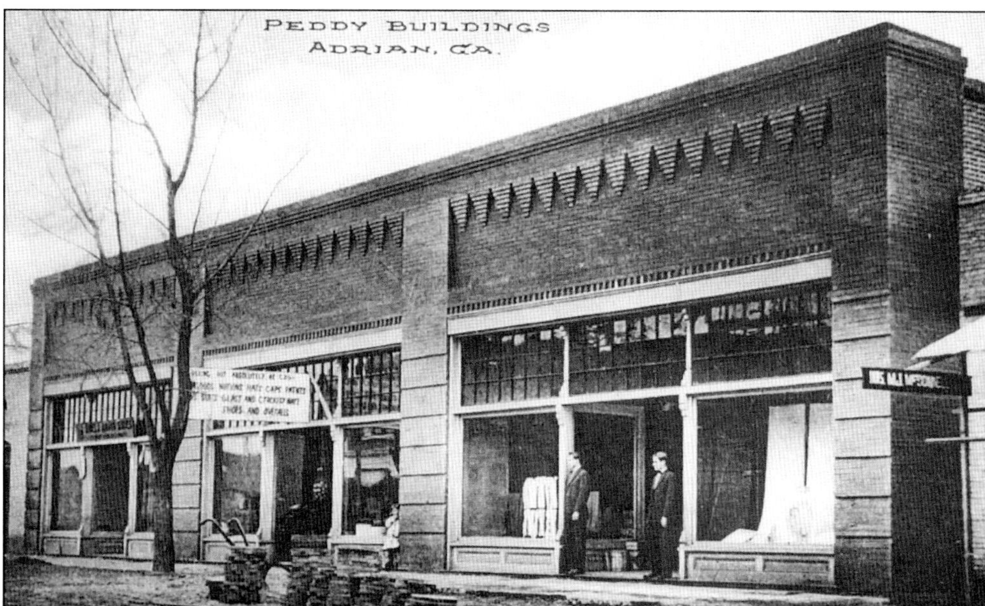

At the Peddy Buildings, in Adrian, a sign over the door said, "Closing out, absolutely at cash. Dry Goods, notions, hats, caps,—glass and crockery, shoes and overalls."

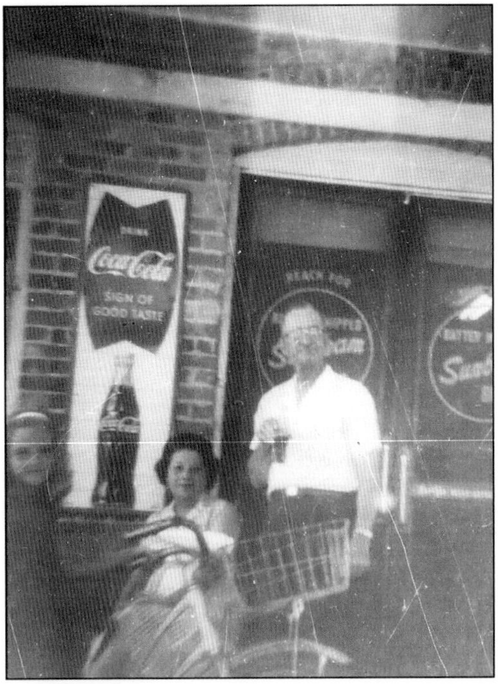

Mr. and Mrs. John H. Moore and granddaughter Melanie are pictured in front of Mr. Moore's store in Nunez. The building, built in 1904 as a Masonic lodge, was occupied as a general store several years later. Mr. Moore acquired sole ownership of the business in 1925 and operated it until he passed away in 1975. It reopened in 1980 and closed permanently in 1983.

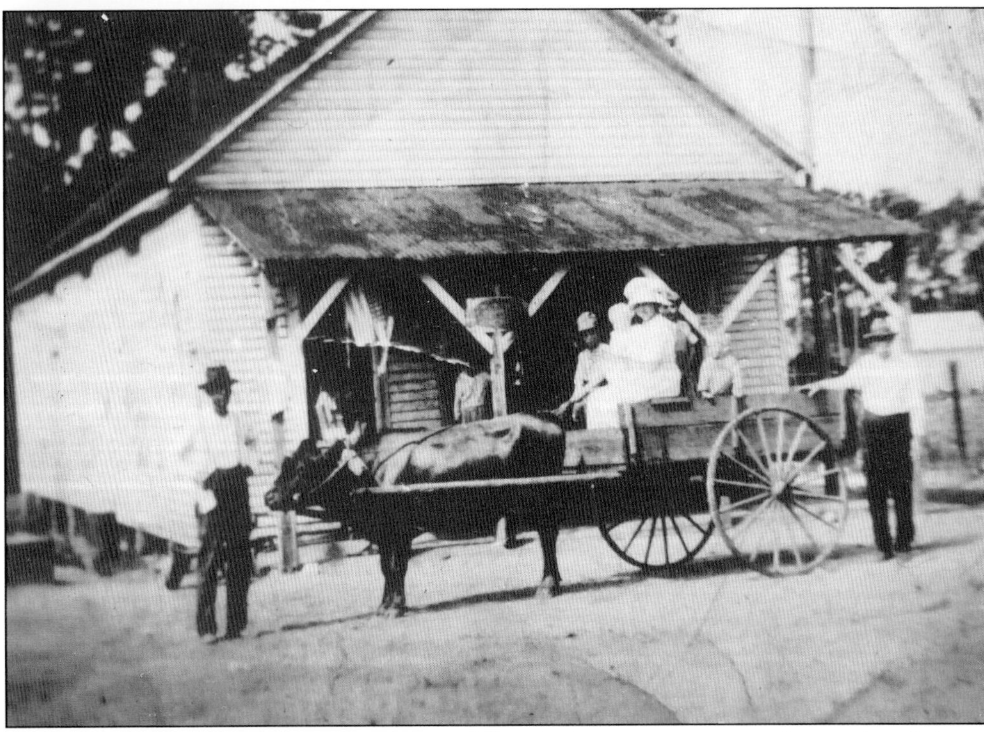

The Ebb Rountree Store was located in McLeod, Georgia, a town with a railroad depot, turpentine still, and this store. The town, largely destroyed by a tornado on May 2, 1929, was located on the present Highway 47 south of Swainsboro (Stillmore Road) near the junction of Mt. Shady Church Road.

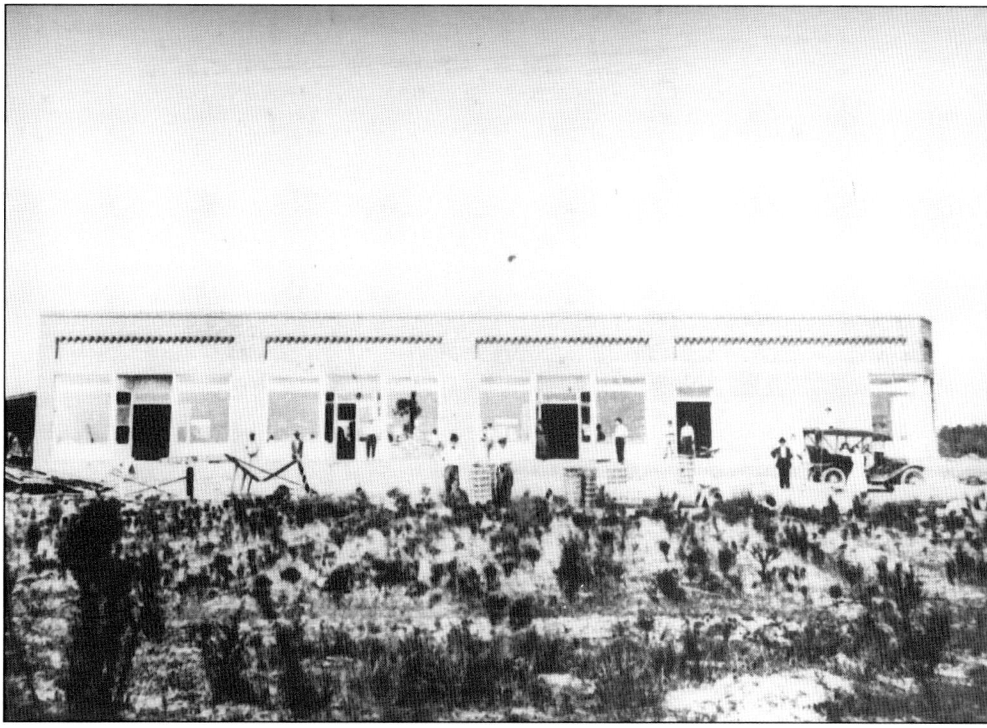

Nunez Mall, constructed about 1910, housed a bank and three storefronts. Nothing remains of that building at present. Among those standing in front are G.A. Fountain Sr. and Will Clark.

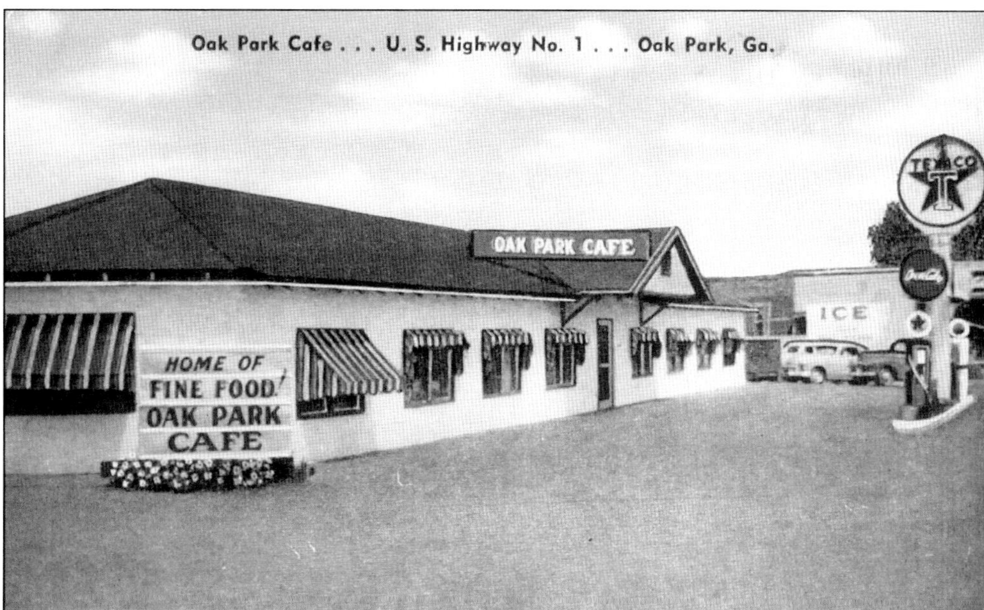

Shown here is the Oak Park Cafe, in Oak Park, Georgia.

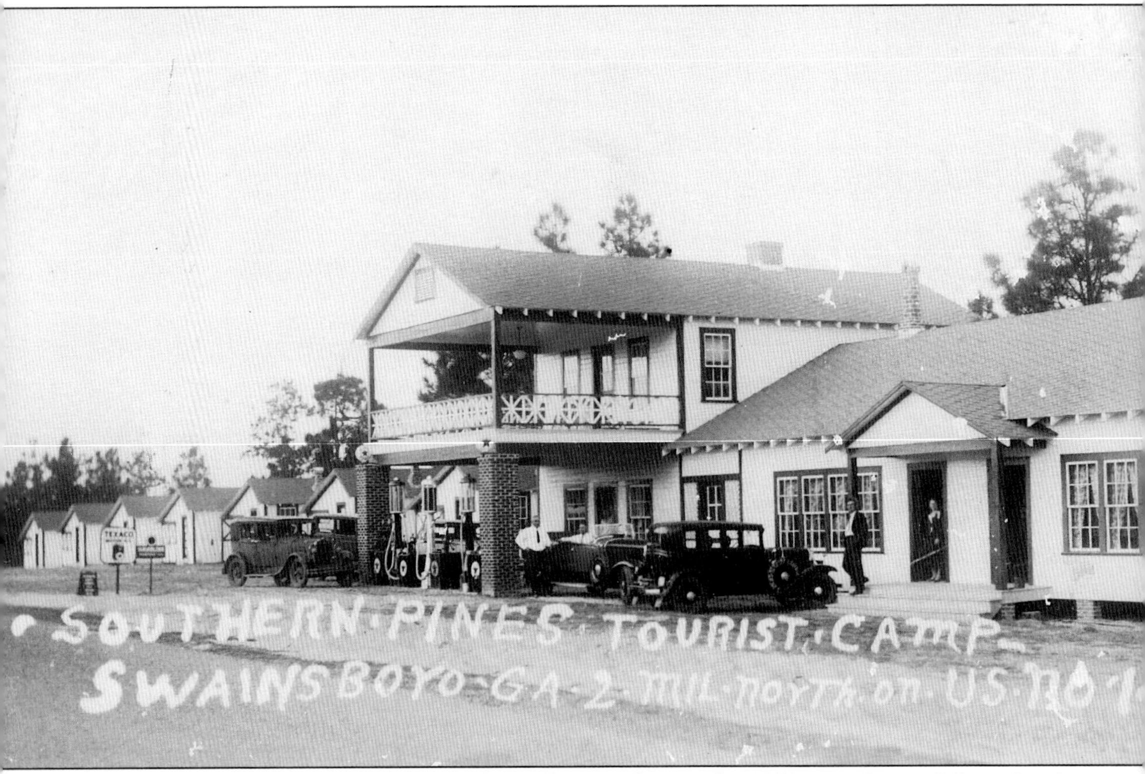

Southern Pines Tourist Camp, a popular gathering place in the 1930s, was located about 2 miles north of Swainsboro. Many civic clubs met there regularly.

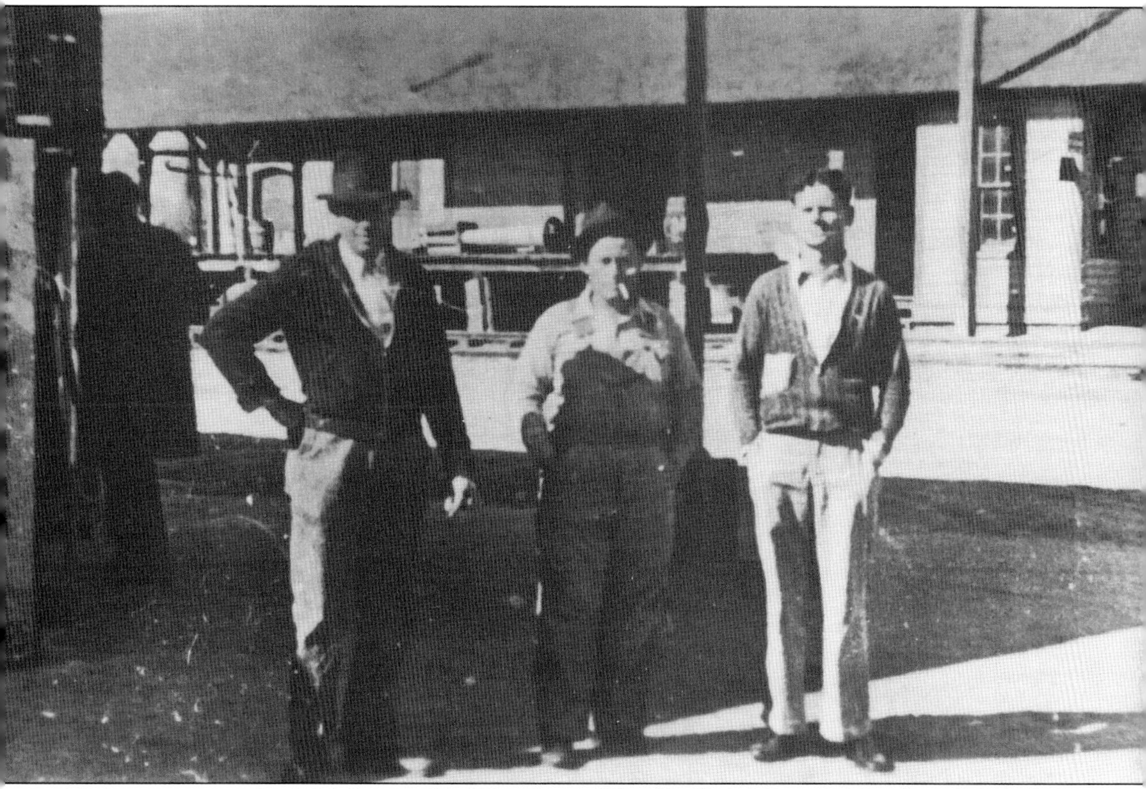

This is a scene in Garfield showing Ted Daughtry, Whit Wall, and Counsel Stephens. Note the railroad depot in the center of town.

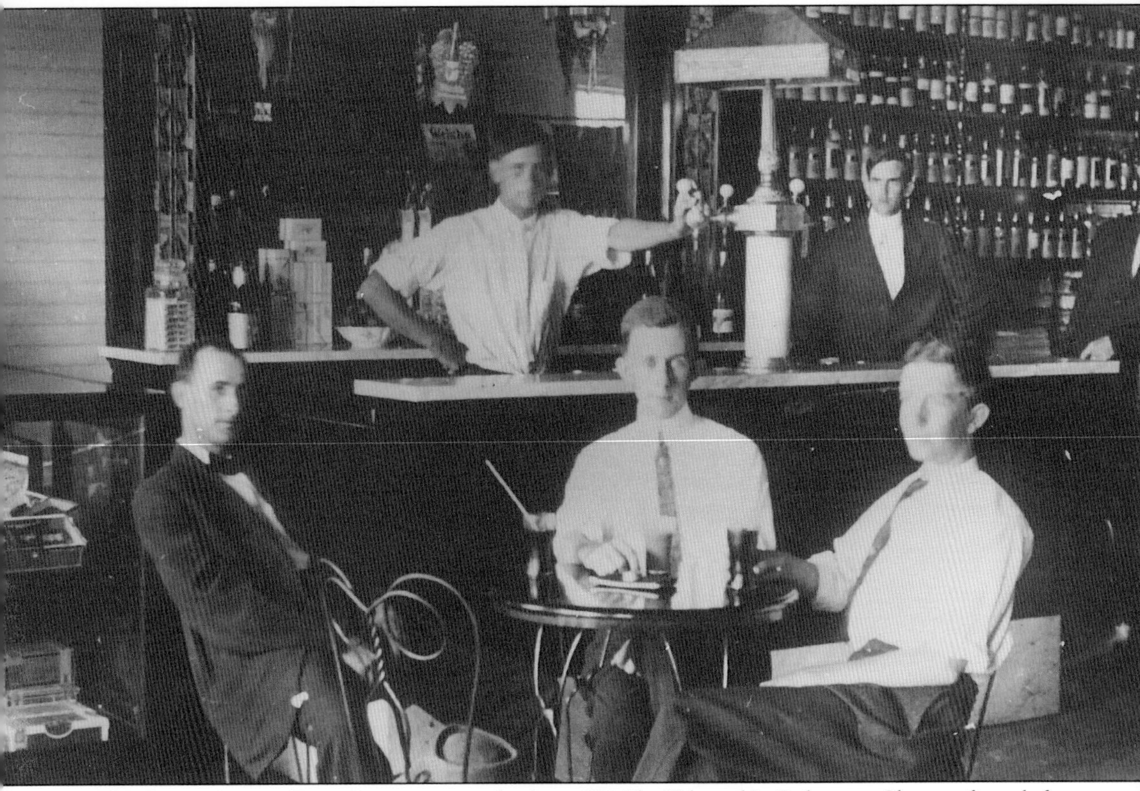

The Summertown Drug Company was built in 1914 by Edward L.Coleman. Shown, from left to right, are: (seated) Dr. David LaGroan, W.T. Adams, and Walle Snellgrove; (standing) Barney Johnson and Mr. Coleman. The building burned in 1960.

Three

Where We Went to School and Church

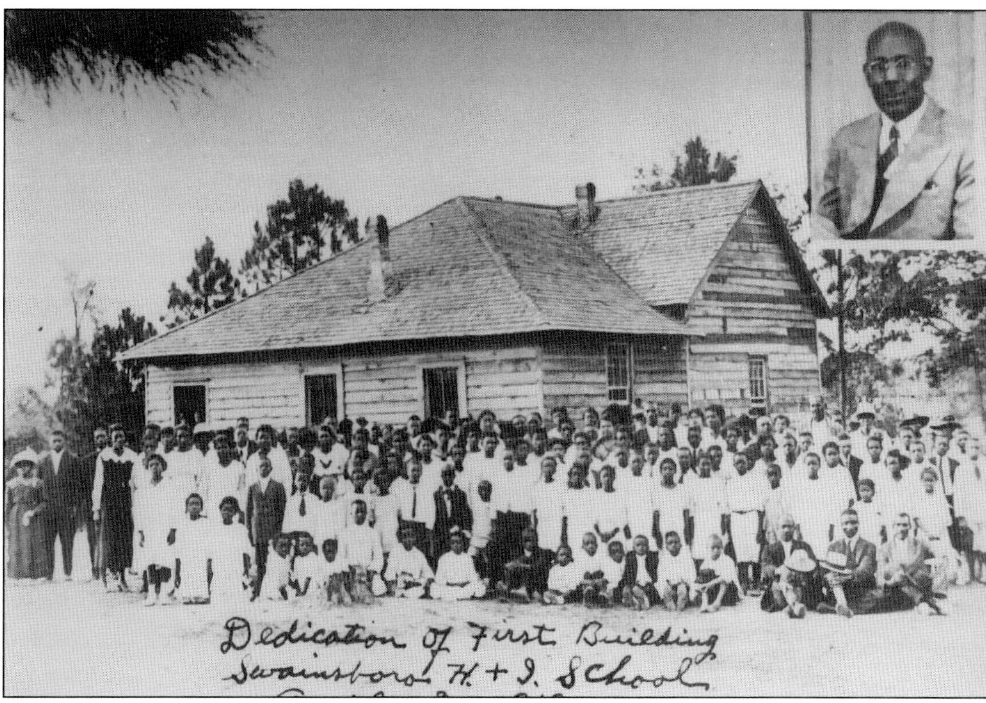

The dedication of Swainsboro High and Industrial School, Swainsboro's first black school building, took place on April 2, 1918. Professor N.F. Williams, born April 2, 1890, was responsible for this and other buildings. He retired in 1955, after teaching for 53 years, 36 of them in Emanuel County.

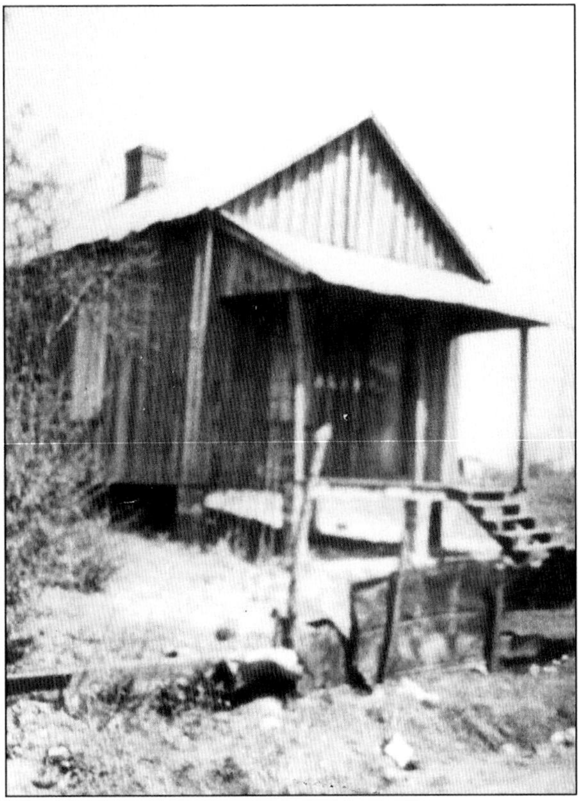

The First Black School Building, 1917, was a rented house near the present Swainsboro City Cemetery. Rented in 1916, it was used until about 1919, when a permanent school was erected. Prior to this, black children were taught in churches or the Society Hall.

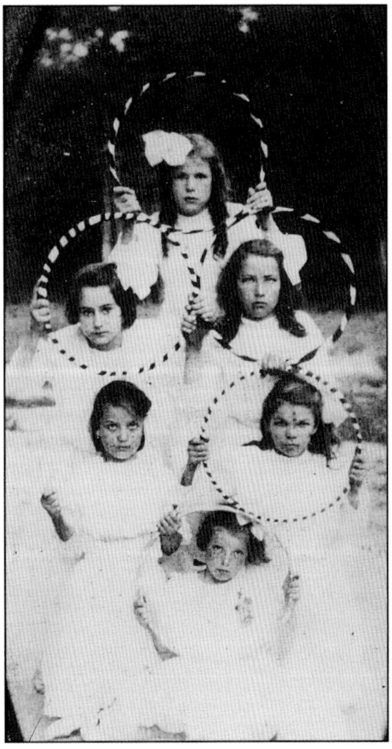

This is the closing program at Coleman Academy, about 1905. Among the girls pictured are: (front row, seated) Ollie Coleman; (middle row) Nannie Lee Turner Walling; (back row) Blanch Turner Lanier.

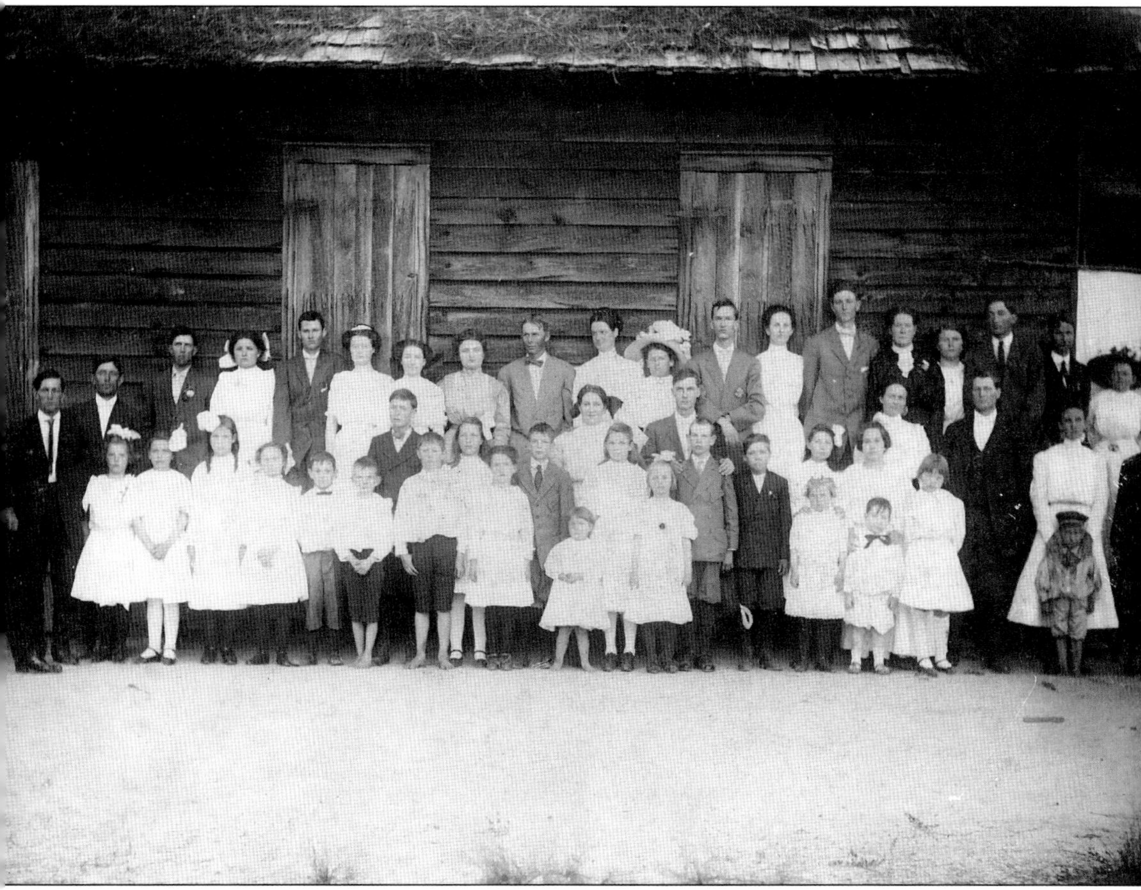

Shown here are students of Coleman Academy, about 1905. In the front row, center, are Remer Young Brinson, Annie Belle Brinson, and John Ivy Brinson. The school still stands on the corner of Lamb's Bridge Road and Old Reidsville Road.

GRADUATING EXERCISES

EMANUEL COUNTY INSTITUTE

TUESDAY EVENING JUNE 8.

8:00 O'CLOCK

Master of Ceremonies .... Lester Roberts

Invocation .... Rev. E. B. Sutton

Duet .... Inez Coleman and Jottie Rountree

The Call of the South .... Hobson Coleman

The Power of Personal Influence .... Nellie Warnock

Class History .... Terah Cowart

Piano Solo .... Deux Polonaises .... Chopin
Inez Coleman.

Naming of Tree .... Annie Belle Brinson

True Nobility .... Cary Bowie

Class Prophecy .... Cora Anderson

Class Song. The Blue and the Gold.

Last Will and Testament .... Ernest Roberts

Character and Hope .... Max Kingery

Address.

Delivery of Diplomas.

This is the Emanuel County Institute 1912 class program.

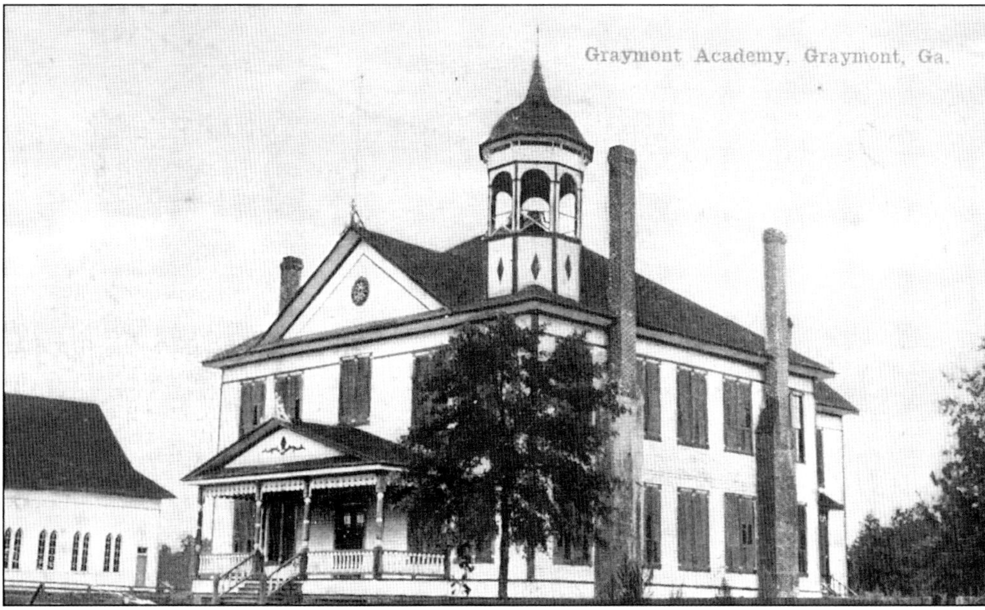

Graymont Academy, later called Emanuel County Institute, was built by Henry Luther of Snellgrove, South Carolina, on land donated by James Rountree. Completed in December 1902, classes began September 1903 with G.E. Usher as principal and Misses May Smoke, Lizzie Byrd, and Ada Bech as teachers. The building burned in 1954.

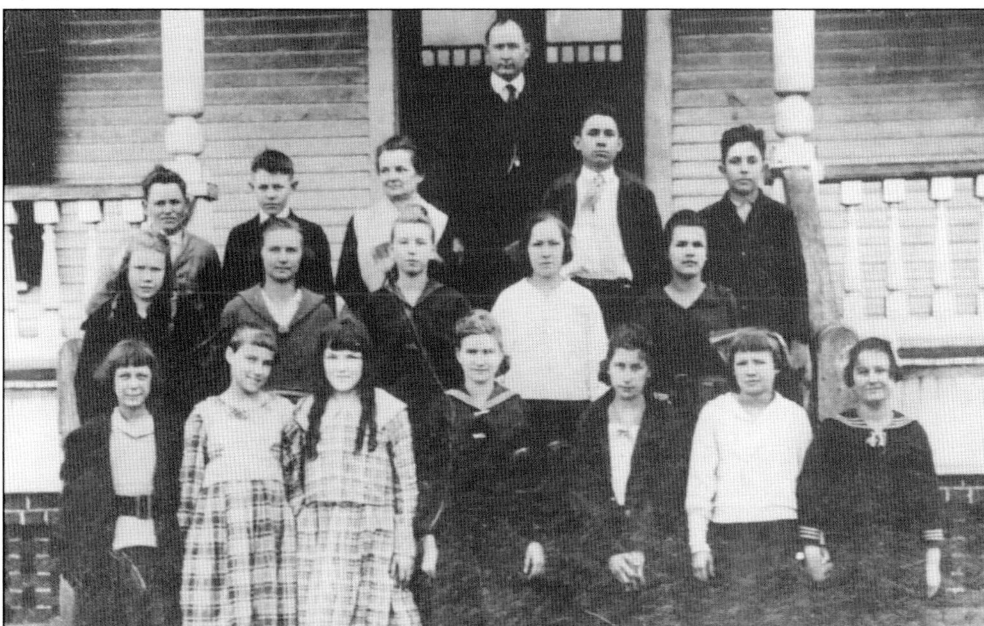

The students of the Seventh Grade Class of 1920, Emanuel County Institute, in Graymont-Summit, are shown here. From left to right are: (front row) Myrtle Weatherford, Josie Aaron, Bonnie New Anderson, Susie Brown, Hortense Roberts, Lillian Morgan, and Lorita Boatright; (middle row) Nadine Hooks, Kathleen Kent, Idel Durden, and Mildred Hooks; (back row) unidentified, Thomas James Cowart, Teacher Dump Lane, Superintendent Earnest Anderson, Horace Samples, and John Giddon Boatright.

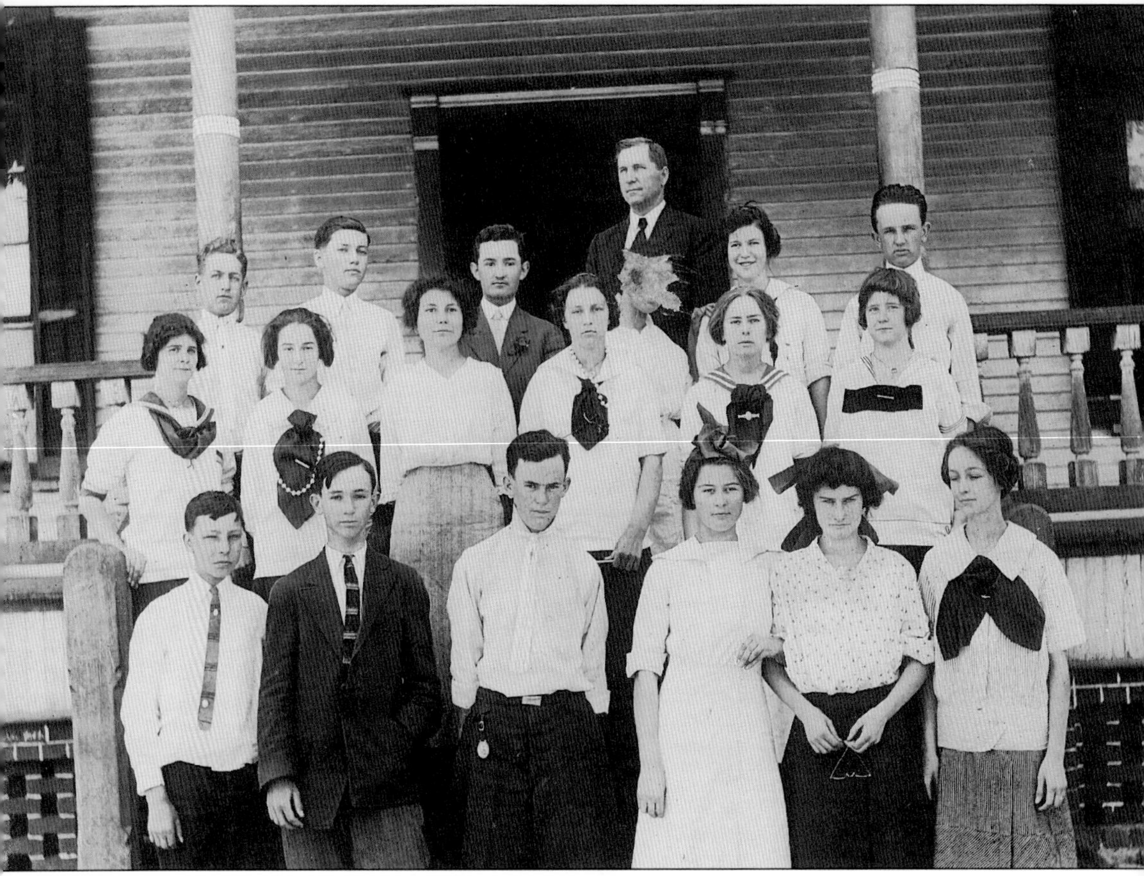

This is the Emanuel County Institute 1912 class picture.

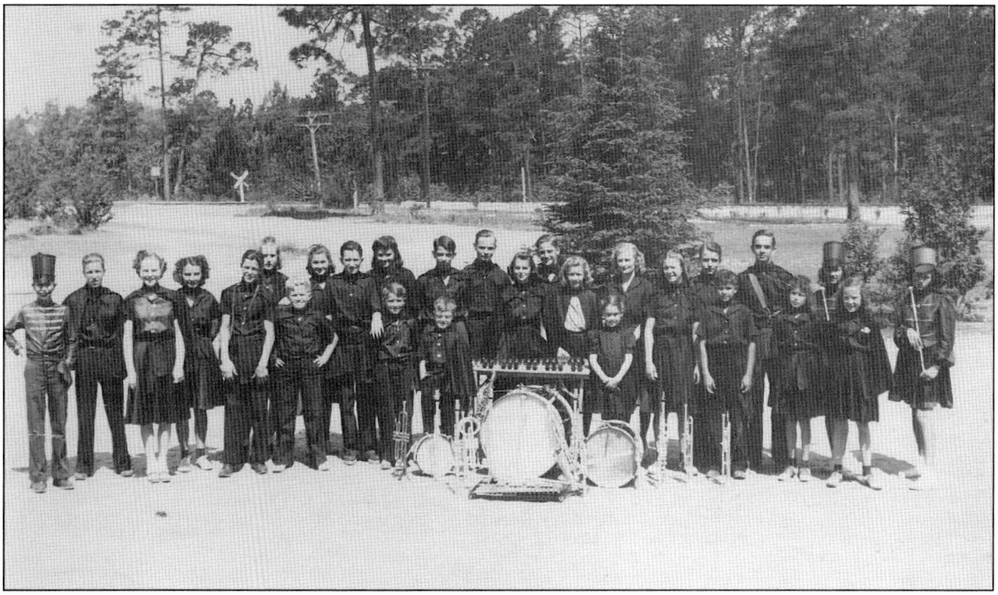

The ECI Band of 1942 posed for this photograph. From left to right are: Remer Brinson, Edwin Coleman, Betty "Pete" Hall, Betty Brown, "Jiggs" Rountree, Mary Hall, Hal Waters, Janice Carmack, Robert Watson, unidentified, unidentified, Bob Tanner, Don Durden, Harold Watson, Helen Doris Proctor, Sam Smith, unidentified, Lydia Higginbotham, Winona Carpenter (band director), Betty Lane Brinson, David Durden, Graham Woodell, Bobby Durden, Bunny Stewart, Dorothy Cumbee, Ninette Sturges, and Mary Anne Bishop.

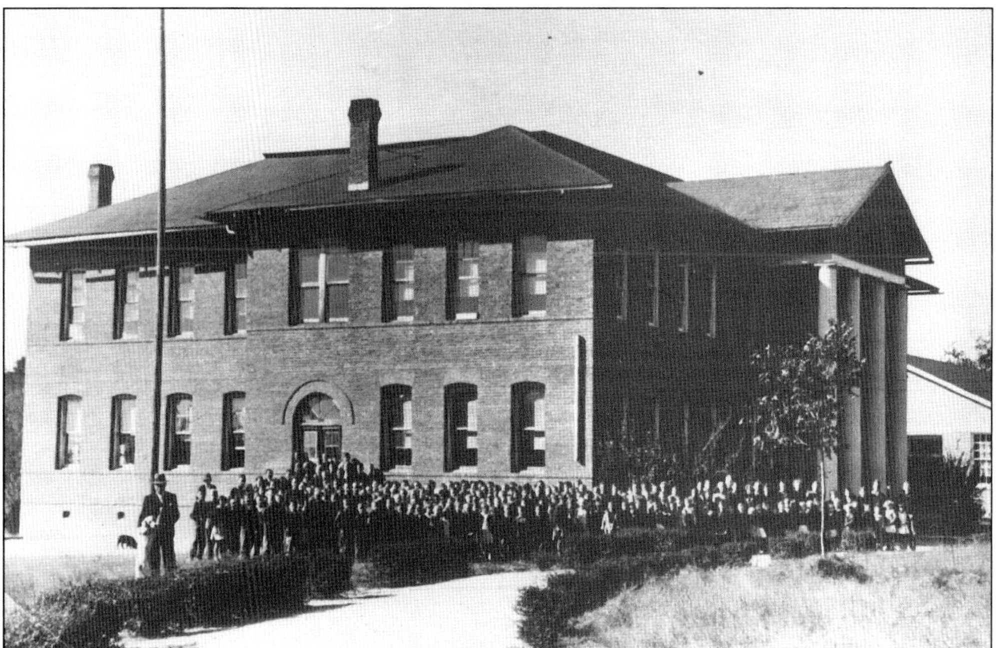

Garfield School was constructed in 1935 to replace a wooden building constructed in 1916. Directing the construction were Trustees H.H. Stewart, chairman, D.L. Bland, and C.B. Johnson. The school was merged with Emanuel County Institute in Twin City in 1962.

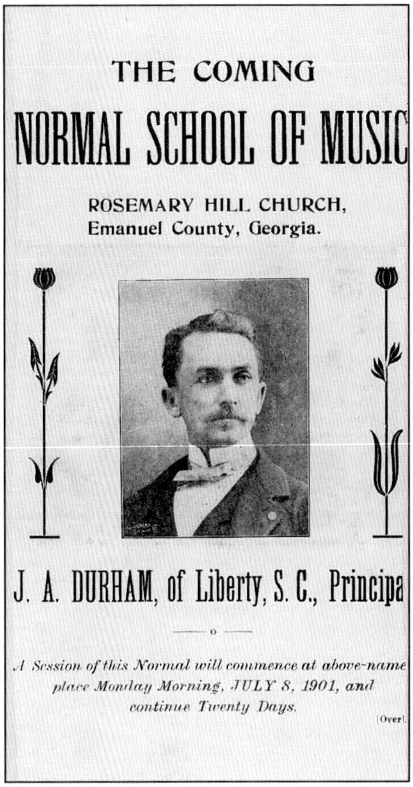

Normal School of Music at Rosemary Hill Church, 1901, was formerly in Emanuel County, and is now in Candler County. The reverse of this card states, "Good Board and Rooms with excellent families, $8.00 for the term; tuition, $2.00 per scholar."

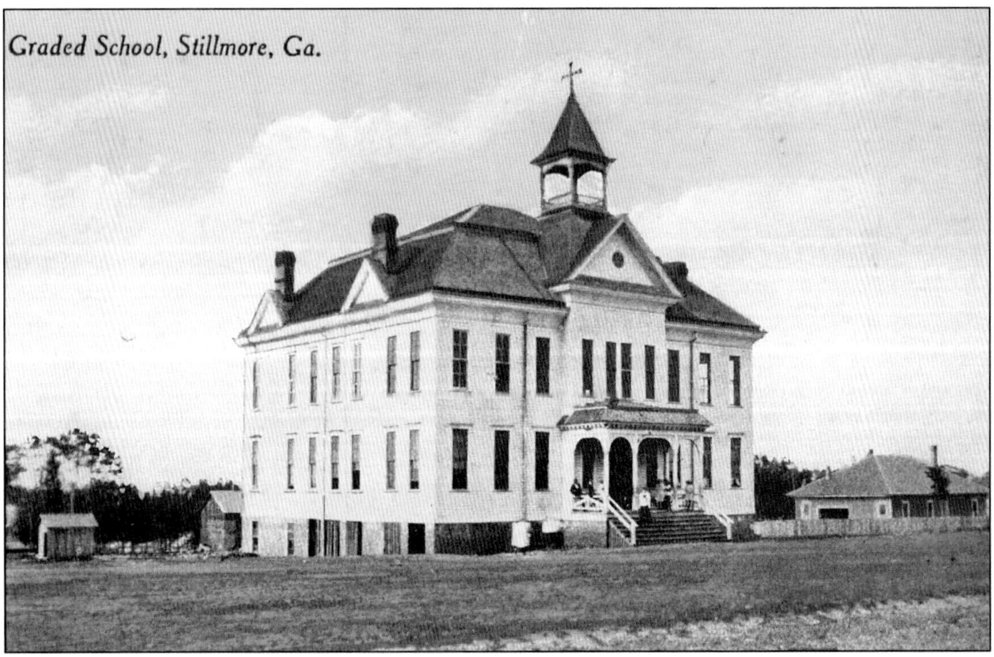

This is the Graded School in Stillmore, Georgia. The notation on the back of the card states it was destroyed by fire on December 15, 1915.

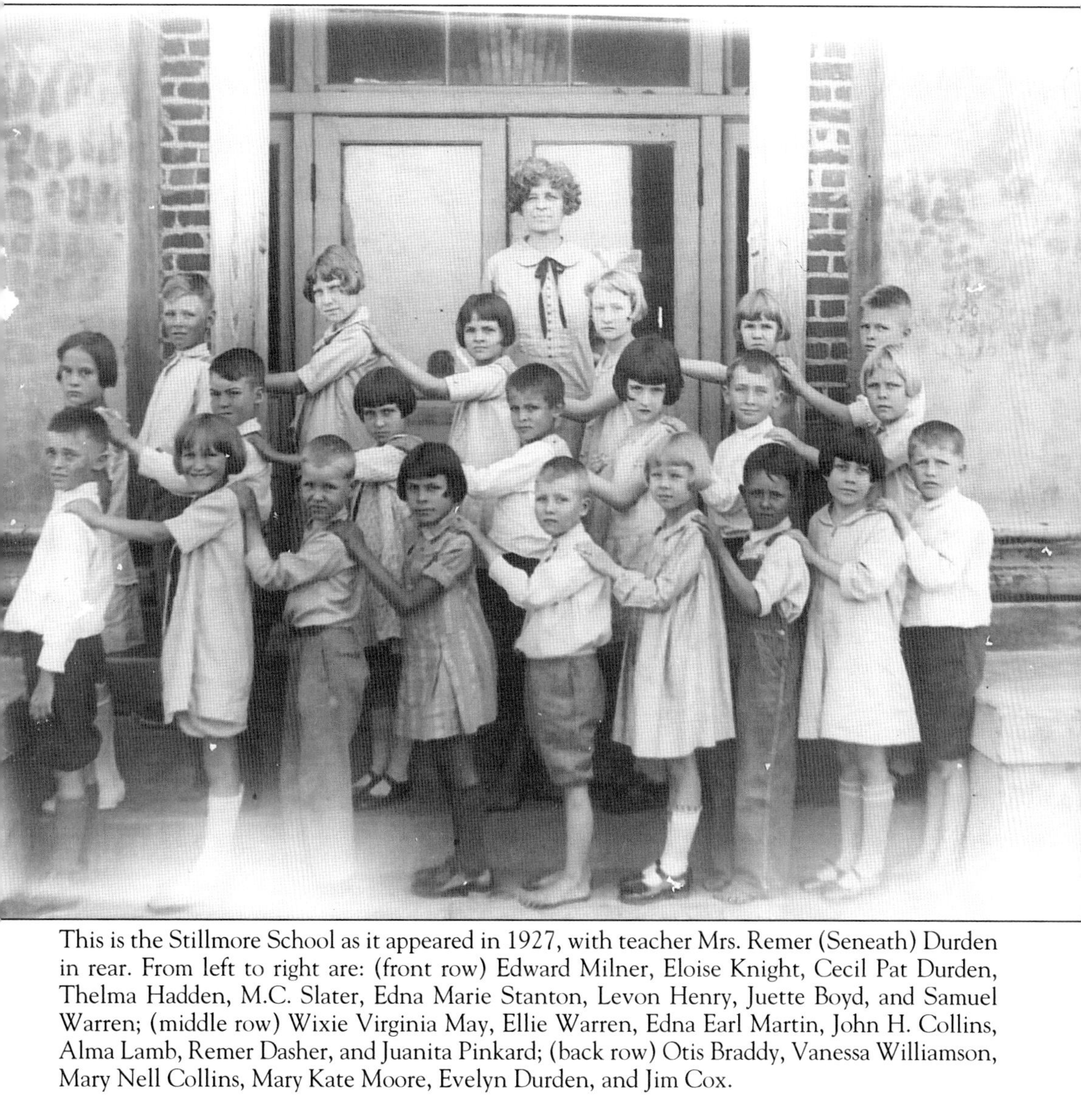

This is the Stillmore School as it appeared in 1927, with teacher Mrs. Remer (Seneath) Durden in rear. From left to right are: (front row) Edward Milner, Eloise Knight, Cecil Pat Durden, Thelma Hadden, M.C. Slater, Edna Marie Stanton, Levon Henry, Juette Boyd, and Samuel Warren; (middle row) Wixie Virginia May, Ellie Warren, Edna Earl Martin, John H. Collins, Alma Lamb, Remer Dasher, and Juanita Pinkard; (back row) Otis Braddy, Vanessa Williamson, Mary Nell Collins, Mary Kate Moore, Evelyn Durden, and Jim Cox.

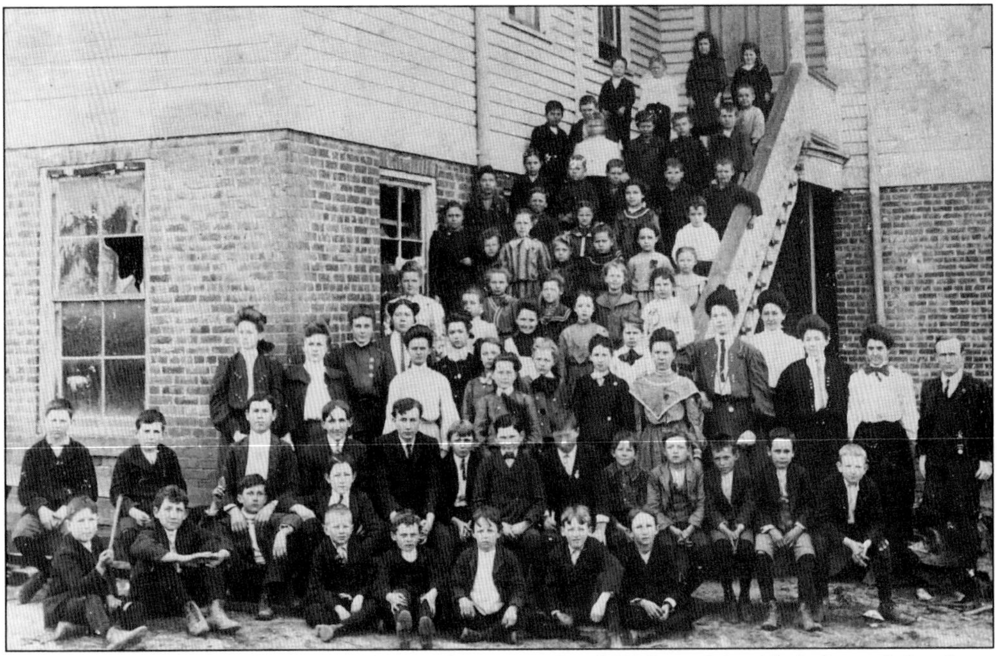

At the Stillmore School in 1907, the teachers were Prof. Wilson, Mrs. Ehrlich, and the three Gunn sisters.

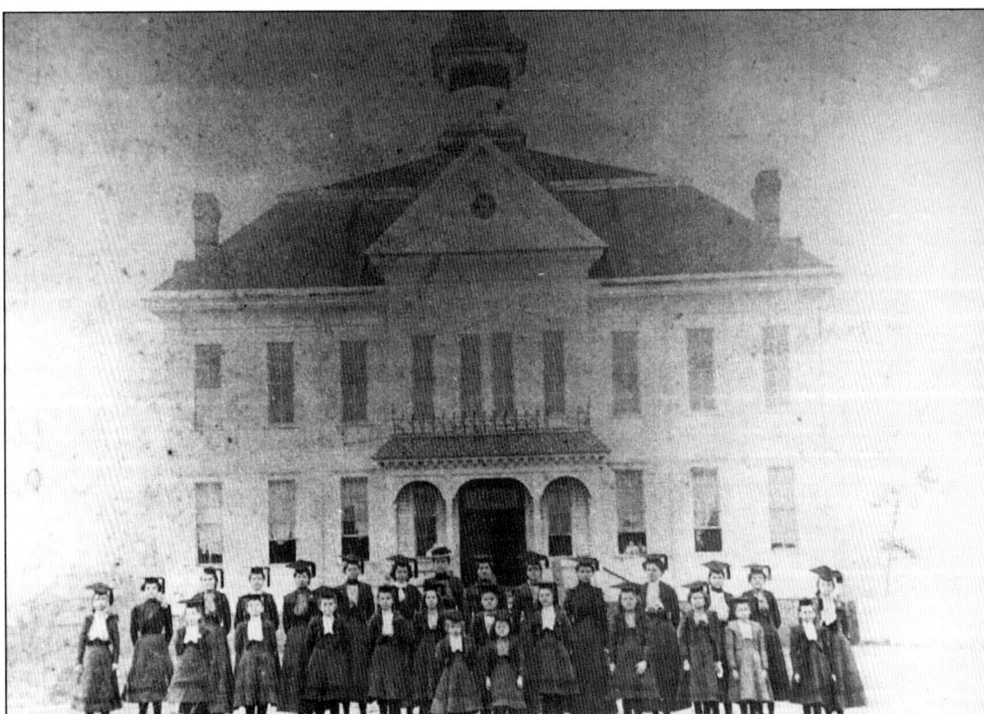

This is the gym class at the Stillmore School, about 1900.

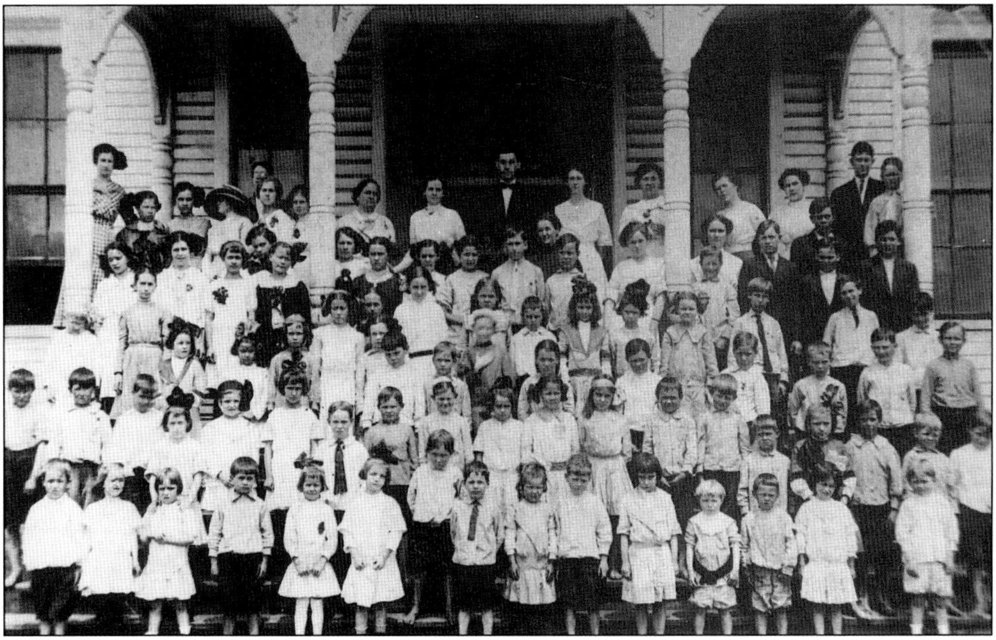

This is the Stillmore School, 1912–13, showing Prof. Twiggs's class.

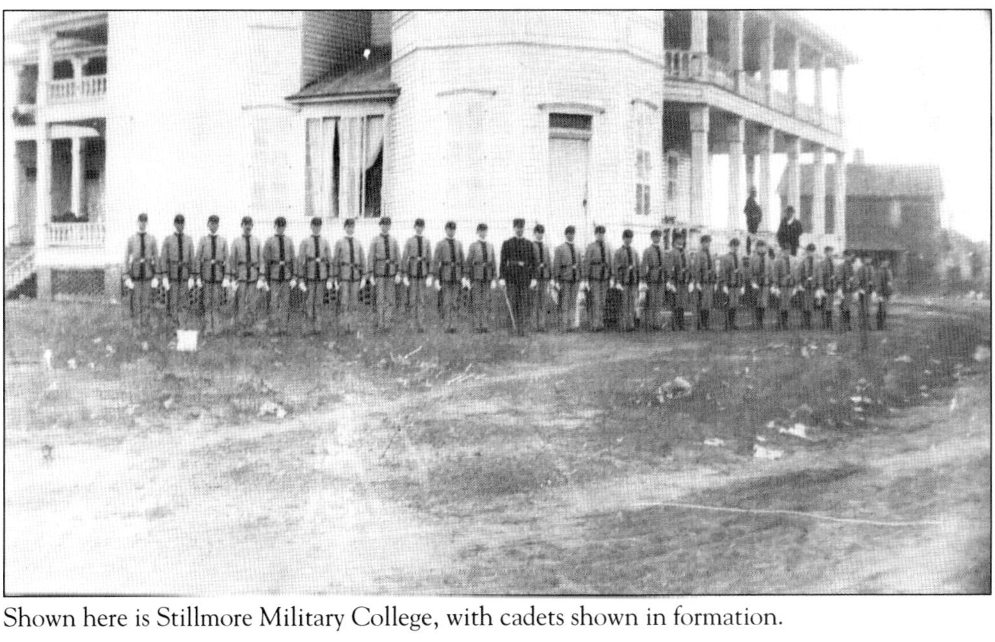

Shown here is Stillmore Military College, with cadets shown in formation.

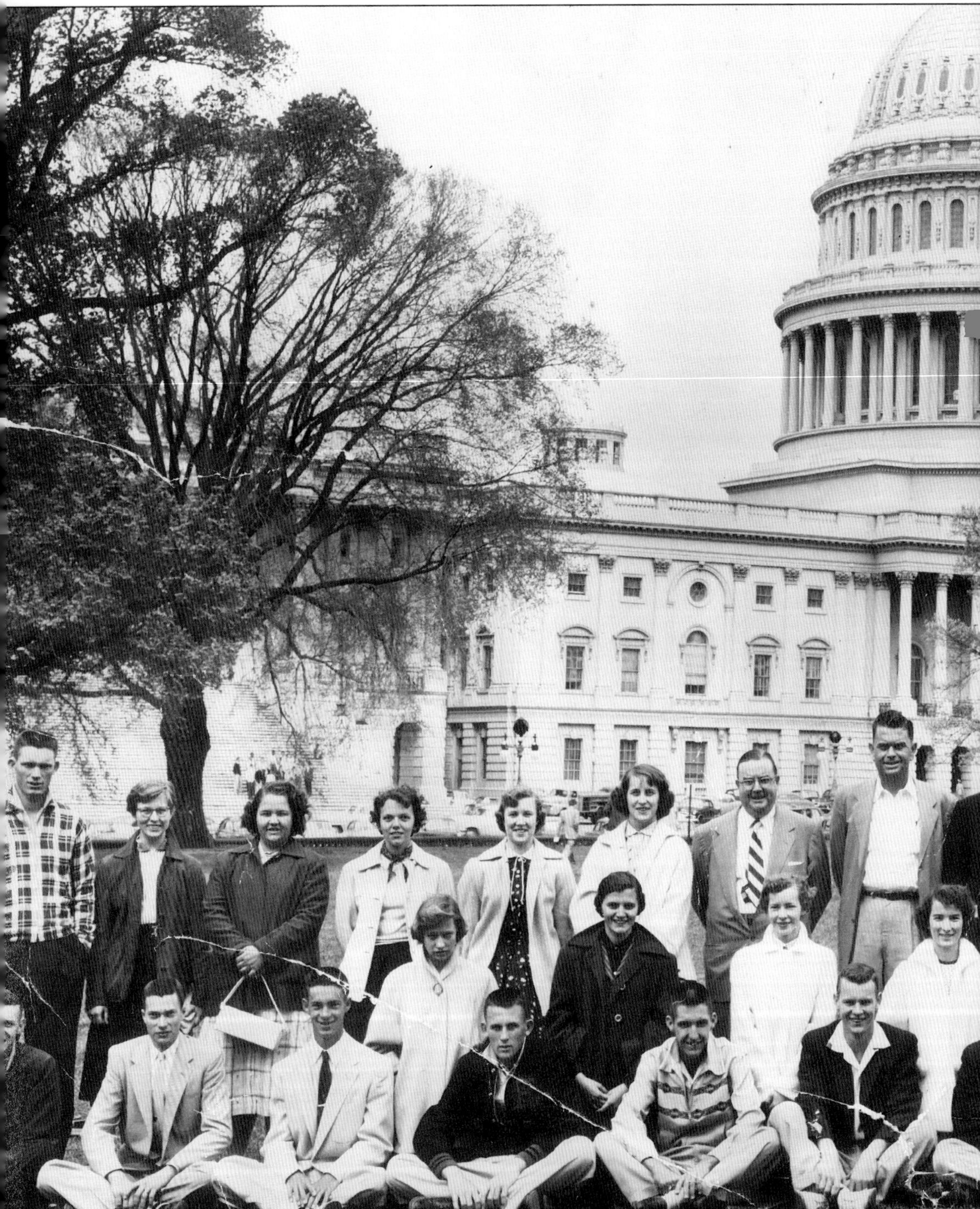

The Emanuel County Institute, class of 1955, posed for this picture. From left to right are: (front row) Luther Bell, C.L. Goodman, Lester Neal, Graham Phillips, Gene Gay, Donald Elkins, Jim Pritchard, Jerry Warren, Jim Cowart, Edward Ellington, David Rowland, Billy Cowart, and Ray Roberson; (middle row) Mary Frances Sutton, Joan Watson, Ann Coleman, Martha

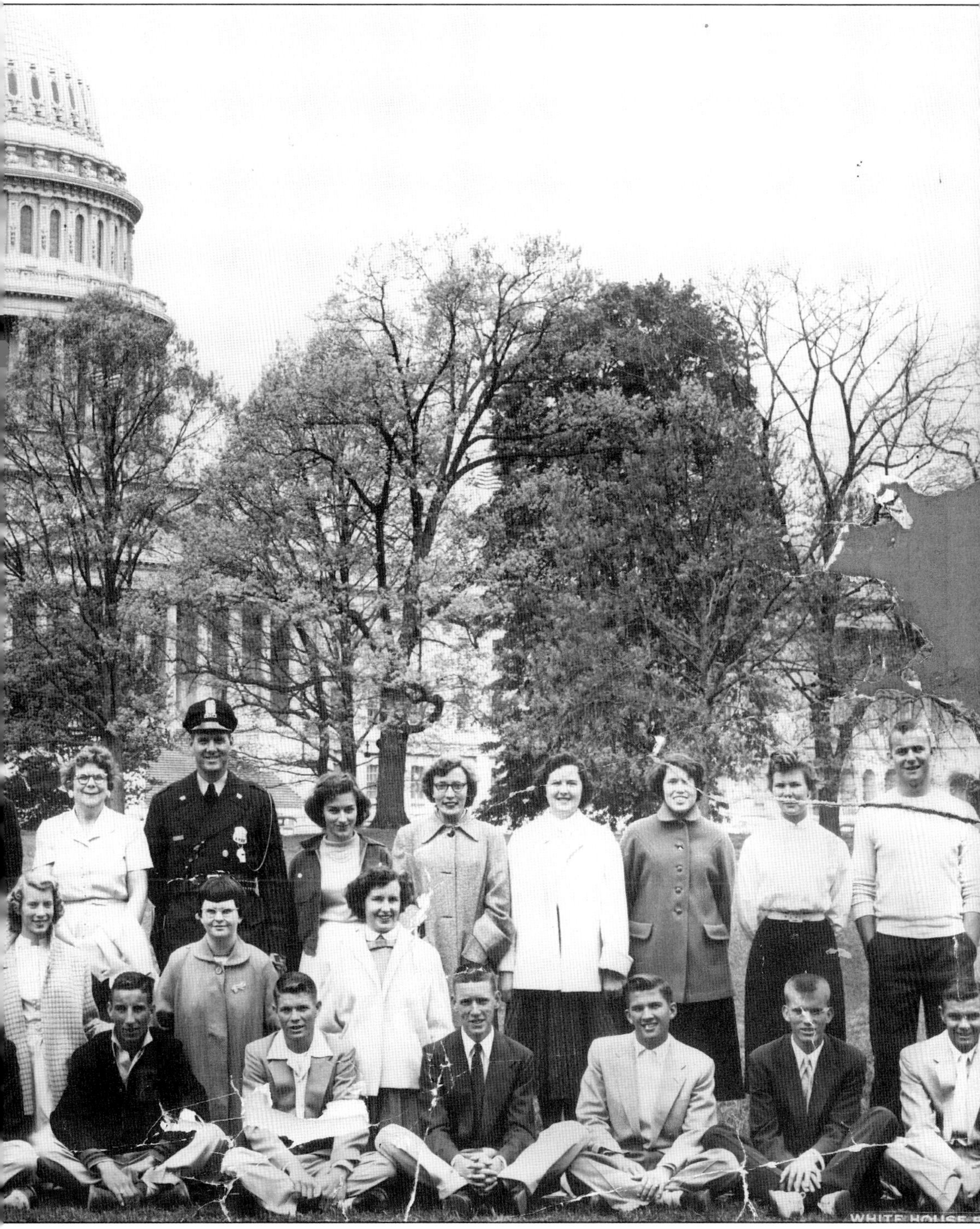

Drew, Roma Roberson, Betty Wheatley, and Arlene Bedgood; (back row) Edd Patrick, Betty Gray, Virginia Hall, Kay Barfield, Juadila Johnson, Mae Brown, Marvin Cox, Carl Grimes, Rep. Prince Preston, teacher Celeste Higginbotham, unidentified, Betty Sue Brinson, Mary Williams, Beth Edenfield, Jean Goodman, Ann Overstreet, and Mickey Gignalliat.

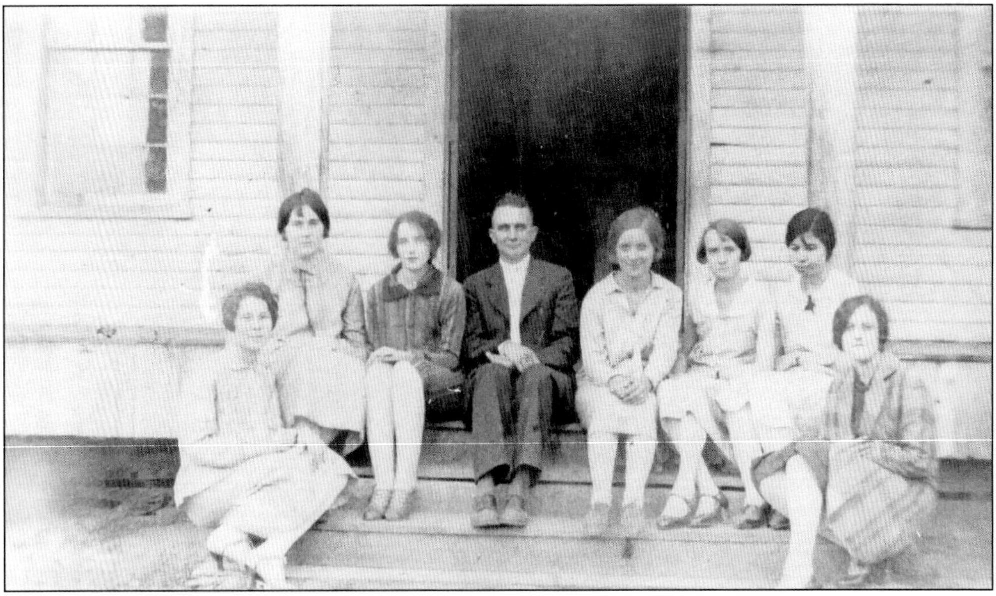

The Blundale School Faculty of 1927–28 included Annie Lee Watkins, ? Brown, Mrs. Silas Fields, John D. Durden, Ella Mae Garrett, ? Flanders, Gladys Hall, and Calene Pierce.

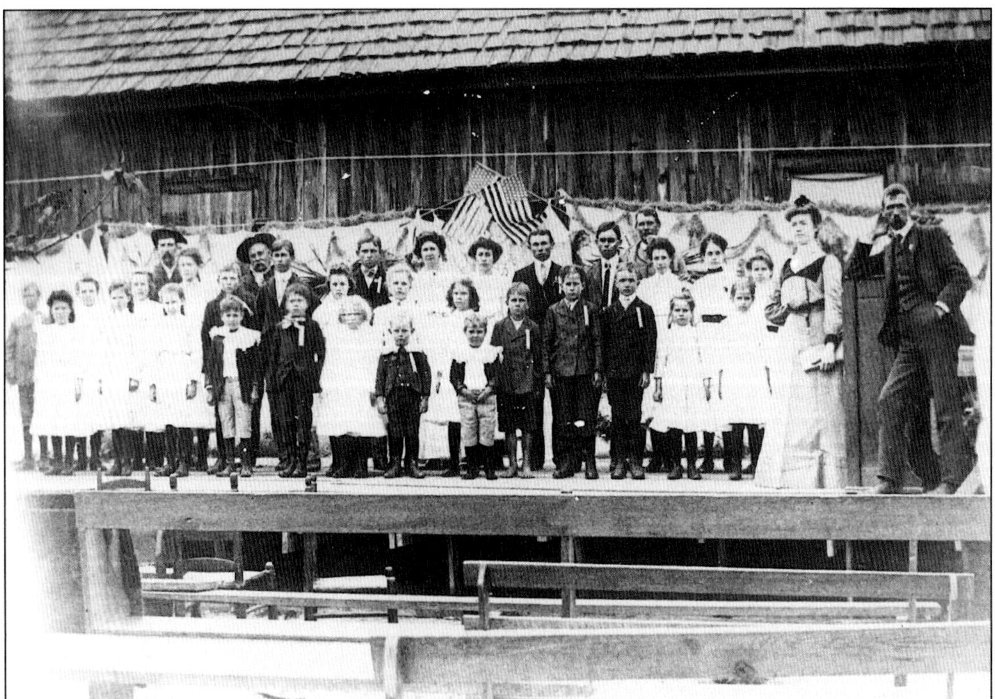

The Edenfield School near Blundale is pictured here.

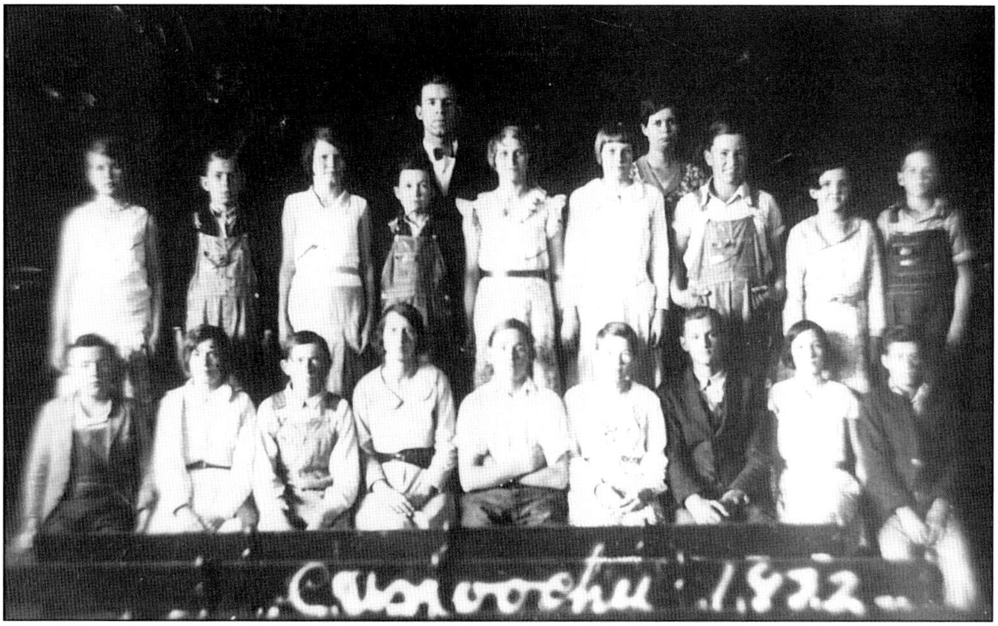

The Canoochee School, with Mr. Phillips, the teacher, was photographed in 1932.

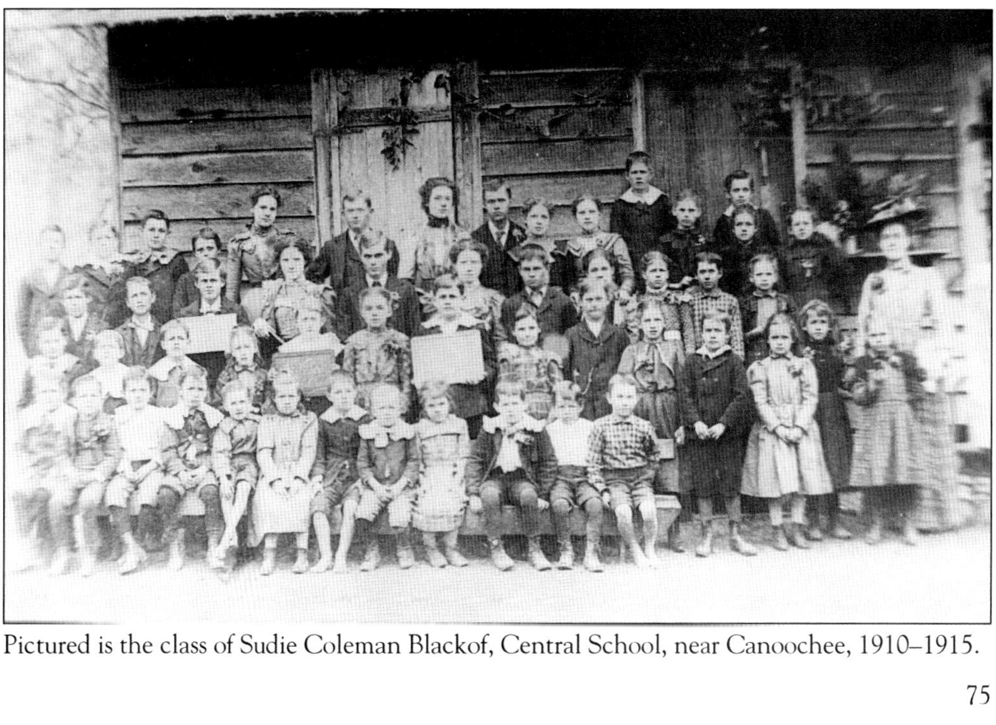

Pictured is the class of Sudie Coleman Blackof, Central School, near Canoochee, 1910–1915.

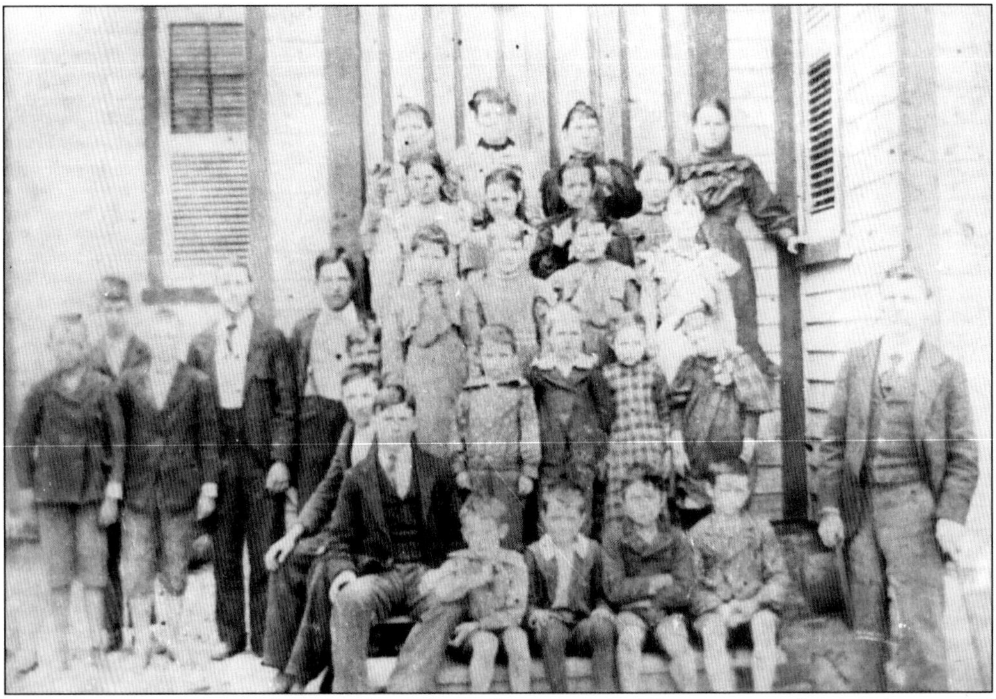

Students of the Lawtonville School are shown here, c. 1898. The picture, taken on the steps of the Lawtonville Church, shows Lena Lewis second from the right, front row, with Ann Adele Clark on her right. Others include Alvin and Cecil Lewis and Ethel Daniel, second from right, top row.

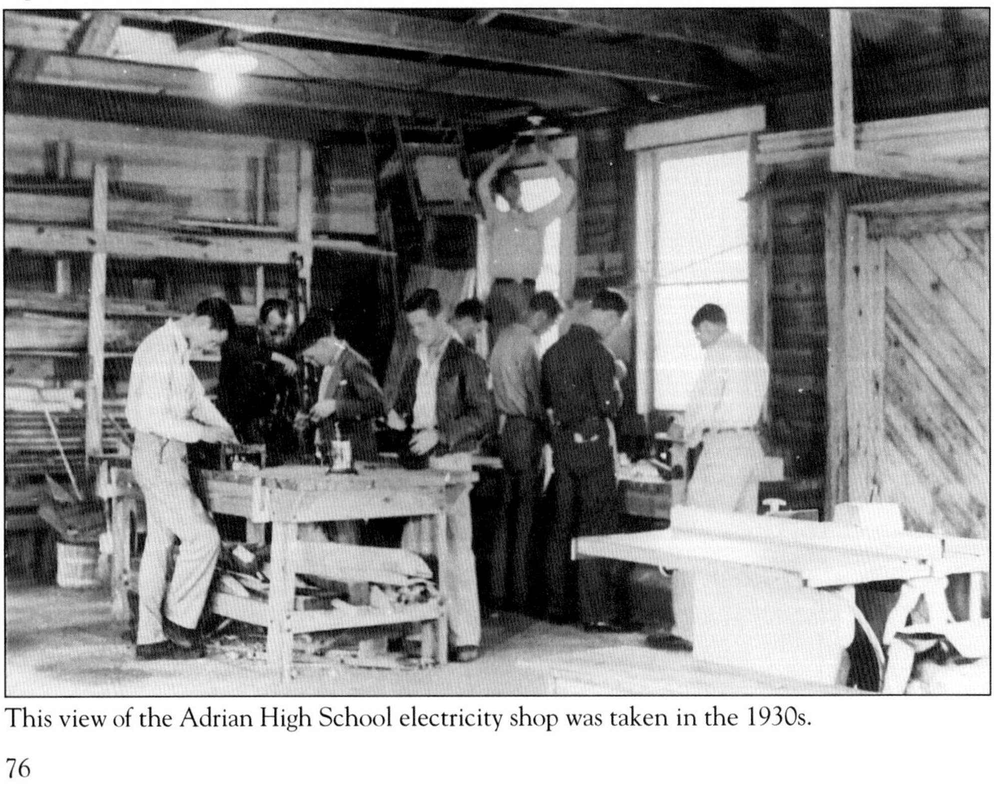

This view of the Adrian High School electricity shop was taken in the 1930s.

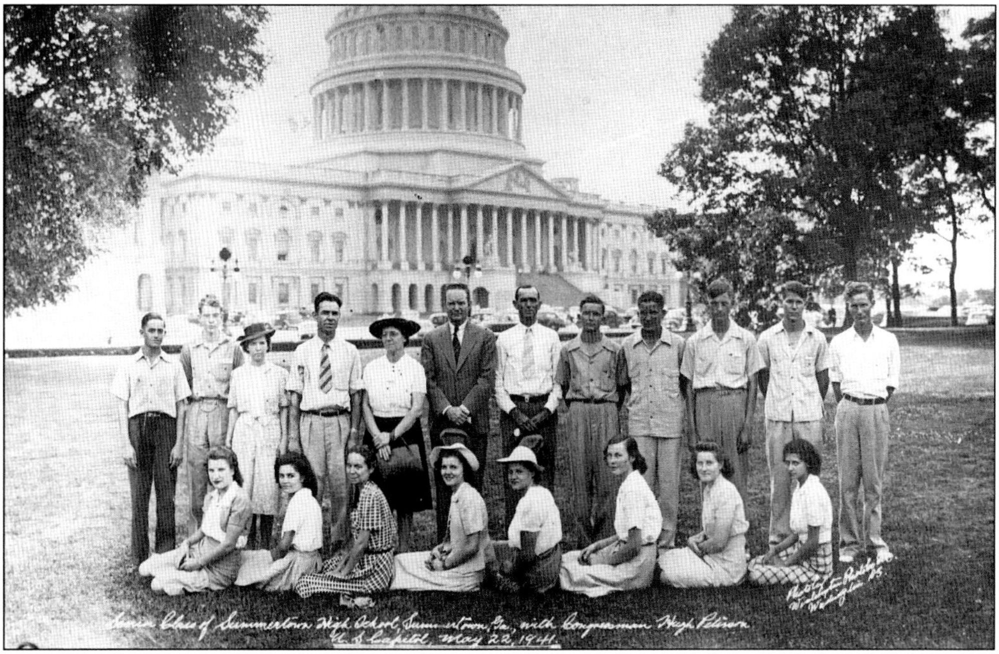

On May 22, 1941, the Summertown High senior class had their picture taken with Congressman Hugh Peterson. From left to right are: (front row) Jettie Cullars, Larina Bishop, Ruth Harris, Grace Williams, Vivian Waye, Janelle Underwood, Virginia Burke, and Inez Nasworthy; (back row) Roy L. Brown Jr., Bobby Boatright, Mrs. J.J. Nixon, Mr. J.J. Nixon, Mrs. J.E. Henry, Congressman Hugh Peterson, Mr. Lott Bishop, Clinton Davis, Paul Davis, Virgil Black, Tobe Henry, and Danny Oglesby.

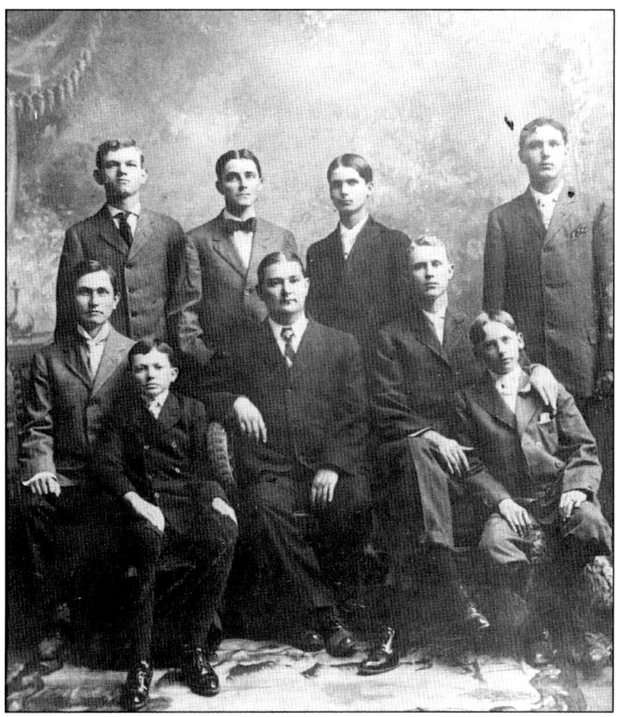

This is the Swainsboro High School and Business Institute, class of 1908. Seated from left to right are: John R. Summers (teacher), Dexter Bird, Prof. York (principal), ? Anderson, and Remer Durden. One of those standing is Frank Coleman.

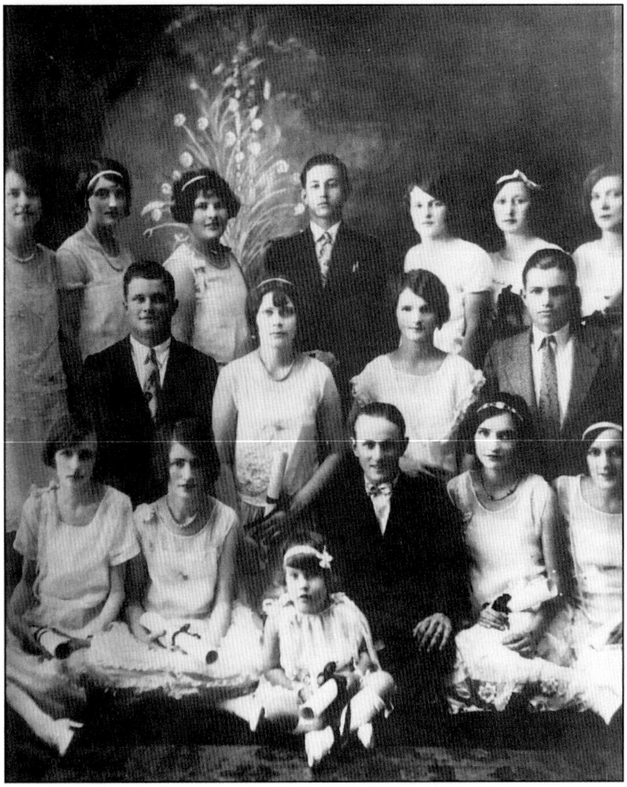

Shown here is the Swainsboro High School class of 1926. Class members include Virginia Williams, Jacqueline Hayslap, Virginia Nunez, Mildred George, Hugh Sconyers, Barney Price, Virginia Giddens, Ruby Sconyers, J.R. Mason, Ella Mae Garrett, Minnie Belle Coleman, Claudia Waller, Aaron Subnotick, Bessie Ehrlich, Eva D. Key, and Gertrude Wilcox.

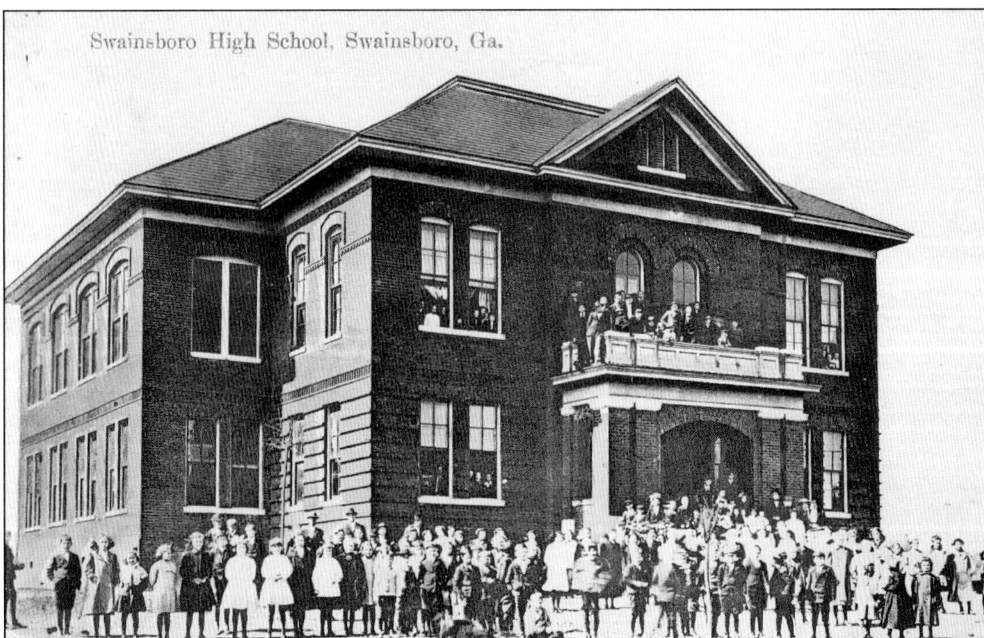

Swainsboro High School, formerly called the Academy, was built in 1905 on what had been the Swainsboro Primary School lot on Lewis Street. The school was torn down in 1968.

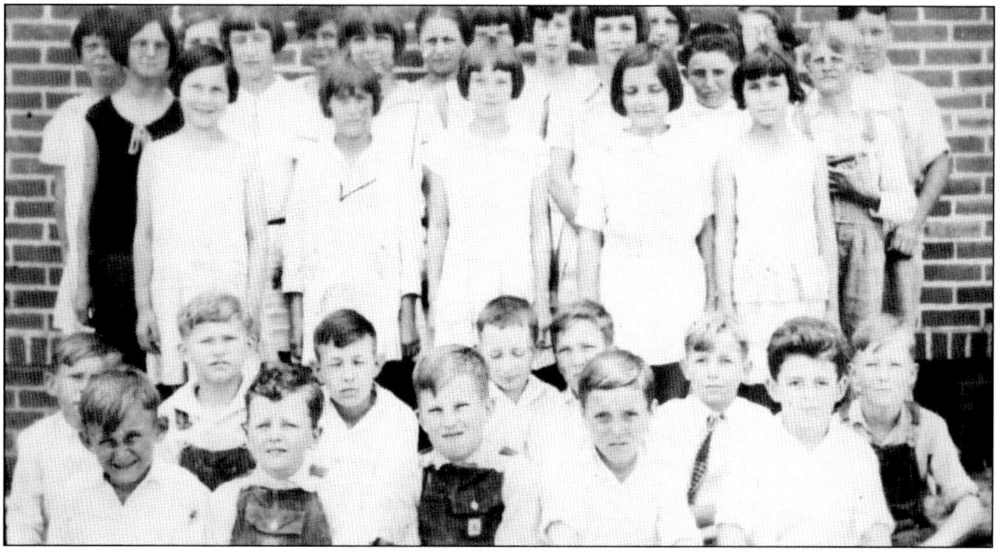

This is the Swainsboro fifth grade class of 1928–29. From left to right are: (front row) Billy Lamb, Rhomiedell Phillips, Harry Bell, Ralph Smith Jr., and Herman Popkin; (second row) Ray Rogers, Frank Price, James Carmichael, Kenneth McGregor, Benny Blackburn, Meredith Price, and Frank Garrett; (third row) Annie Maude Sherrod, Johnnie Lorid Overstreet, Hilda Brown, Dottie Bradley, and Sibyl Moxley; (fourth row) Elizabeth Parker, Bernice Scott, Clyde Rhiner, Lucille Frost, Mildred Waller, ? Strange, and Fred McDaniel; (fourth row) Nell Lawson, Marjorie Smith, Pauline Paige, Sarah White, Leila Fields, Annie Jim Davis, Evelyn Tyson, and James Bradshaw.

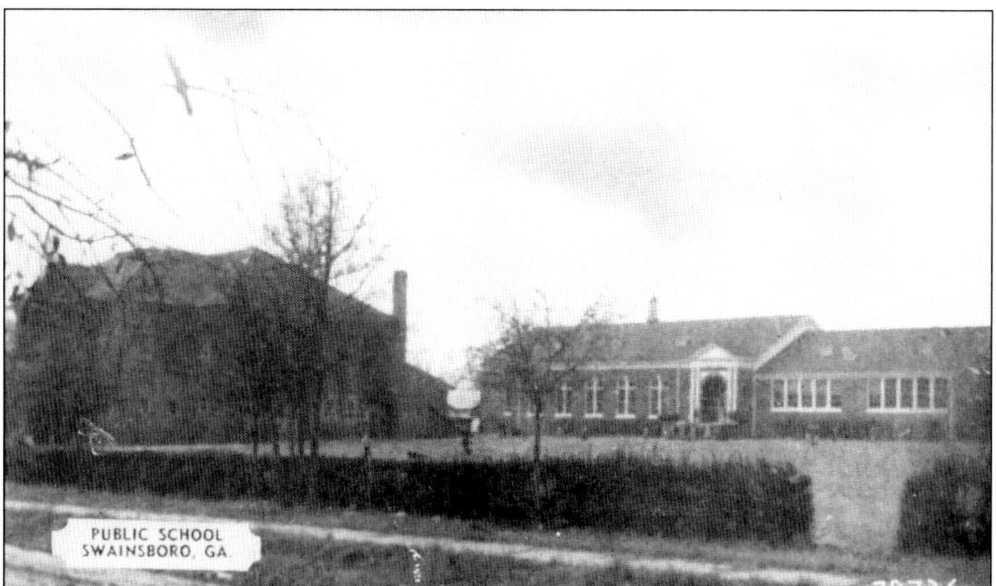

Swainsboro Primary School is shown with the old high school building in the foreground. This building is now occupied by the Head Start Program.

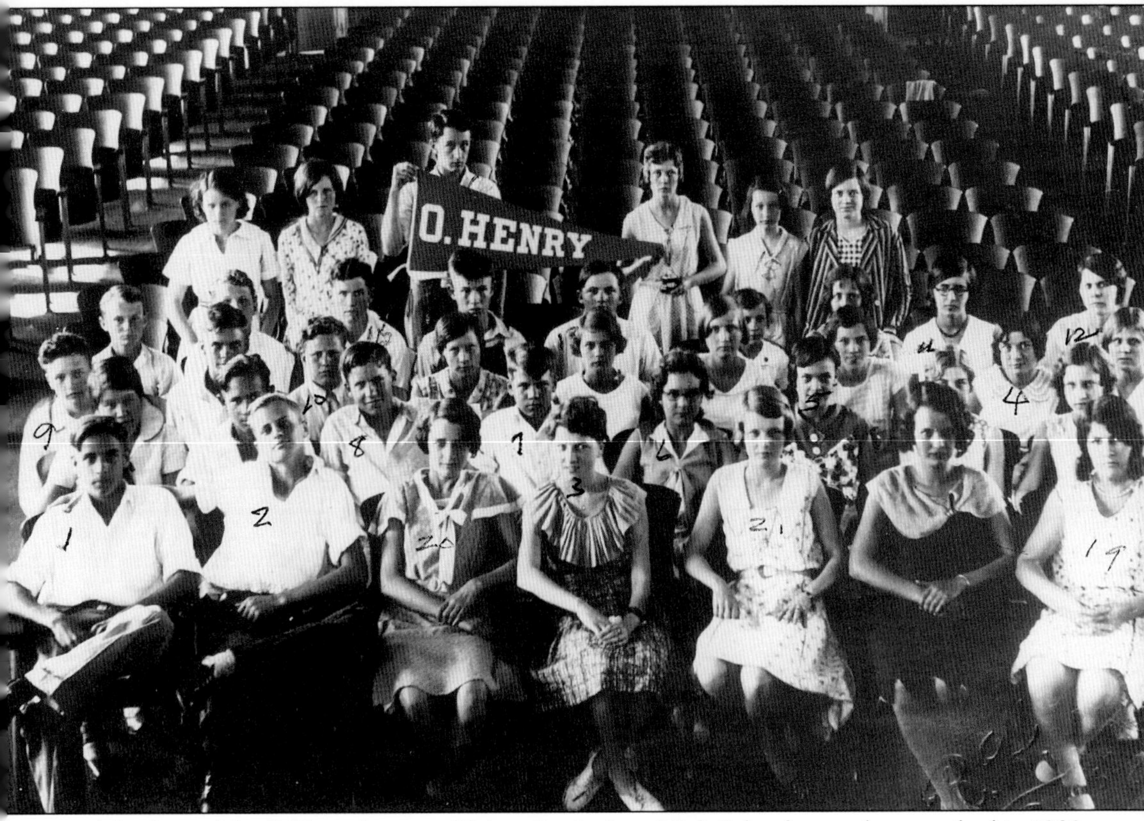

Members of the O.Henry Literary Club at Swainsboro High School were photographed in 1930. From left to right are: (front row) Charles Elliott, Bill Walden, Christine Lindsey, Aileen Reed, Jane Holloman, unidentified, and Nell Lewis; (second row) Martha Cork, Earl McCullough, Wm. Kitchens, Louis Proctor, Maurice Rountree, Madge Durden, Suzzanne Mason, and Helene Thompson; (third row) John L. Kent, Reid Watson, Jerry Rich, ? Fields, Jeanette Youman, Ethel Rich, Louise Harmon, Robbie Scott, and Maggie Thompson; (fourth row) Woodrow Peeples, Clinton Garrett, ? Roy Bell, F.H.Cadle, William Kitchens, Ada Walden, unidentified, Christine Langford _____, and Eva Crenshaw (teacher); (fifth row) Frances Grimes, unidentified, Bob Pound, Gaynelle Franklin, Virginia Shearouse, and Margaret Rountree.

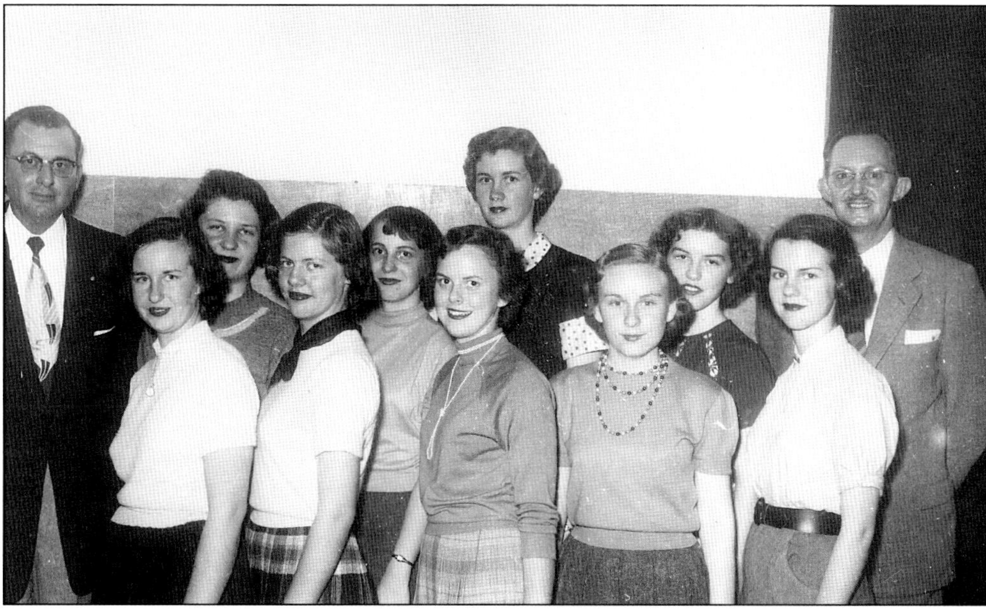

A Swainsboro High School group from 1955 is shown here. From left to right are: (front row) Arlene Bedgood, Gayle Page, Ann Kennedy, LaNelle Bishop, and Nancy Williams; (second row) Sarah Youngblood (second from left), Bobby Sasser (far left), and Leroy Williams (far right). Others are unidentified.

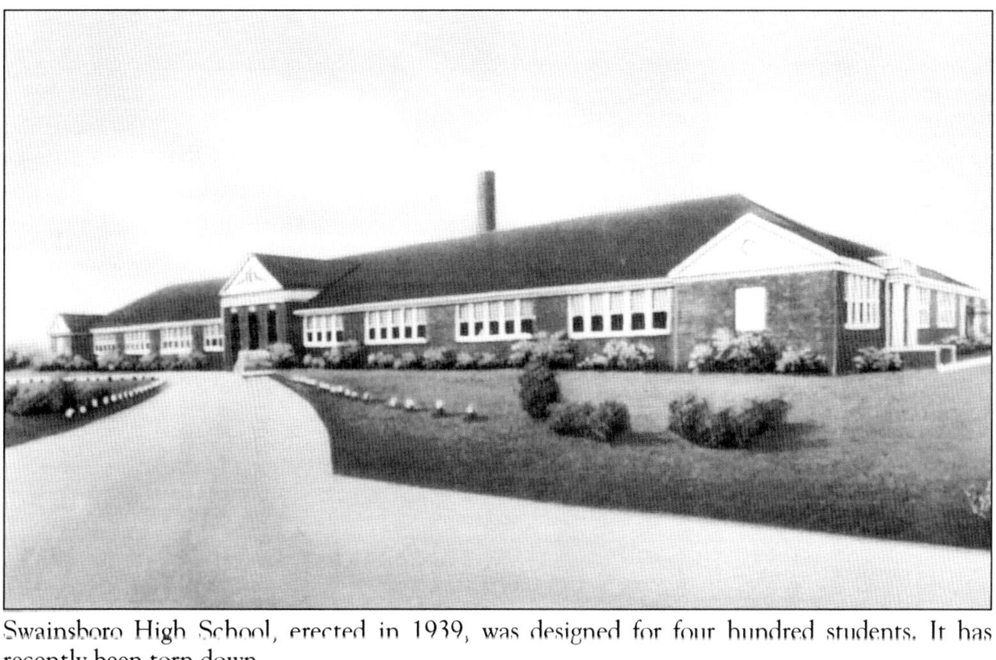

Swainsboro High School, erected in 1939, was designed for four hundred students. It has recently been torn down.

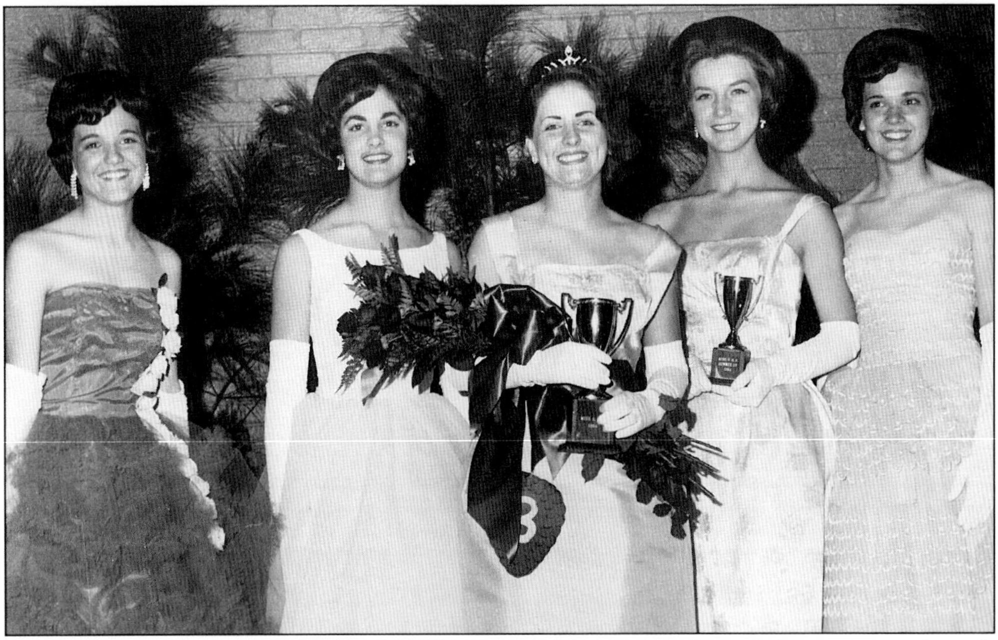

This is the Miss Swainsboro High School Beauty Contest of 1964. From left to right are: Brenda Davis, Martha Smith, Bobbie Fagler (Miss Swainsboro High School), Nancy Layton, and Sara Steinberg.

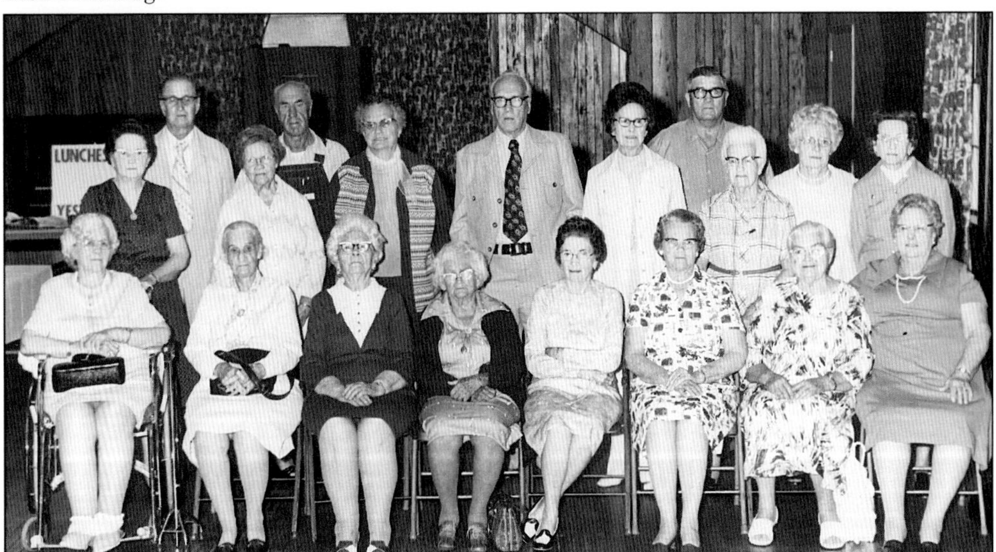

Hales Chapel School, formerly located about 5 miles south of Summertown, had a class reunion in September 1976. From left to right are: (front row) Mrs. Rossie Sherrod Hall, Mrs. Goy Sherrod Boatright, Mrs. Gertrude Bunn Phillips, Mrs. Pinkie Durden Chance, Mrs. Ollie Brinson Hill, Mrs. India Muns Edwards, Mrs. Clyde Rogers Rackard, and Mrs. Estelle Bishop Parnell; (middle row) Mrs. Sudie Brinson Roberts, Mrs. Eunice Ridgdill Bishop, Mrs. Mae Underwood Howell, Mrs Anna Underwood Pound, Mrs. Julia Fanning Brinson, Mrs. Madie Boatright Waters, and Mrs. Mattie Bishop Brinson; (back row) the Rev. Fran Brinson, Marvin Fanning, Greene Underwood, and Cecil Sherrod.

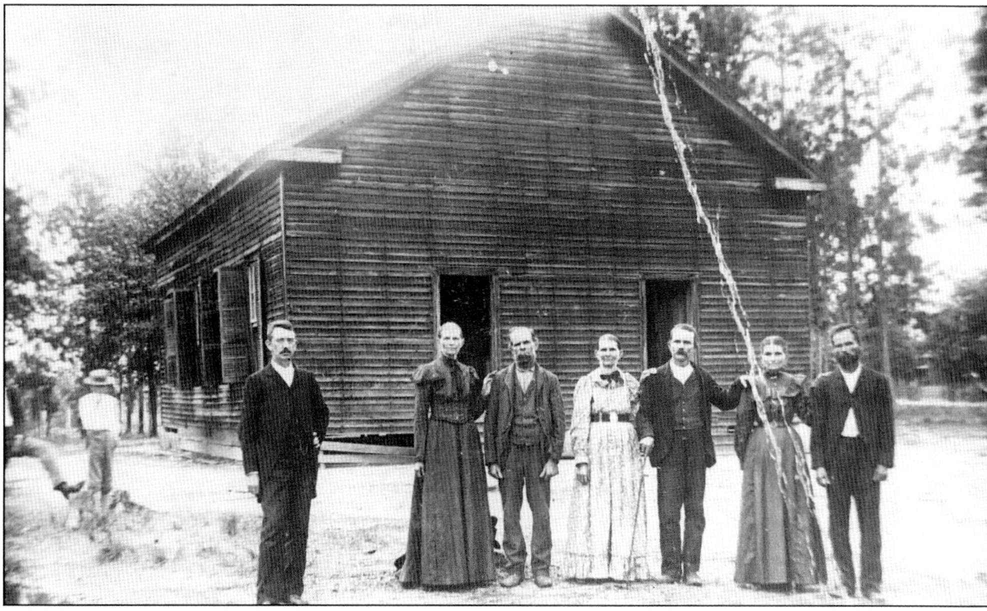

Ebenezer Church, located in the Kemp community, was constructed in 1877. Prior to that, the church was in a log building 3 miles away, built in 1800. The preacher is J.M. Foster.

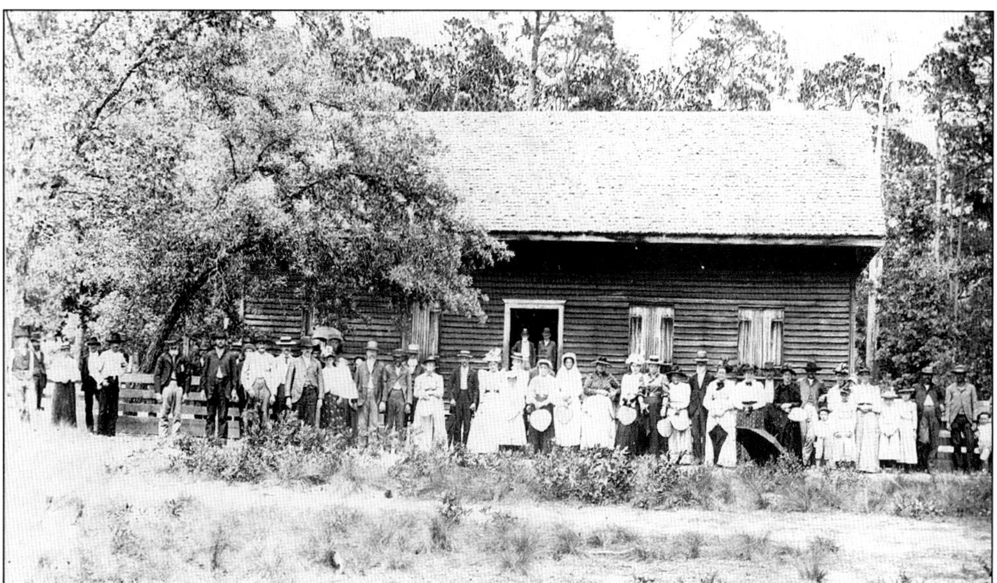

Antioch Primitive Baptist Church was constituted in 1842, with John H. Cowart as pastor. The present building, shown here, was constructed in 1865 by William Coleman. It is located off Lamb's Bridge Road, and services are still held regularly there.

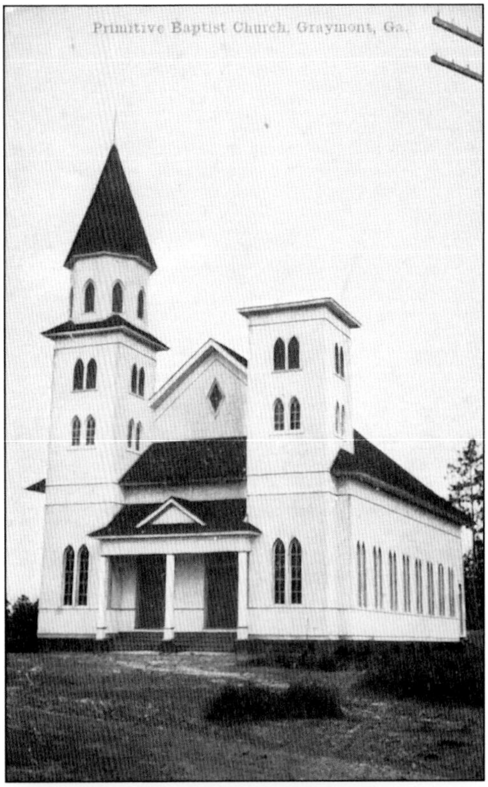

Baptist Rest Primitive Baptist Church, in Graymont, was founded on July 27, 1907. The first pastor was Elder W.H. Crouse, and the first clerk was W.L. Durden. This picture was taken about 1916.

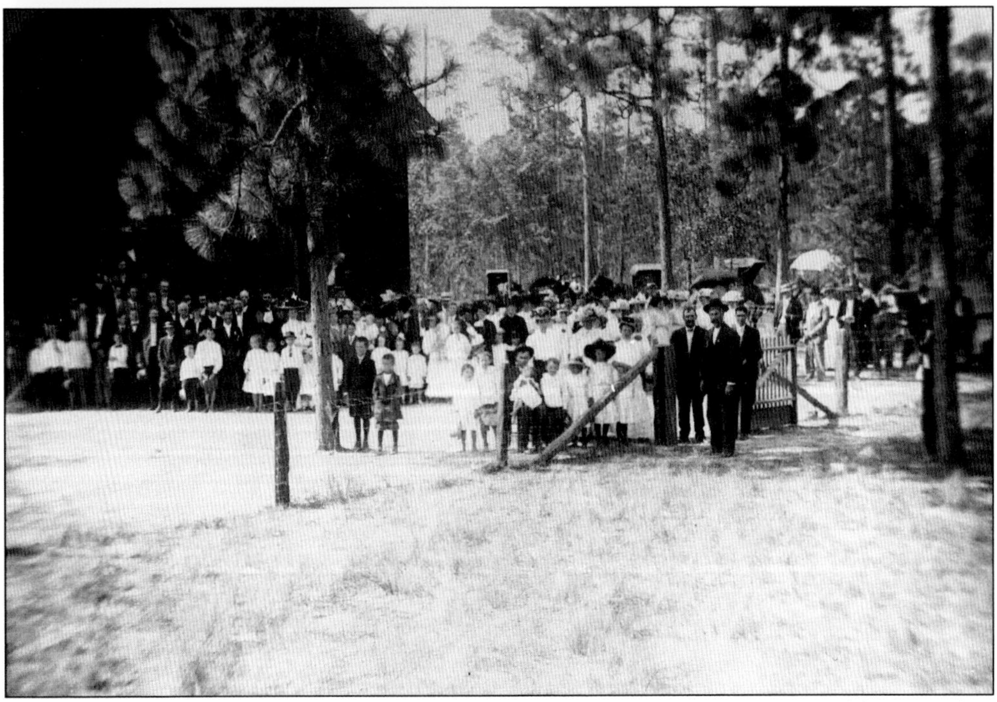

Shown here is the Old Canoochee Baptist Church on Church Day, c. 1910. Old Canoochee Church, constituted in 1818, is located 3 miles west of Twin City on U.S. 80.

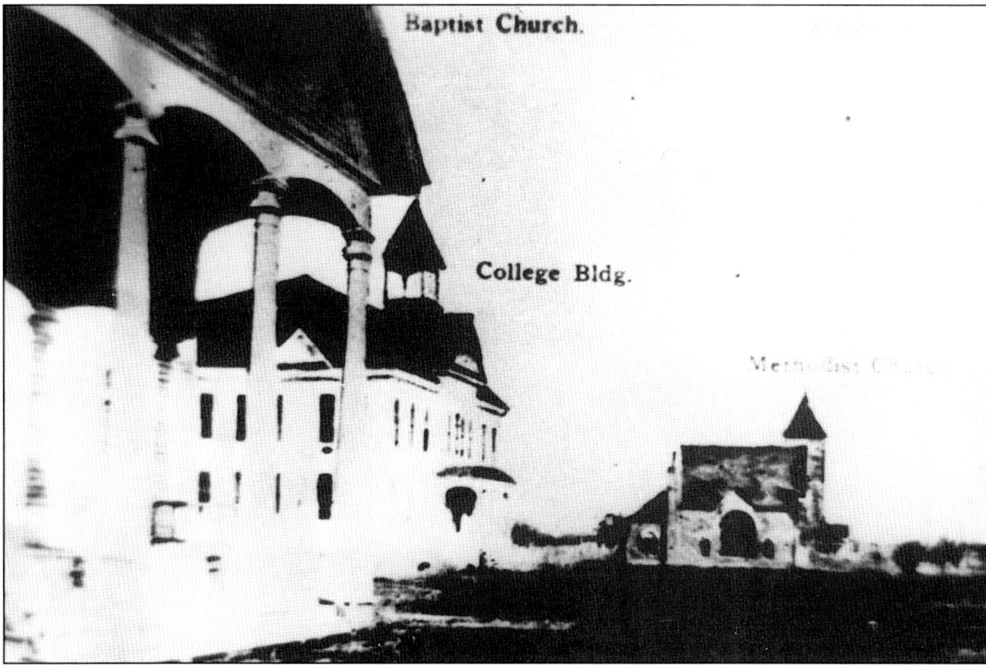

This is a Stillmore scene with the Baptist church in the foreground, college building in middle, and the Methodist church in rear.

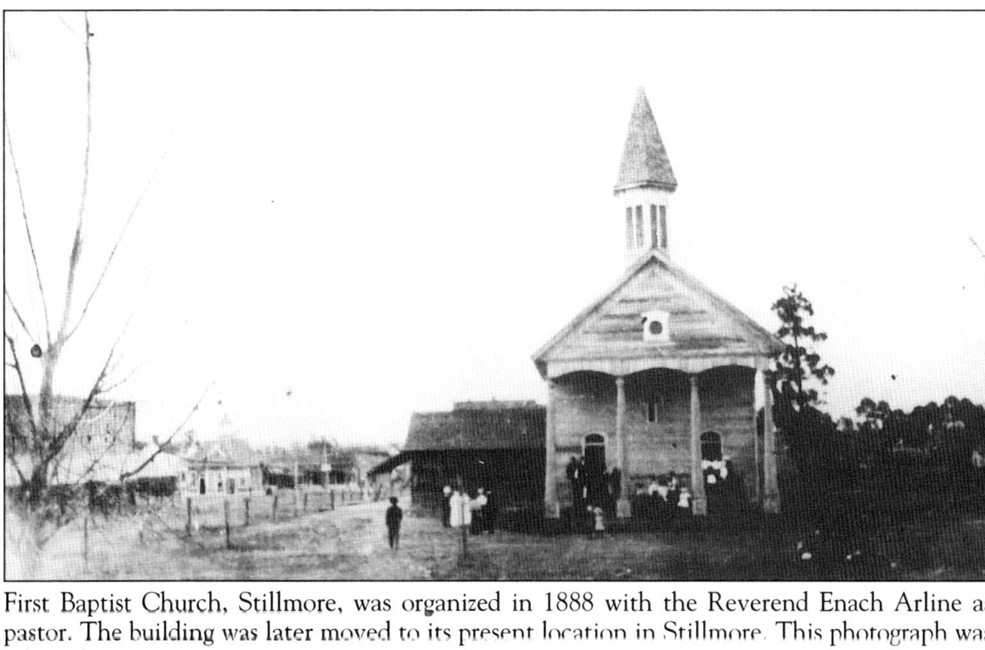

First Baptist Church, Stillmore, was organized in 1888 with the Reverend Enach Arline as pastor. The building was later moved to its present location in Stillmore. This photograph was taken about 1910.

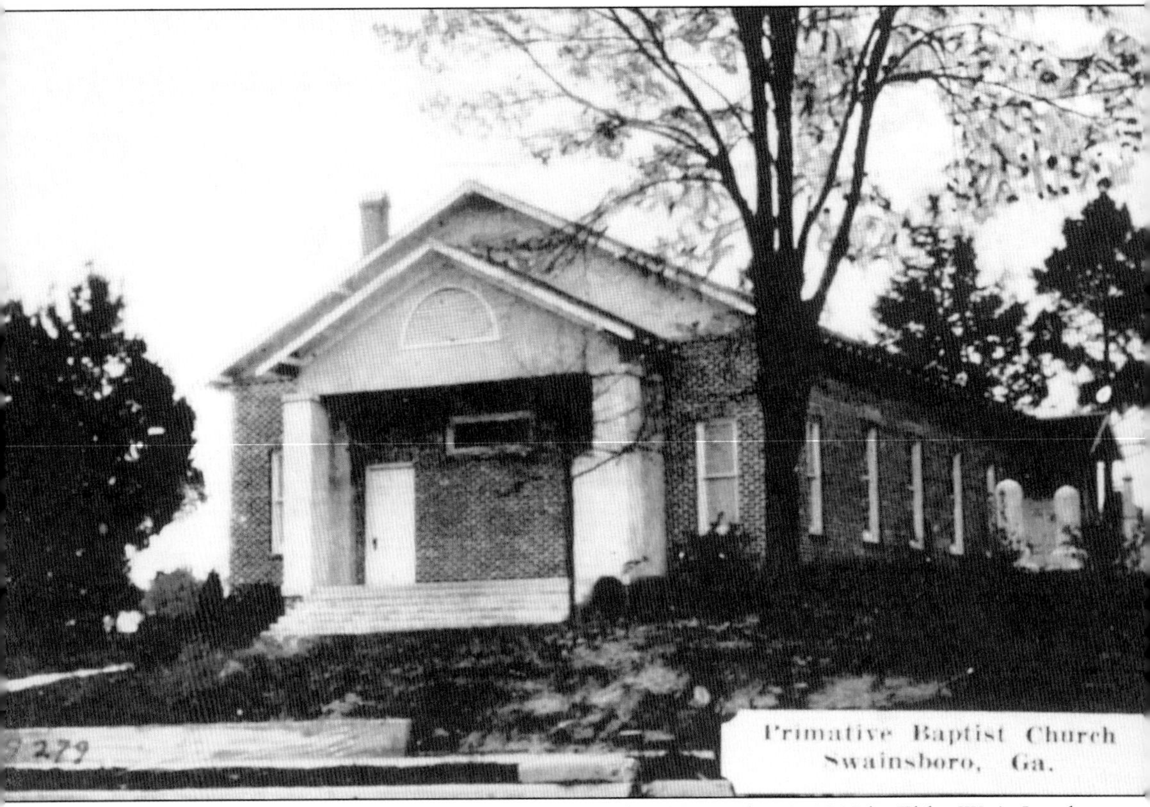

Swainsboro Primitive Baptist Church was organized on November 9, 1907 by Elder W.A. Lamb. The congregation occupied the above building, built prior to 1875 and occupied originally by the Swainsboro Baptist Church. In 1930 the building was renovated with brick construction and enlarged.

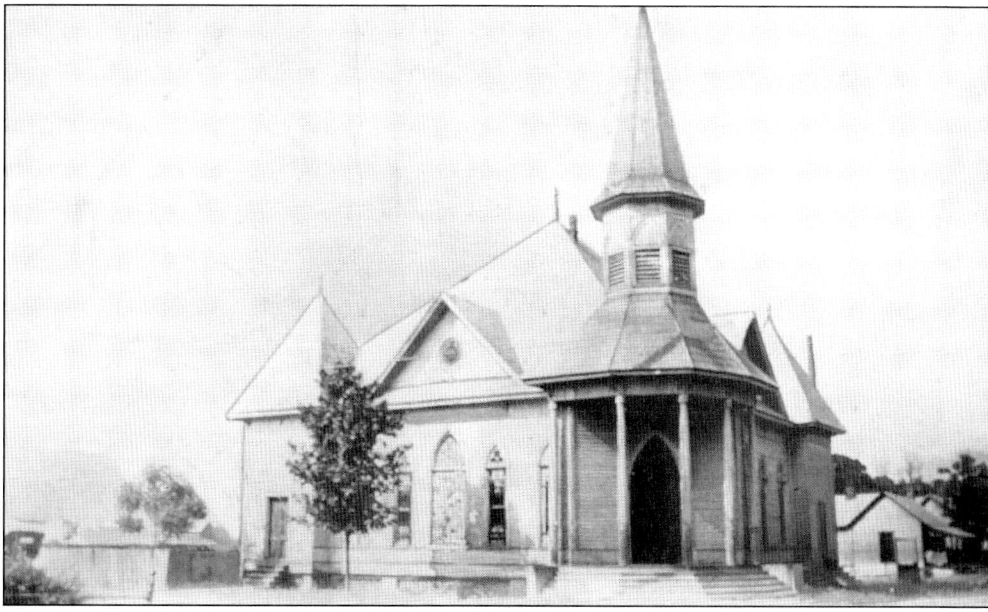

Swainsboro First Baptist Church was originally constituted in 1875 with Rev. George Washington Smith as pastor. The church was located in what is now the Swainsboro Primitive Baptist Church. In 1900 a new church was erected near the site of the Founders Cemetery and the Wadley Southern Depot. In 1914, the church was moved to the site shown above, at the northeast corner of North Main and Church Streets. A new church building was consecrated on March 6, 1949.

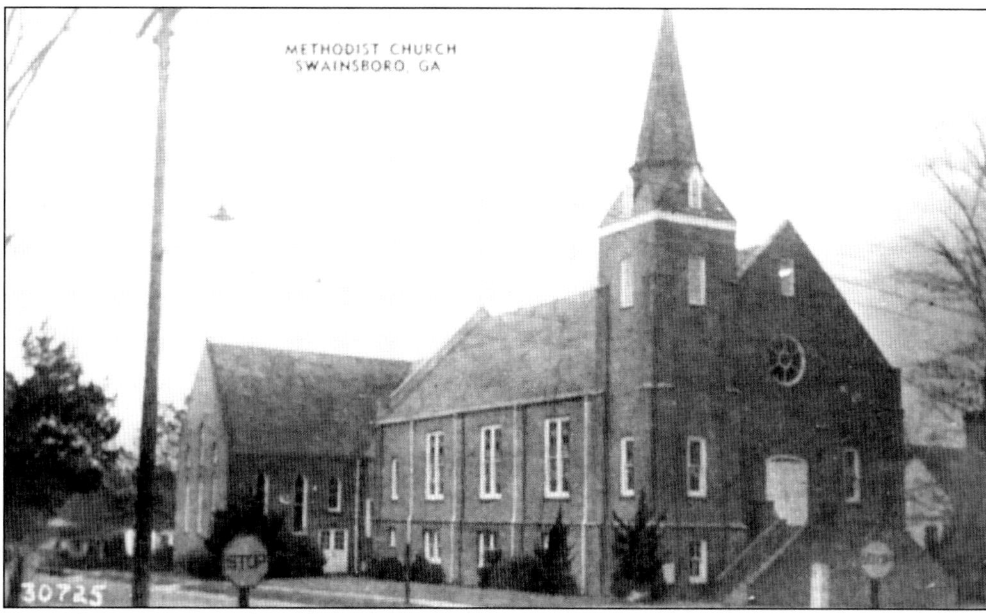

Swainsboro First United Methodist was organized as early as 1863. The building shown above was originally constructed as a wood structure in 1896. In 1937, the building was remodeled and a new sanctuary was constructed. When a new church building was constructed in 1957, this building was occupied by the First Church of the Nazarene. At present it houses the Emanuel County Arts Council.

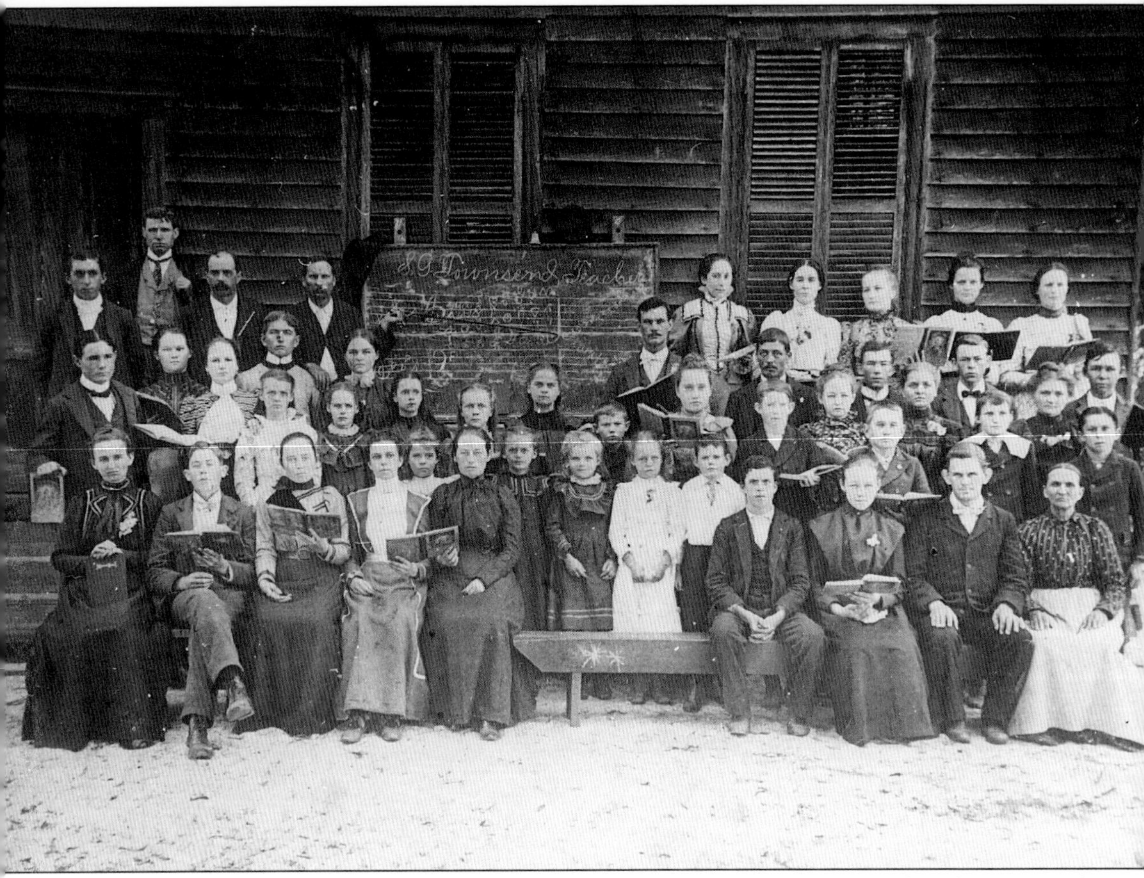

S.G. Townsend was the teacher at a music school held at Oak Chapel Baptist Church. Organized on September 14, 1873, services were first held under a huge red oak tree. The building was constructed shortly thereafter. The Reverend J.M. Donaldson was the first pastor, and the building was also used as a school. Note the blackboard shows music with old-fashioned-shaped notes. Everyone appears to be dressed in their best.

Four

This is How We Got Around

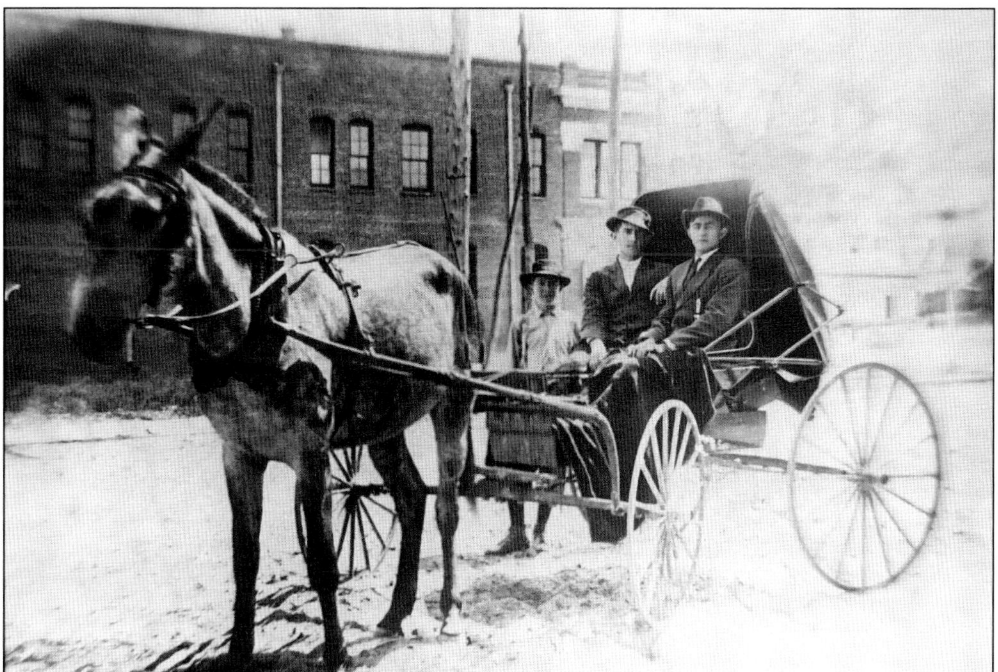

Shown here is a buggy ride in Adrian in the early 1900s with Septus Thigpen on the left and Newton Meeks on the right.

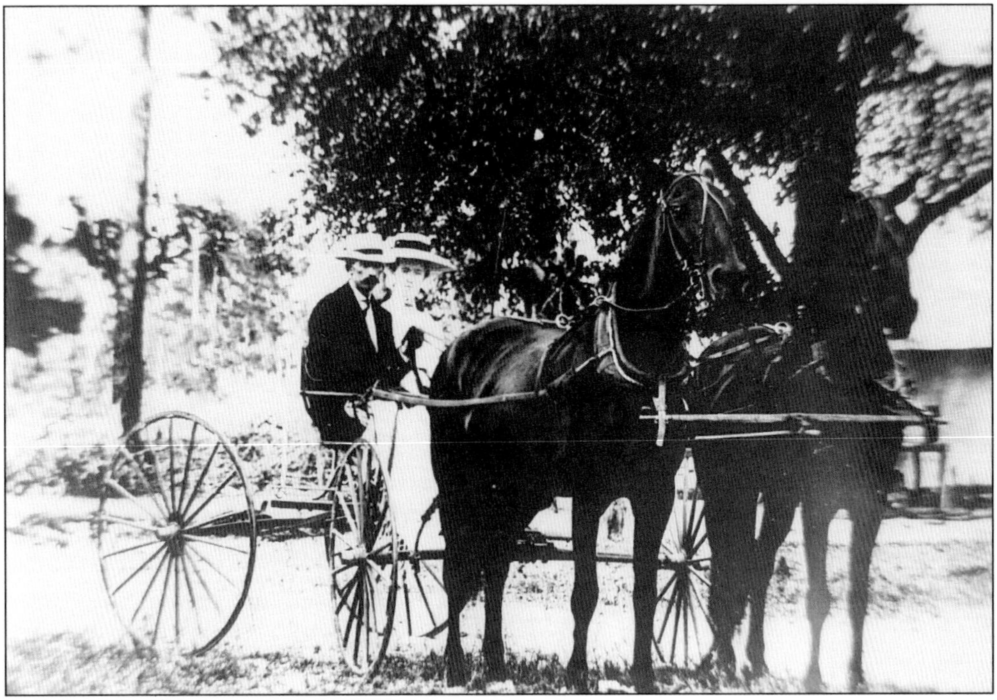

Mr. and Mrs. Thomas L. Black are shown on their wedding day, in 1909.

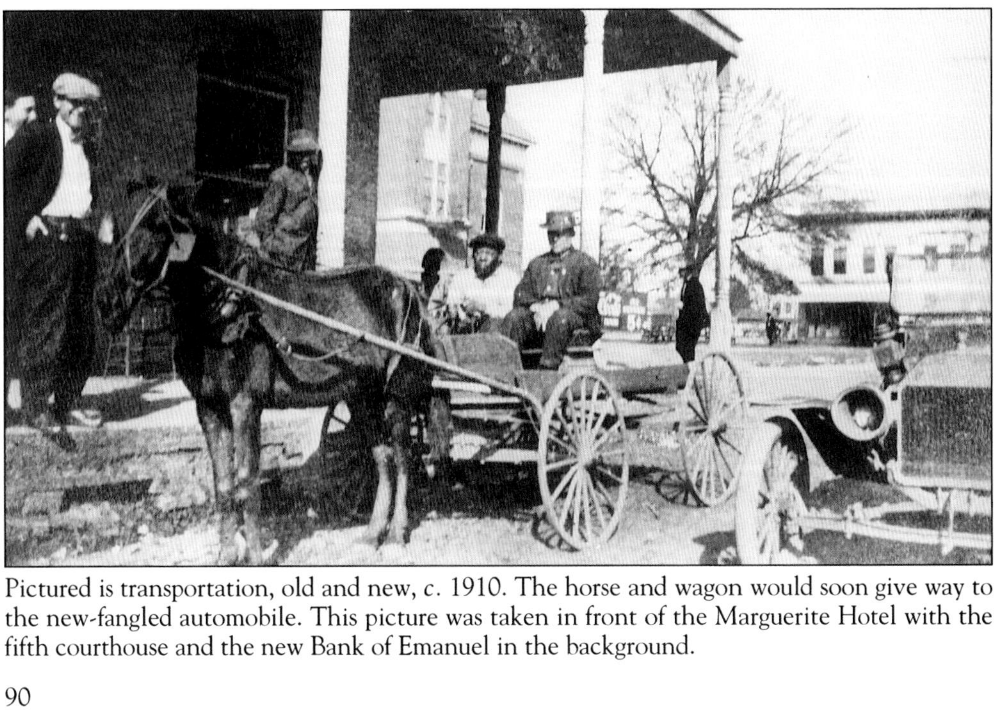

Pictured is transportation, old and new, *c.* 1910. The horse and wagon would soon give way to the new-fangled automobile. This picture was taken in front of the Marguerite Hotel with the fifth courthouse and the new Bank of Emanuel in the background.

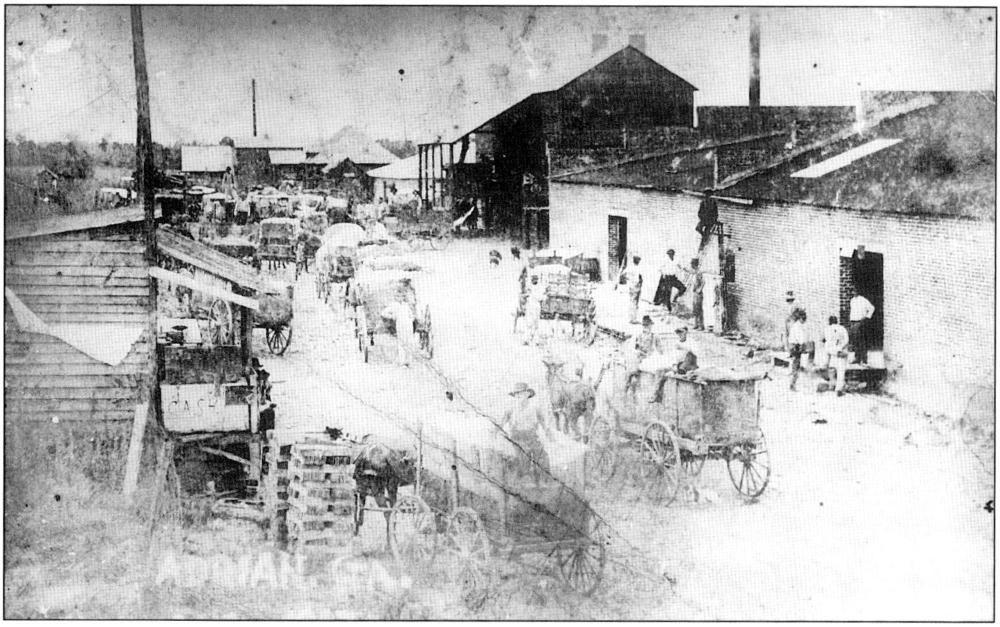

These men were bringing cotton to the gin in Adrian in 1917.

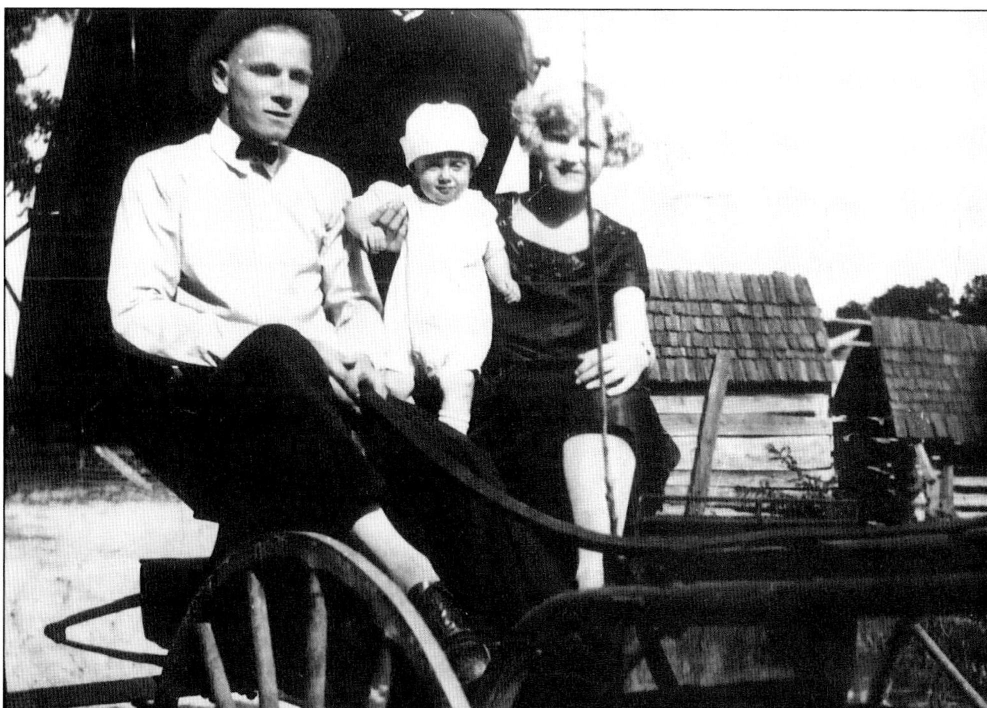

Ernest McArthur, his sister Lucille McArthur Edenfield, and their nephew "Doc" McBride, are pictured in the early 1920s. "Doc" McBride operated Swainsboro Hardware for many years.

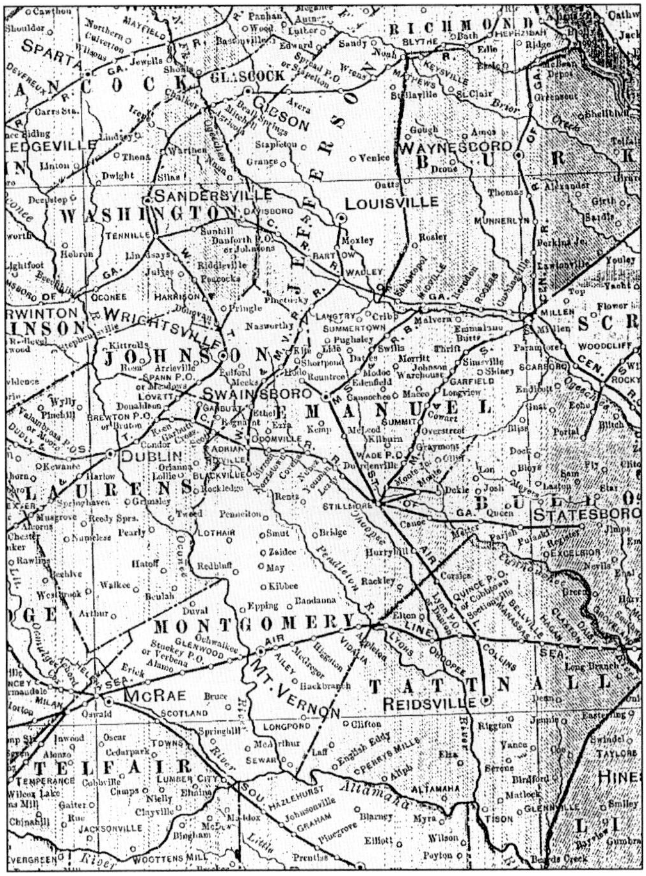

A 1900 railroad map of Emanuel and surrounding counties is pictured here. Three railroads crossed in Stillmore; the Millen & Southwestern, from Millen through Summit-Graymont; the Stillmore Air Line, from Midville to Reidsville; and the Central of Georgia, from Adrian to Register. Many villages listed here have since disappeared. Hodo, Shortpond, Lide, Pughsley, Langtry, Cribb, Maceo, Merritt, Longview, Kilburn, Monte, McLeod, Hurryhill, and Canoe no longer exist.

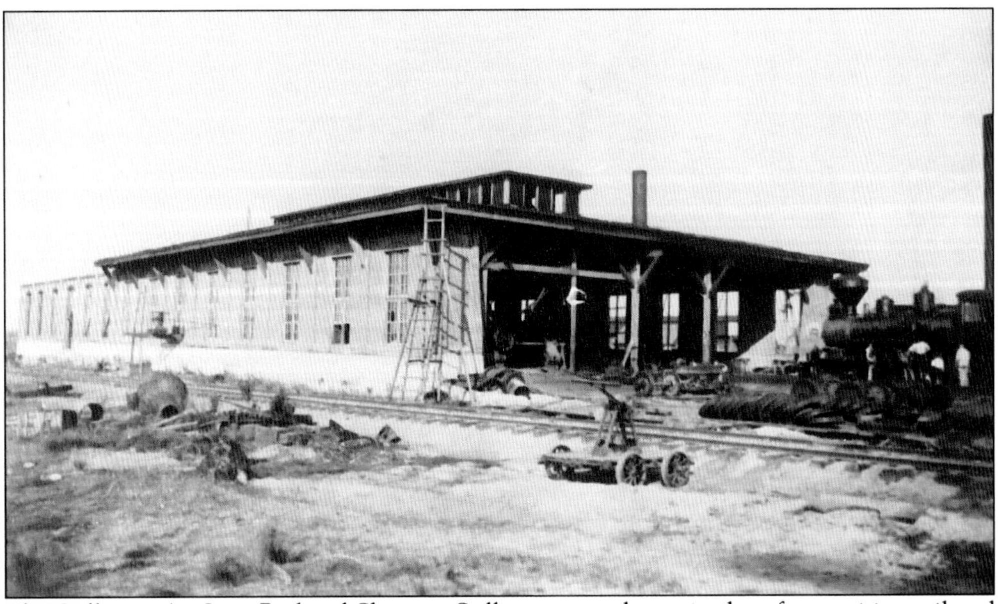

The Stillmore Air Line Railroad Shop, in Stillmore, was the main shop for repairing railroad equipment. Note the steam engine at right.

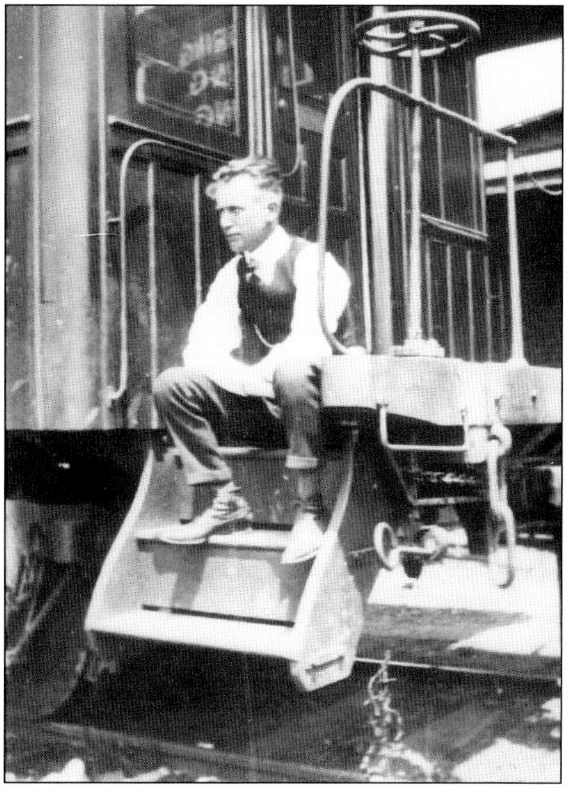

This is the Stillmore Air Line Railroad Engine #444. George M. Brinson, born in 1861 in Emanuel County, was the builder and president of this railroad and later made a fortune in building railroads, sawmill operation, banking, naval stores, and sugar refining. He died in 1941 in Brooklet, Georgia.

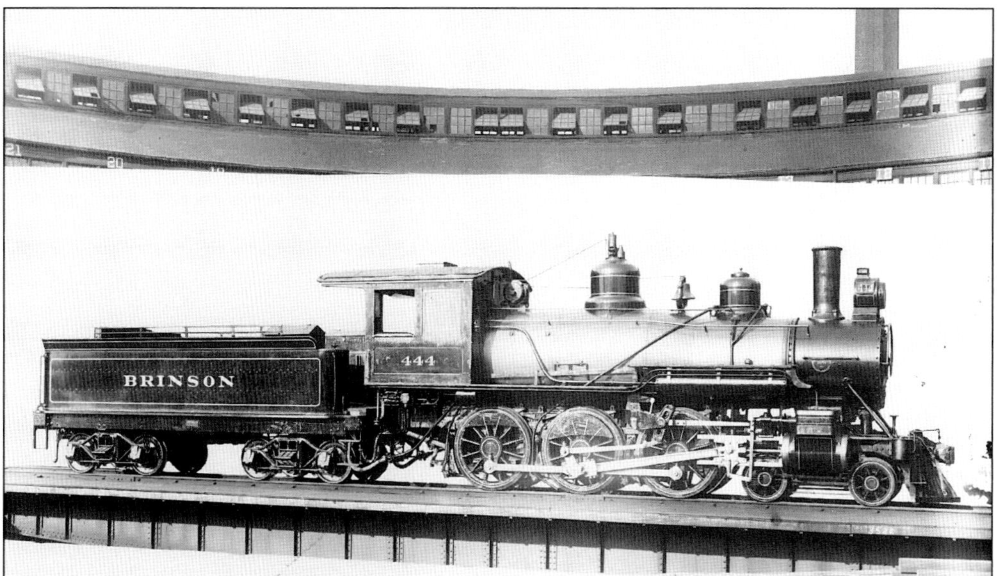

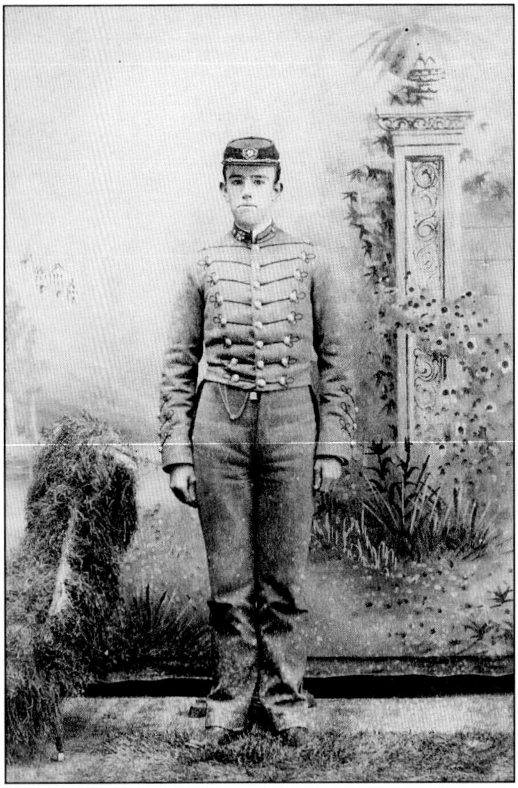

Frank R. Durden married Carrie Harris in 1894. The younger brother of Mathew and Dennis Durden, he was involved in many of their enterprises and was general manager of the Millen & South Western Railroad.

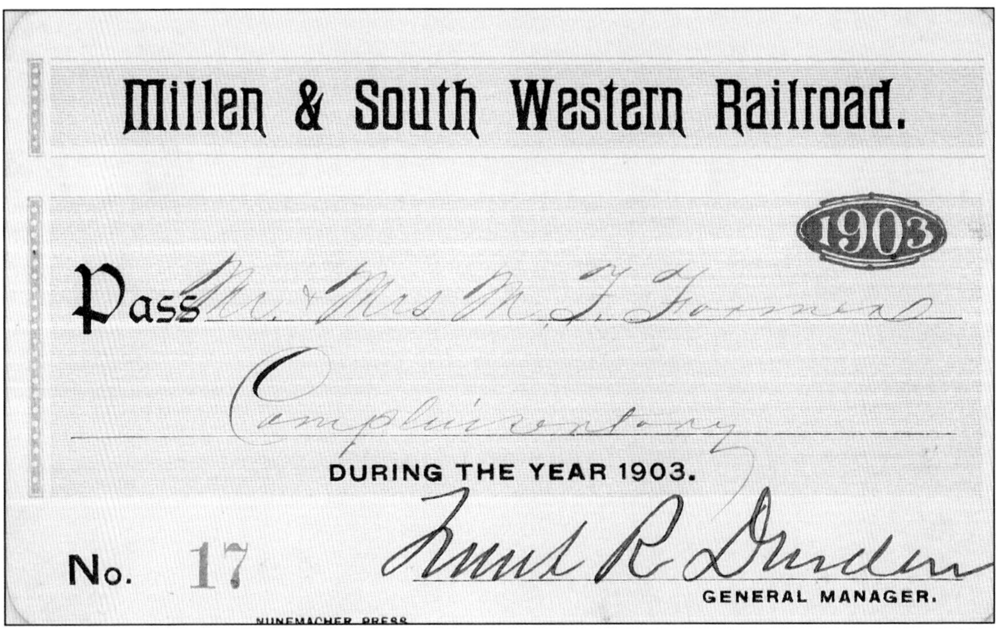

Shown here is a 1903 pass for the Millen & South Western Railroad. The pass was signed by Frank R. Durden, general manager.

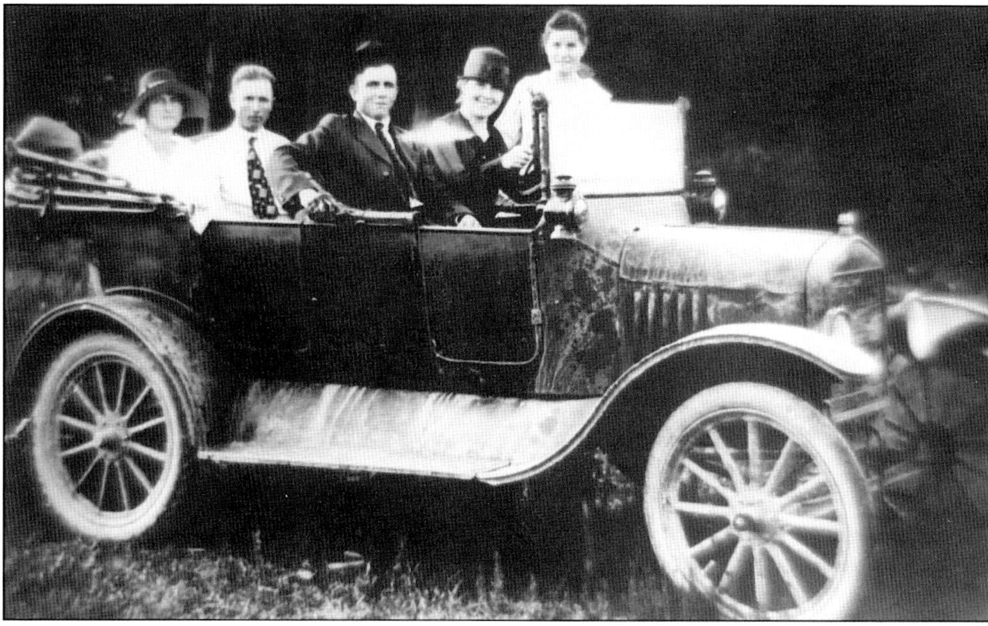

These people are cruising in a Model T. Ford about 1915. Orin Braswell is in the front seat at left, and Mae Reynolds is in the back seat.

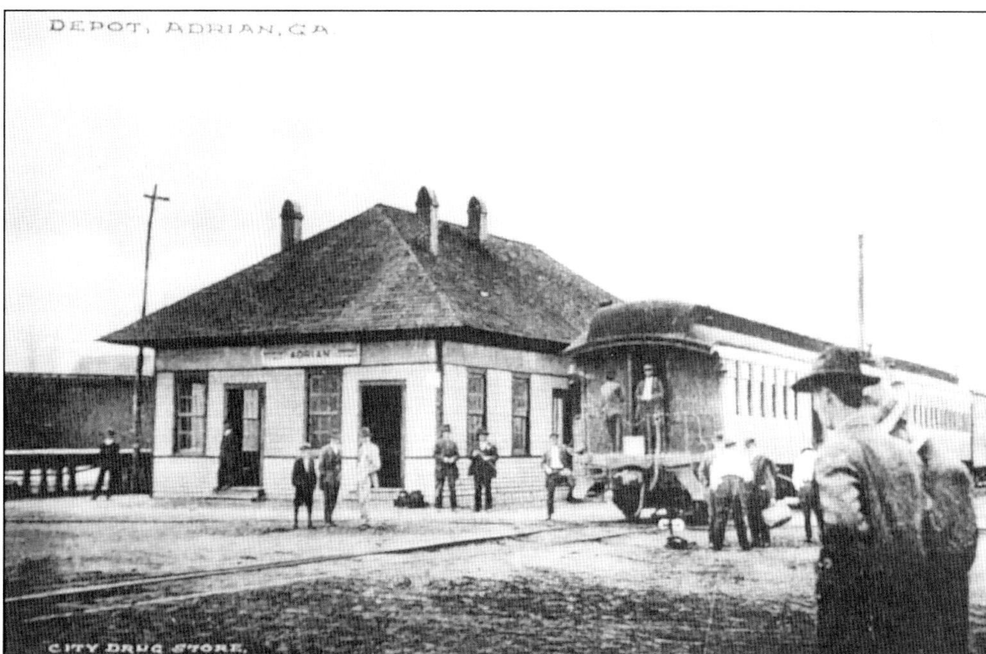

This was the railroad depot in Adrian. Both the Wadley-Southern and the Central of Georgia Railroads ran through Adrian, but service was discontinued by 1937.

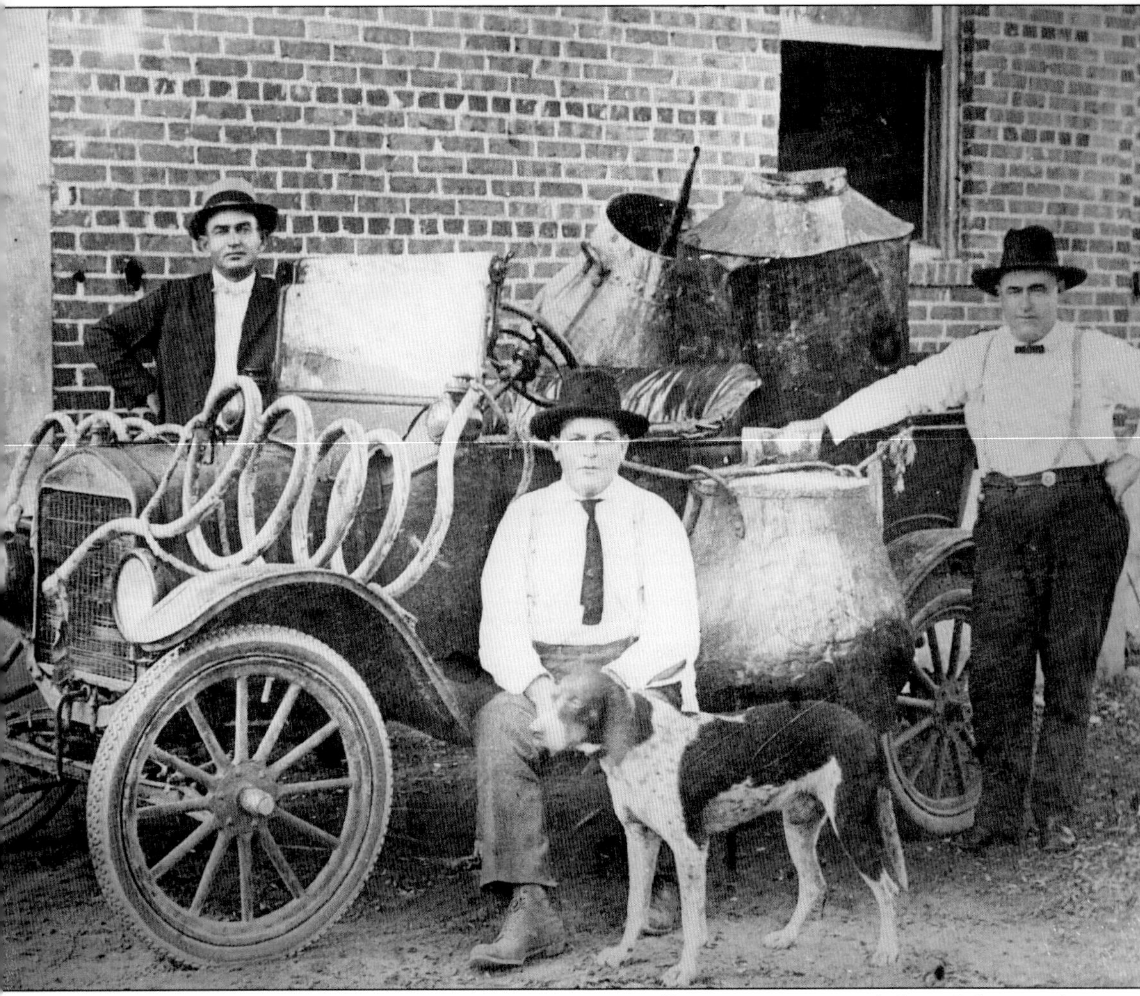

These revenue officers are confiscating a copper still, *c.* 1920. Pictured from left to right are: Thomas S. Tyson, Thomas Brown, and Enoch Oliver. The name of the hound dog is not known.

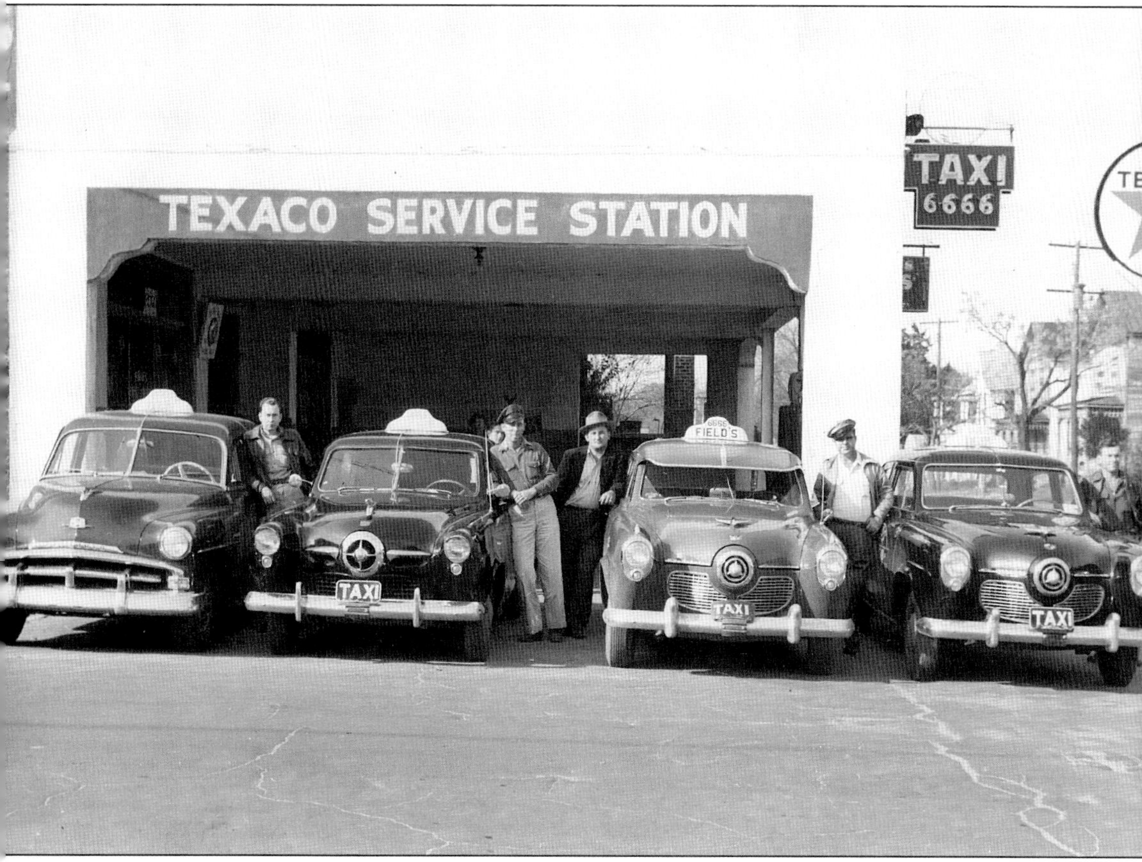

Fields Taxi Service, shown here as it appeared about 1952, was located at the corner of West Pine and North Main Streets. Pictured from left to right are: Frank Coleman, Paul Farmer, W.E. Fields, Jordan Fennell, and Ray Peebles.

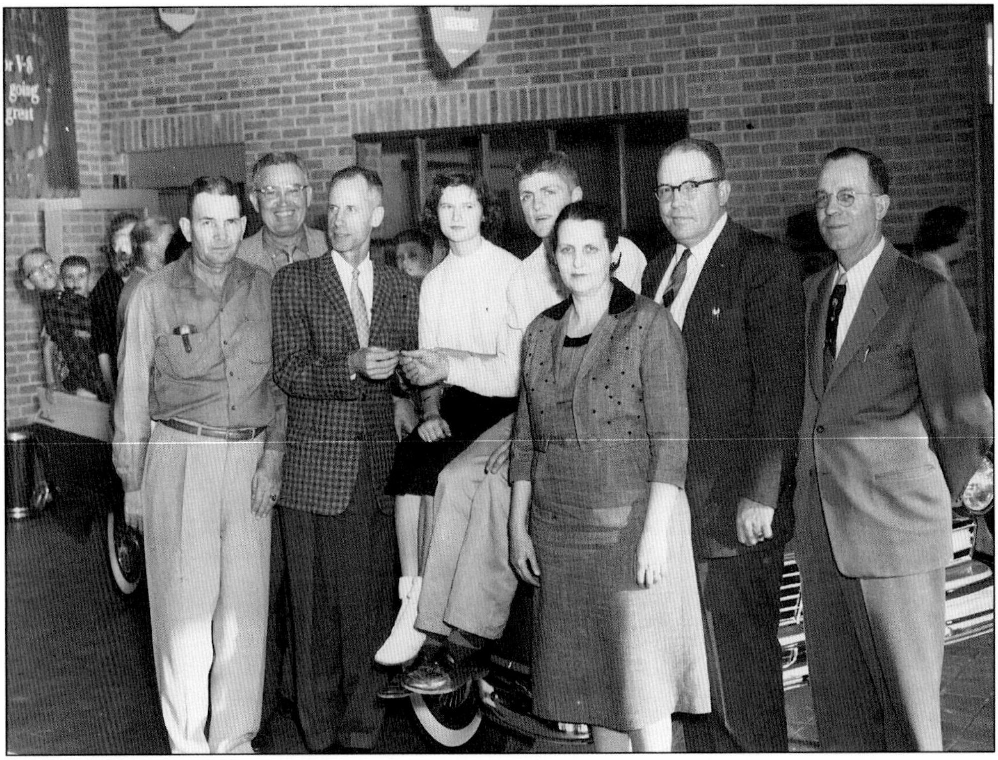

This ceremony was the presentation of a Ford driver training car to the 4-H Club. From left to right are: Olan Rountree, Earl Varner, Jimmy Morgan, handing over keys, Emily Brown, Charles Hutchinson, Louise Cowart, Darius Brown, and W.O. Phillips.

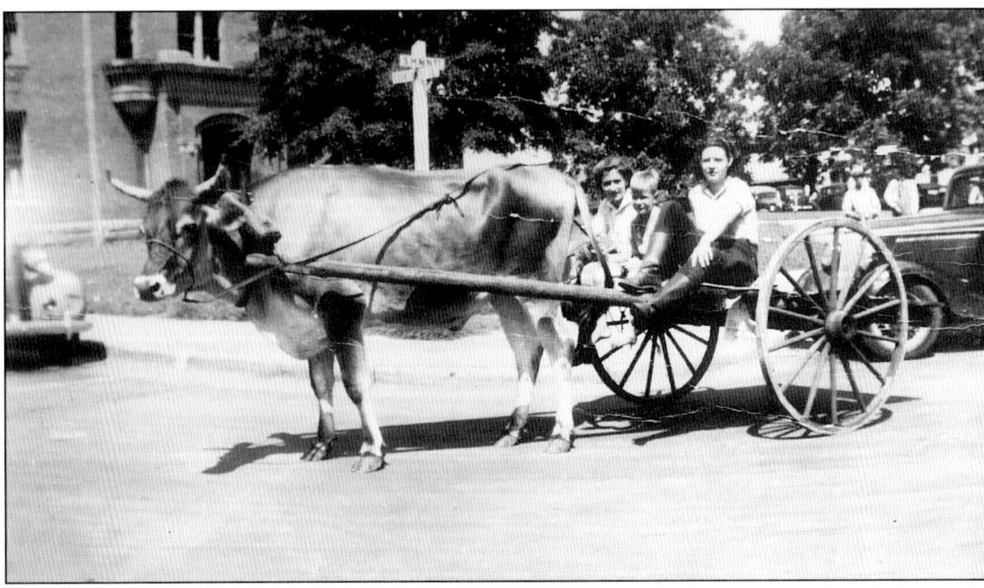

Here, an oxcart is shown in downtown Swainsboro, about 1935. On the cart, from left to right are: Ary MacMillan, Josh Hunnicutt, and Jeanette Lindsey.

Five

This is Who We Were

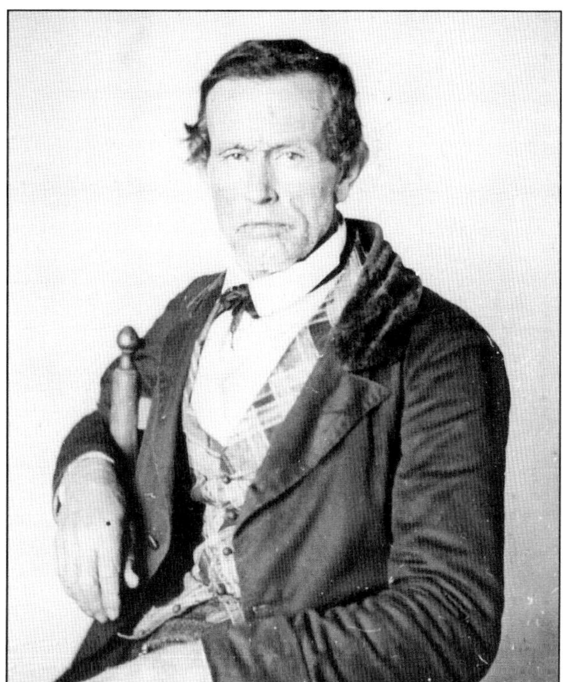

Benjamin E. Brinson, born January 1, 1800, was the son of Adam Brinson II and Mary Sheppard. One of the earliest settlers in the county, his house was the first post office, and he served as judge of the Inferior Court and a member of the Georgia House of Representatives in 1843. The picture is a rare ambrotype taken before his death in 1861.

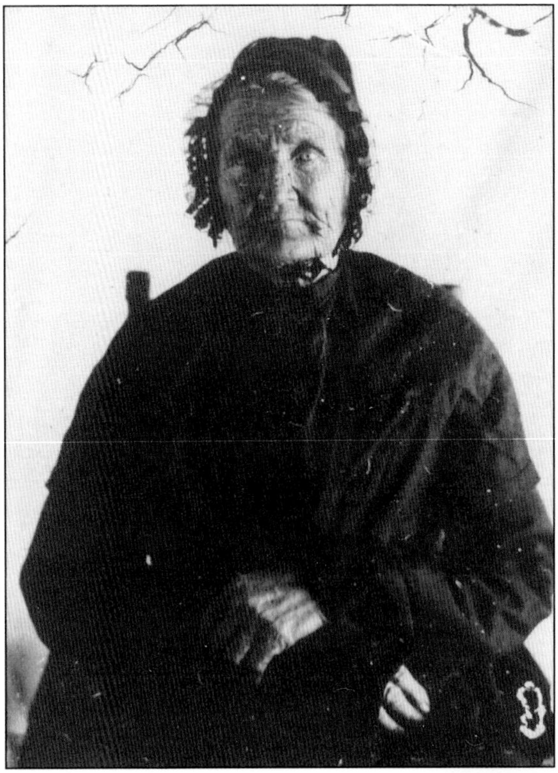

Mary Lewis (6/26/1804–4/14/1870), wife of Benjamin Brinson, was the daughter of Jesse Lewis, veteran of the War of 1812, and Mary Clifton. Soon after her father died in 1817, Mary Lewis was living with her mother and three sisters. She remembered bears coming in their yard and a panther trying to tear off their roof shingles. Mary Clifton had to blow a hunting horn to summon help.

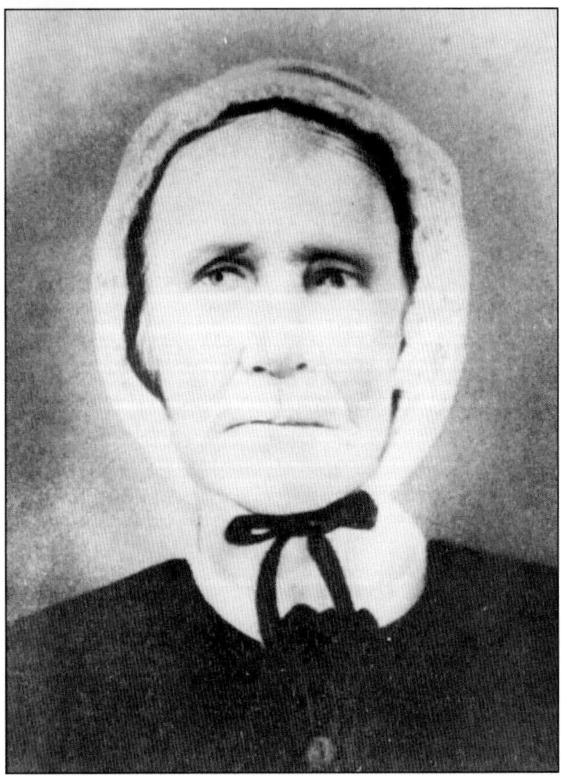

Mary Lucretia Scott (1797–1878), daughter of Gen. John Scott and Eliza Coleman, was married to Rev. Elisha Coleman. She was said to be a woman of imagination and talent, acting as a caterer to plantation owners, but she was also outspoken and independent, traits difficult to accept in a minister's wife. She and her husband later moved to Emanuel County, near Canoochee.

Rev. Elisha Coleman, born April 2, 1789 in Burke County, was the son of Jonathan Coleman and Milly Pittman. He married Mary Lucretia Scott, his second wife, in 1829. The marriage proved to be a stormy one. Rev. Coleman served with the 8th Brigade, 1st Division, Georgia Militia of Burke County. Originally a member of Bark Camp Church, he later attended Old Canoochee Church in Emanuel County and was one of the organizers of Hawhammock Church on July 23, 1842. He died on October 30, 1860, while living with his daughter, Lucretia Virginia Coleman Edenfield. His wife lived down the road with a son.

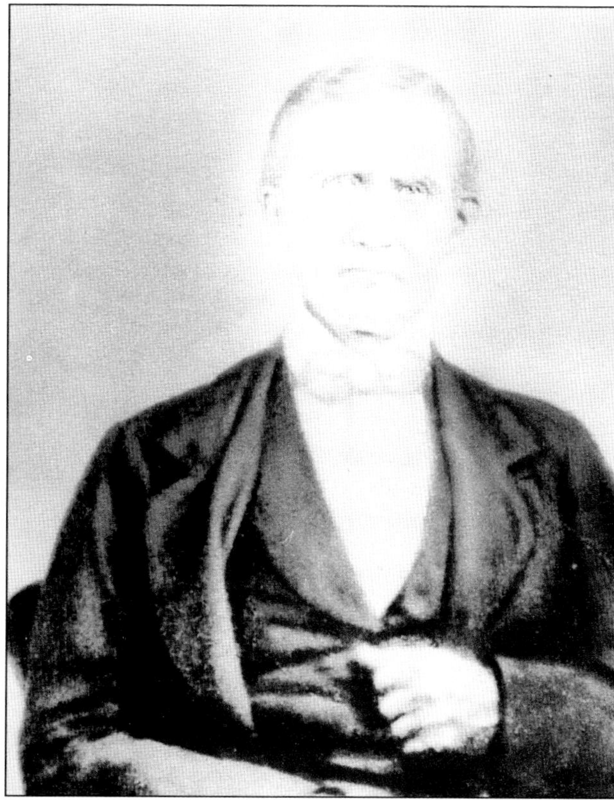

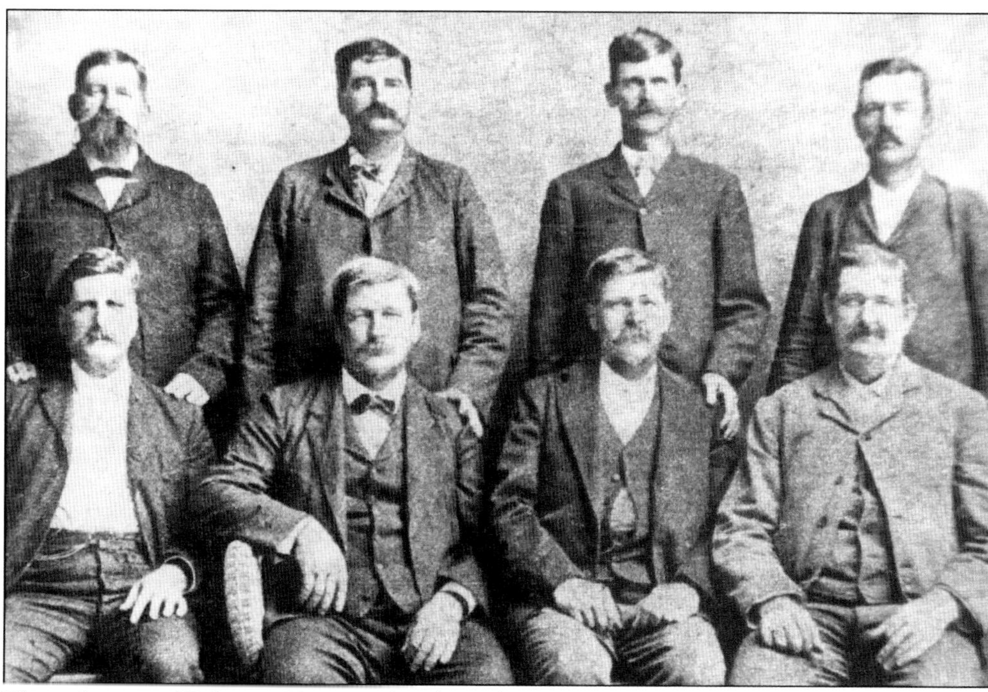

The eight sons of Solomon Youmans lived on adjoining farms in the "Youmans' Settlement." In this 1903 photograph are: Ebb, George, Lott, Lawson, Nathan, Sewell, Norwood, and John.

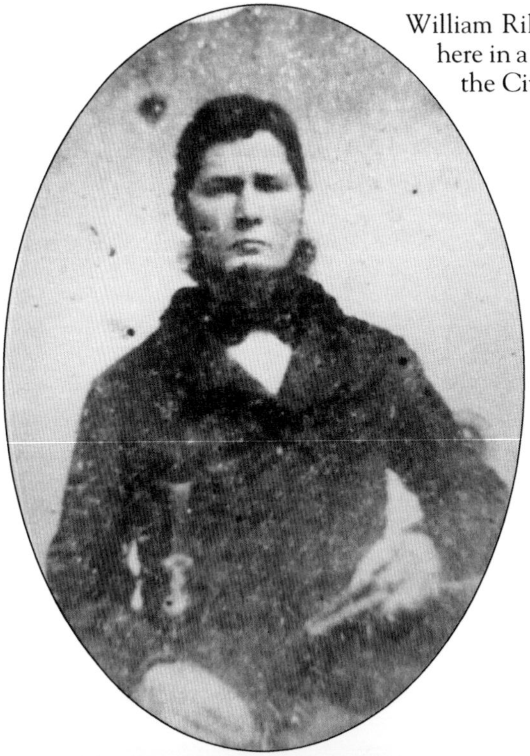

William Riley Adams (2/21/1829–4/11/1918) is shown here in a very early photograph, probably made before the Civil War.

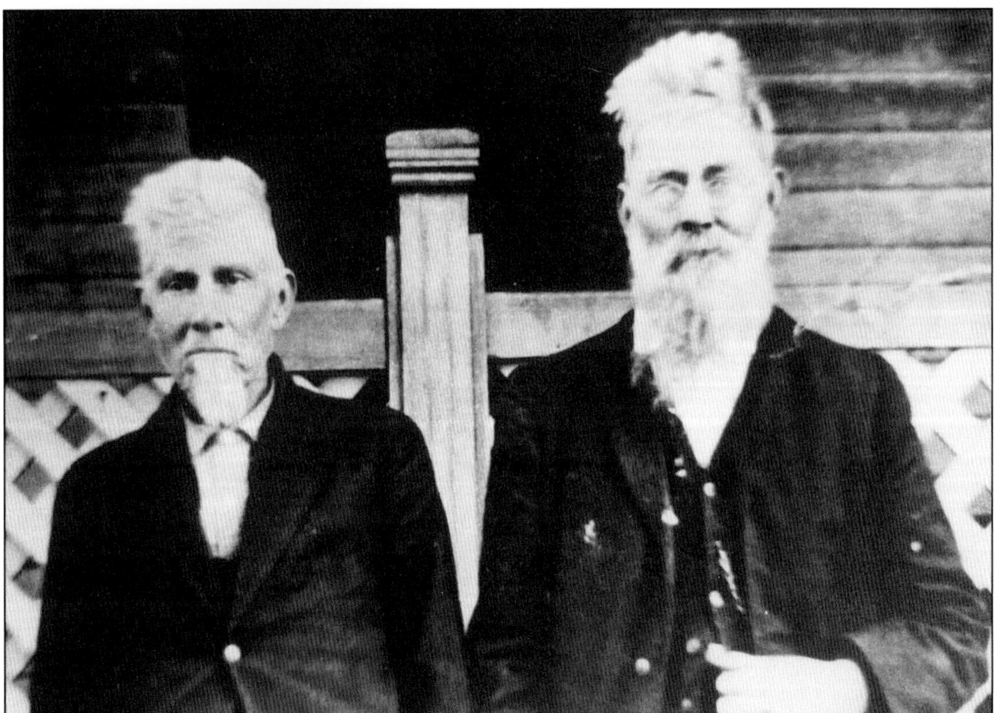

A much older William Riley Adams (right) and his brother Nathan Adams had their picture taken before 1918.

Pictured here are an older Augustus Lewis Cowart (6/15/1832–8/29/1910), son of Augustus Miles Cowart, and his wife, Nancy Ann L. Barwick Cowart (12/27/1835–11/19/1911), daughter of Lott Barwick. The Cowart's house was located off Highway 80 East near Twin City.

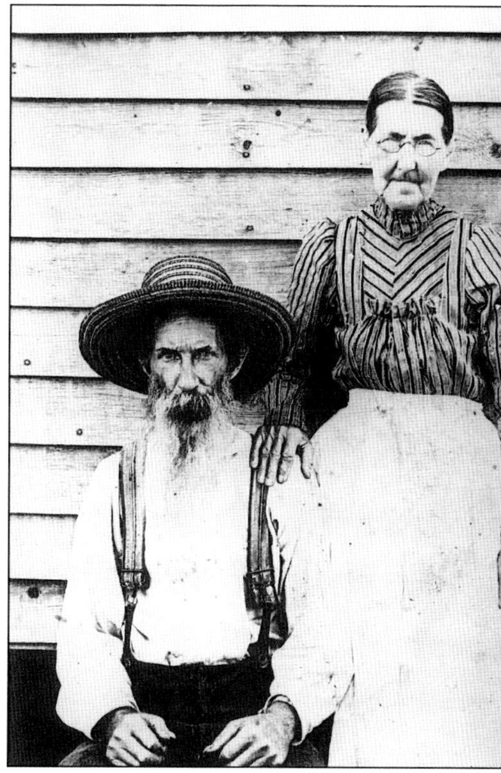

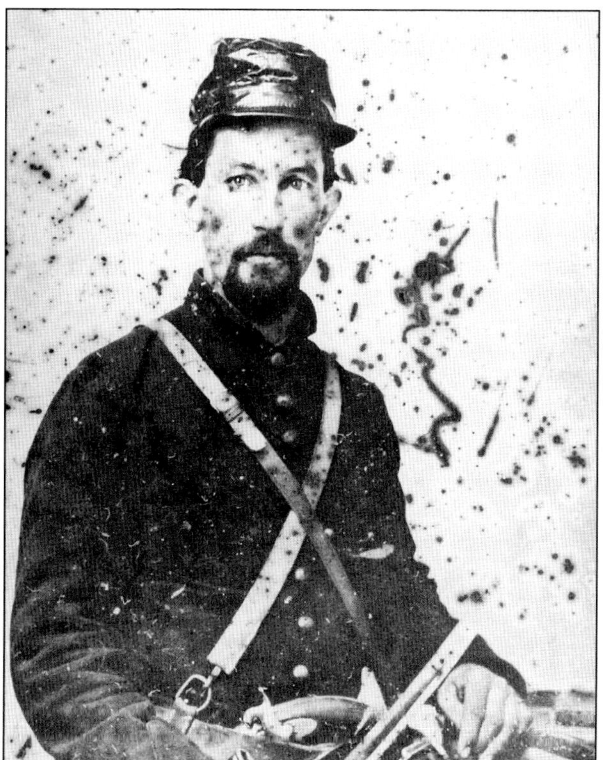

Augustus Lewis Cowart was photographed while a young man serving with the Bulloch Troop, Confederate Army during the Civil War.

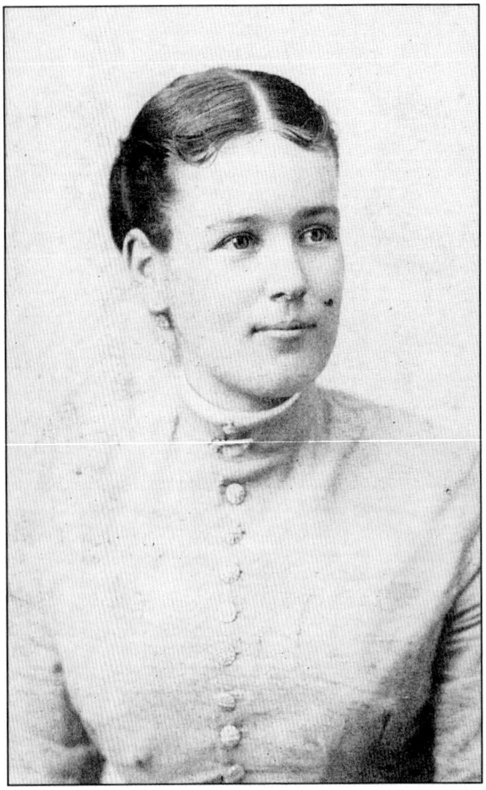

Mary Evelina (Sis Moll) Brinson Perkins, daughter of Mary Durden and Jesse Adam Brinson, had her picture taken while a young woman in 1886. She was an infant in November 1864 when a detachment of Sherman's troops came through the Brinson Farm.They were delighted with the baby and wanted to hold her. At the same time they had no qualms about killing every cow, hog, and chicken on the place.

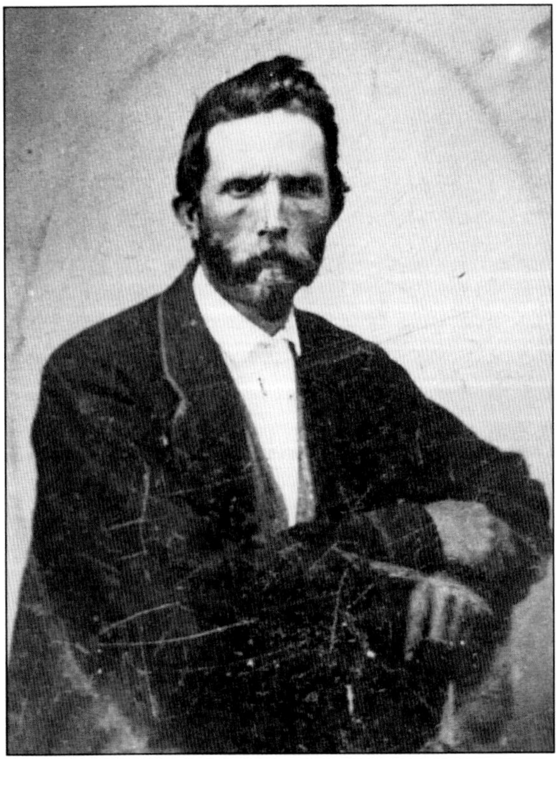

Rev. Joe Black, Methodist Minister, was the grandfather of Louise Black. This image is from an old tintype.

This is Zilphia Rountree as she appeared as a young woman.

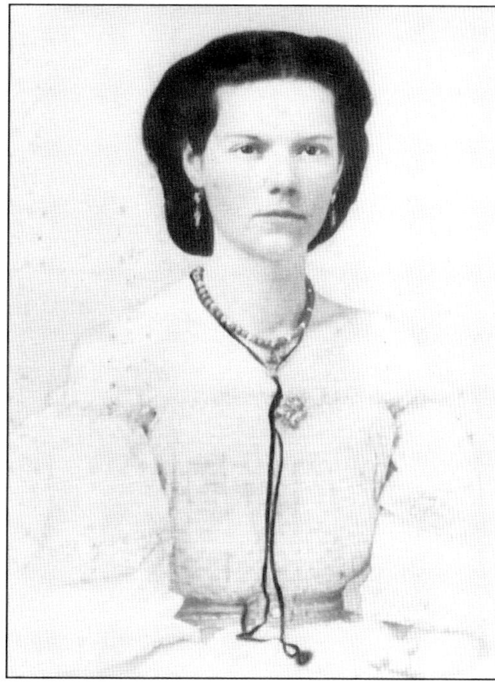

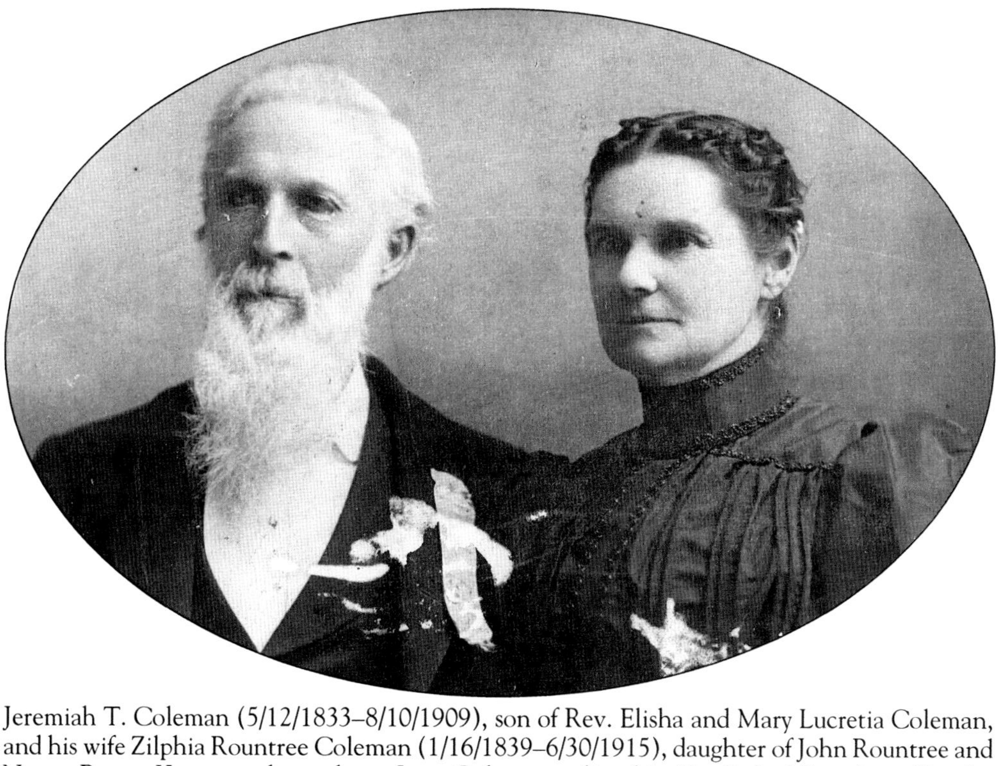

Jeremiah T. Coleman (5/12/1833–8/10/1909), son of Rev. Elisha and Mary Lucretia Coleman, and his wife Zilphia Rountree Coleman (1/16/1839–6/30/1915), daughter of John Rountree and Nancy Brown Kent, are shown here. Jerry Coleman enlisted in Co. B, 2nd Battalion, Cavalry in 1862. He was a farmer and store owner before and after the Civil War. His home, "The Sycamores," has been moved to the First Baptist Church Recreation area in Twin City.

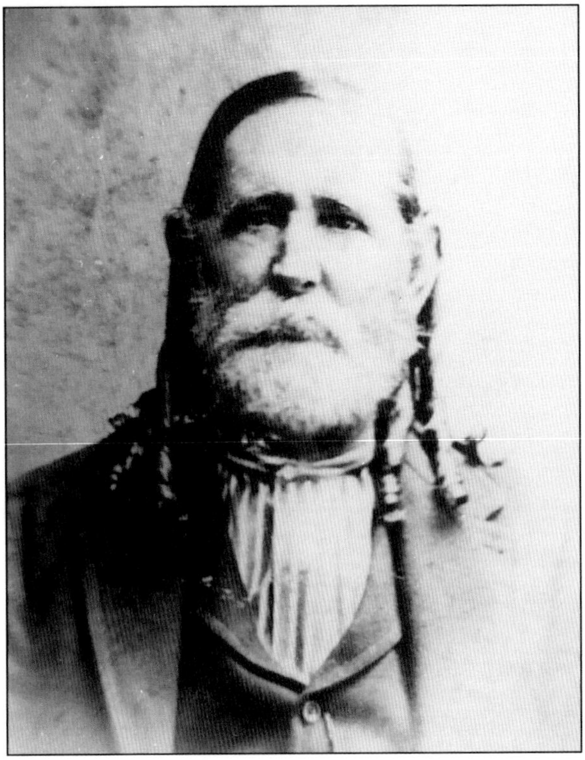

James Ellison, owner of Ellison & Coleman lumber yard, had his picture taken about 1890.

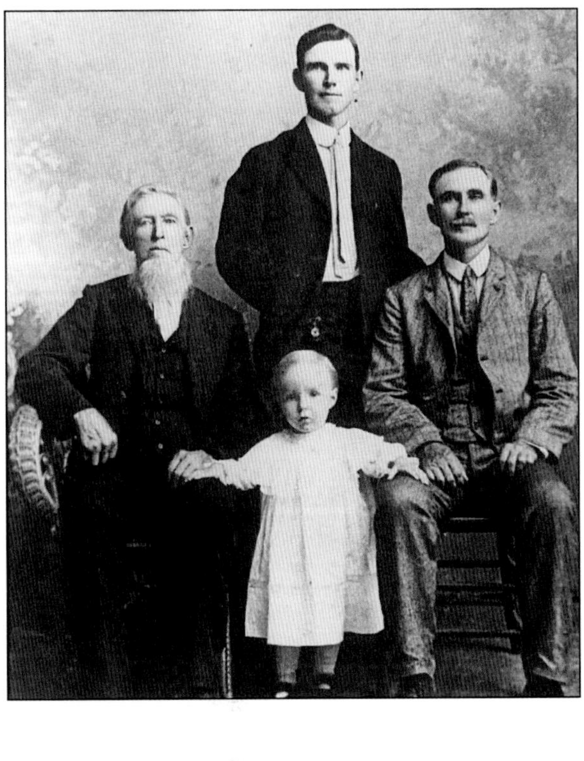

Pictured here is the Hall family. From left to right are: Houston Henry Hall (11/30/1839–2/13/1914), Charlie Iverson Hall (6/22/1880–6/25/1944), James Wright Hall (3/27/1861–7/15/1936), and Gordon Hall (3/2/1905–11/1/1970), age 2. The picture was taken in 1907.

Clara Virginia Coleman (2/16/1865–3/12/1945) was the daughter of Jeremiah T. Coleman and Zilphia Rountree and the granddaughter of John Rountree. She married Dennis Brinson Durden on October 31, 1881. Her home is presently located at the Twin City Baptist Church Recreation area. John Rountree's log cabin has been restored at the Carilee Coleman Walsh Historic Park in Twin City.

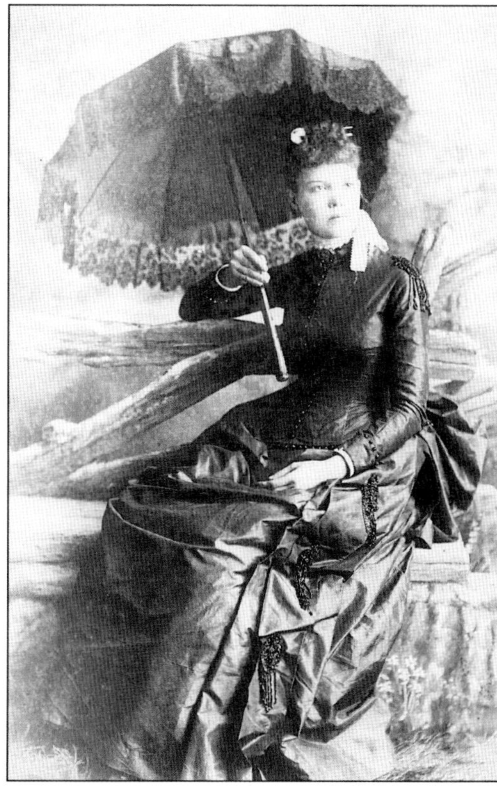

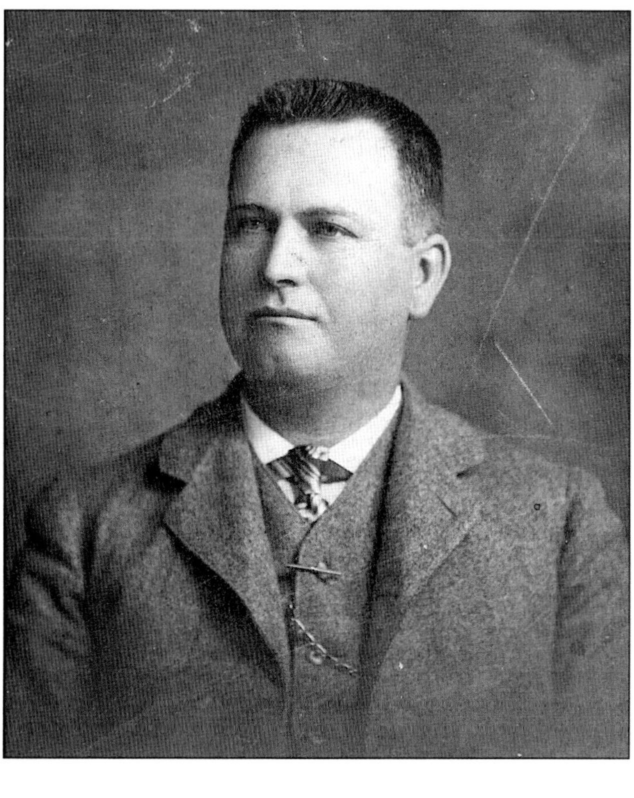

Dr. Edward Thaddeus Coleman (1/20/1863–9/18/1929) was the son of Jeremiah Thaddeus Coleman and Zilphia Rountree. He was a graduate of the University of Georgia, operated a hospital in Graymont, and was, at one time, president of the Medical Association of Georgia.

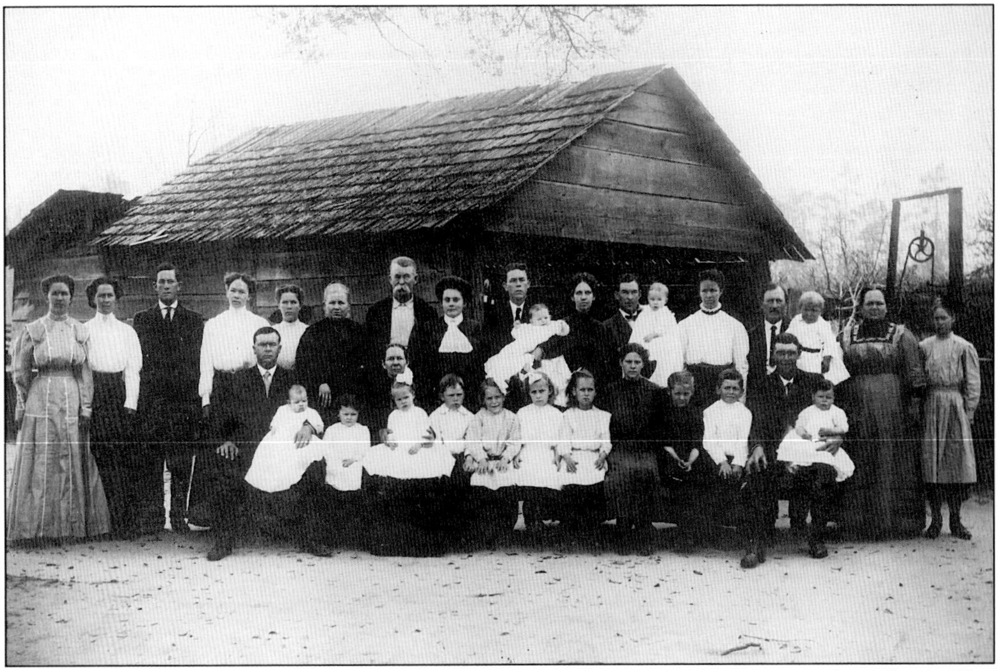

James Albert Neal, his wife, Sarah J. Turner Neal, and their children, Arminda, Julia, Lilllie, Lewis, Lizzie, Rufus, Ida, James Albert, Sarah, Jane, Ben, Sidney, Mary, Nannie, Herschel, Paul, Ruby, and Ruth.

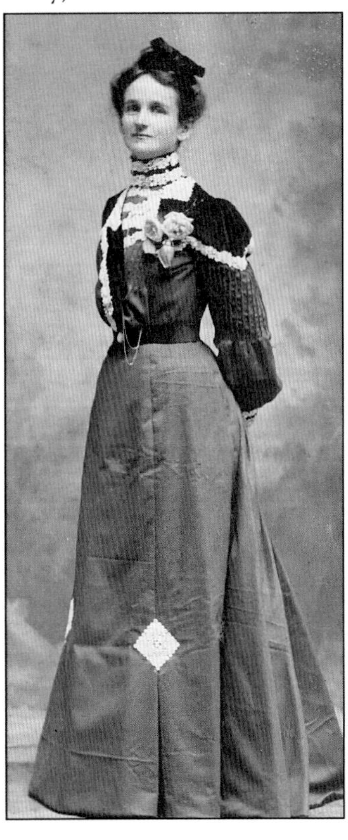

Margaret "Maggie" Durden (1/19/1872–2/14/1960), daughter of Algerine T. Durden and Millicent Moore of Stillmore, married Dr. Edward T. Coleman in 1890. They lived in Graymont.

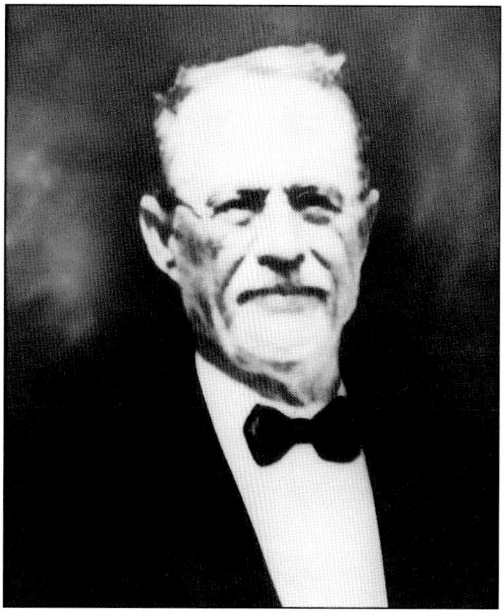

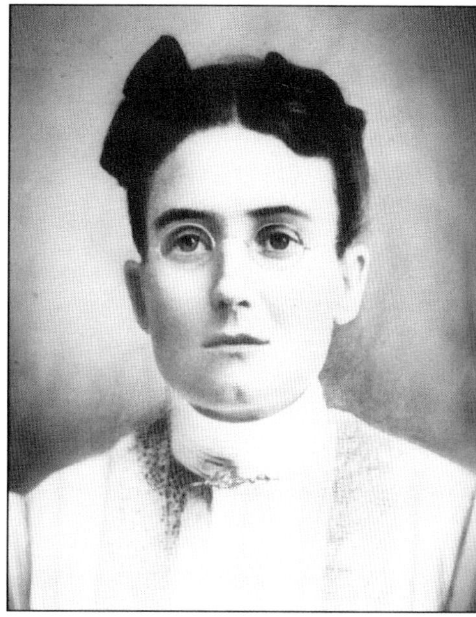

Left: James Amascus "Tobe" Coleman (3/26/1848–4/24/1928) married Fannie Lake in 1884. He served with the 2nd Georgia Militia, Stapleton's Regiment, during the Civil War. Afterwards he farmed and rafted timber for several years, joined his brother John C. in a general store business, and, in partnership with James Ellison, operated a sawmill and the Coleman & Ellison Railway. In 1894 he was elected to the Georgia Legislature and in 1900 formed the Citizens bank. *Right*: Fannie Lake (3/31/1869–11/2/1962), wife of James Amascus Coleman and daughter of Enoch Maybon Lake and Susannah Ethridge, is shown here. Their former home is now the Coleman House Inn.

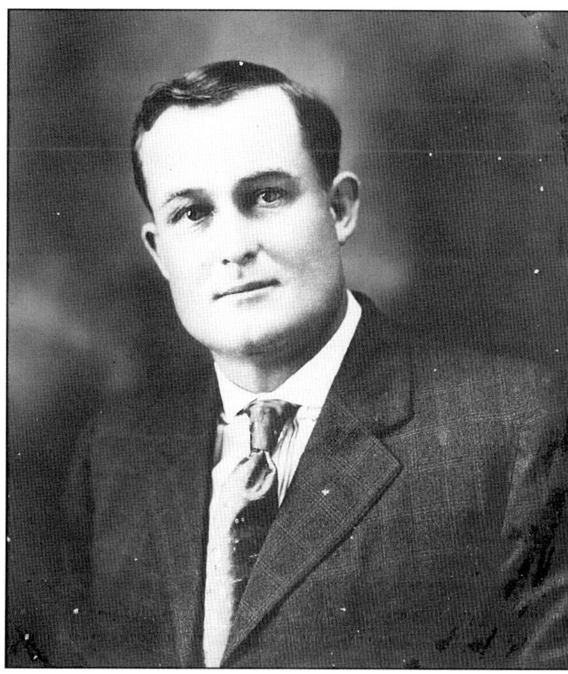

John Randolph Coleman (5/30/1887–1/19/1952), son of James Amascus Coleman and Fannie Lake Coleman, married Aline Forehand. He was president of the Citizens Bank from 1928 until his death, chairman of the Emanuel County Commissioners, director of the Wadley & Southern Railroad, member of the mercantile firm of Coleman, Elliott, & Clark, and involved in naval stores business.

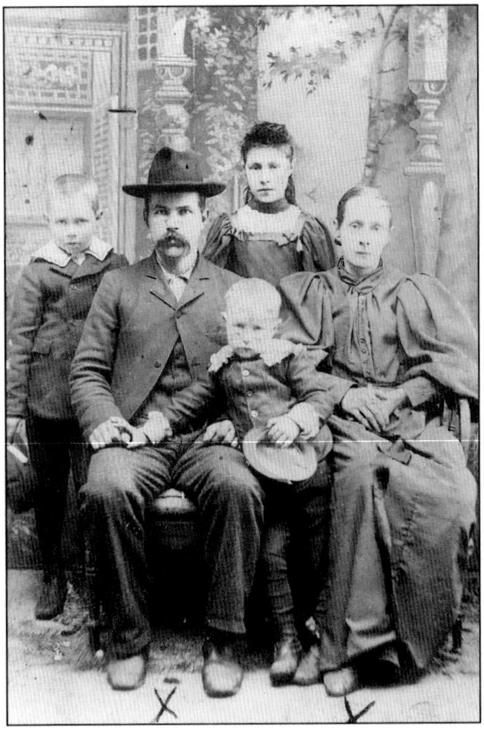

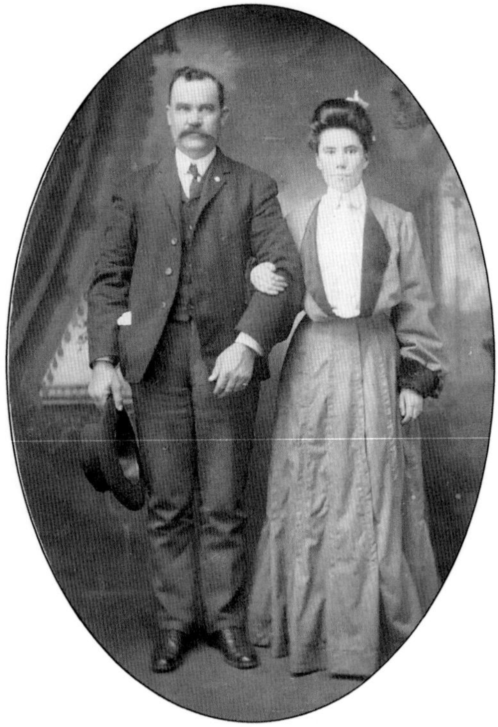

Left: Shown here are Madison Lewis Cowart, Susan Ann Woods, and their children Annie, born 1884, Claude William, born 1890, and Remer Y., born 1892. *Right*: Lott Cowart and his wife, Bertha Ellington Cowart, posed for this photograph.

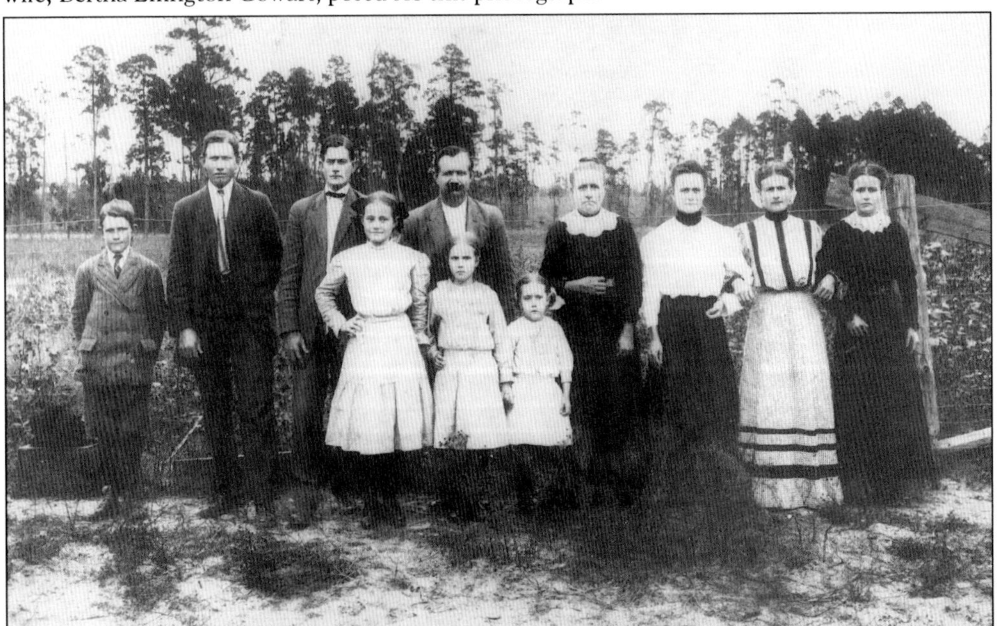

This is the Spencer Douglas family at their homeplace near Norristown Junction *c.* 1910. Pictured from left to right are: (front row) Elizabeth (Lizzie), Ada, and Lou; (back row) Wylie, Clint, Gordon, Spencer (father), Mozelle (mother), Minnie, Nancy, and Emmie Douglas.

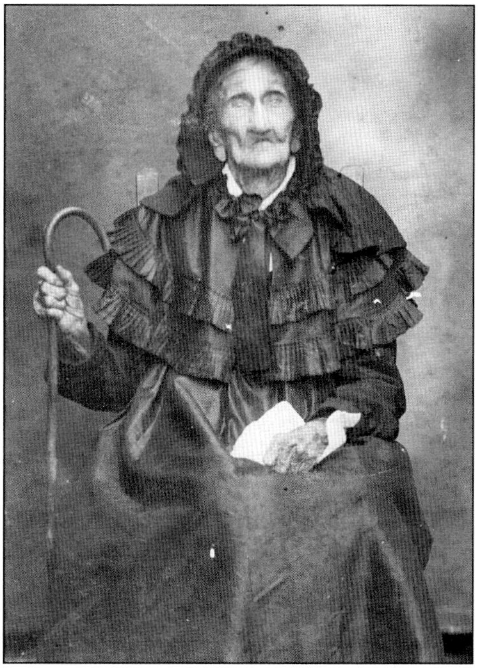
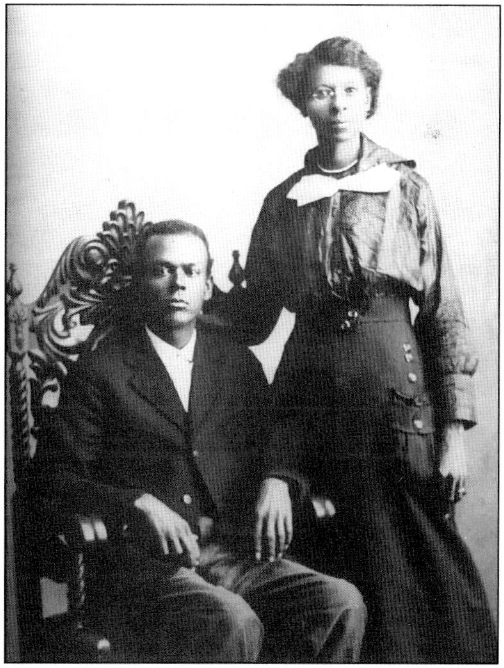

Left: Elize Collins Adams, the matriarch of the Adams family and wife of Mathias Adams, was photographed at a very advanced age. *Right*: This is Arsula Brinson and her husband, Sol Chance. He was the son of Pherabe Chance; she was the daughter of Peter Brinson.

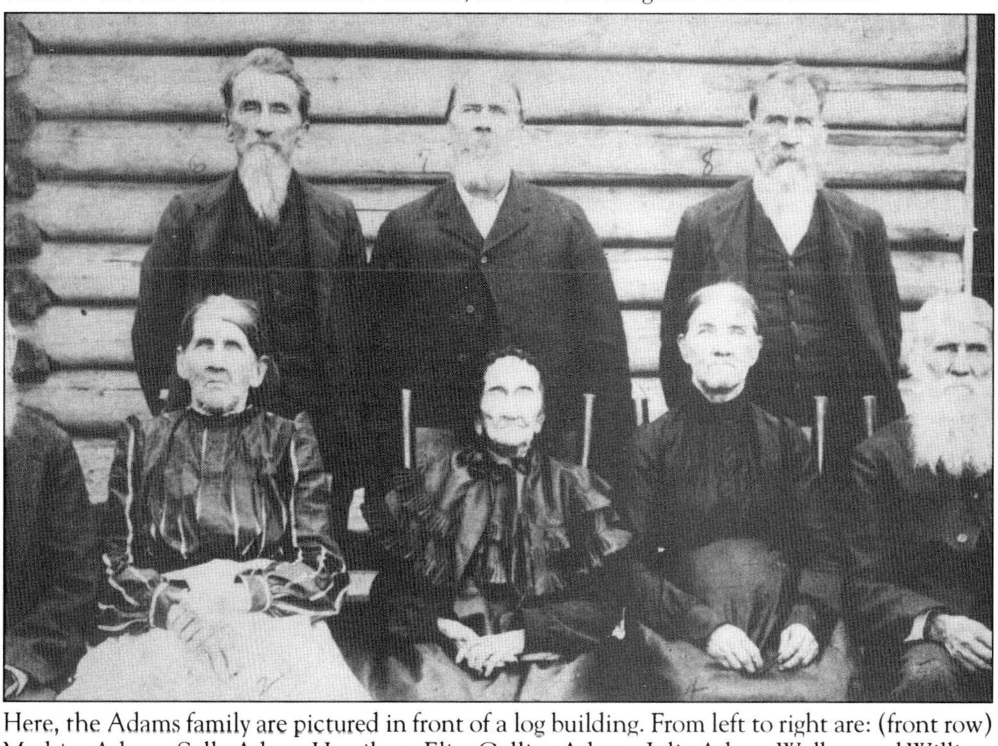

Here, the Adams family are pictured in front of a log building. From left to right are: (front row) Mathias Adams, Sally Adams Hamilton, Eliza Collins Adams, Julie Adams Walker, and William Thomas Ezekial Adams; (back row) Jasper Adams, Robert Adams, and Charlie Adams.

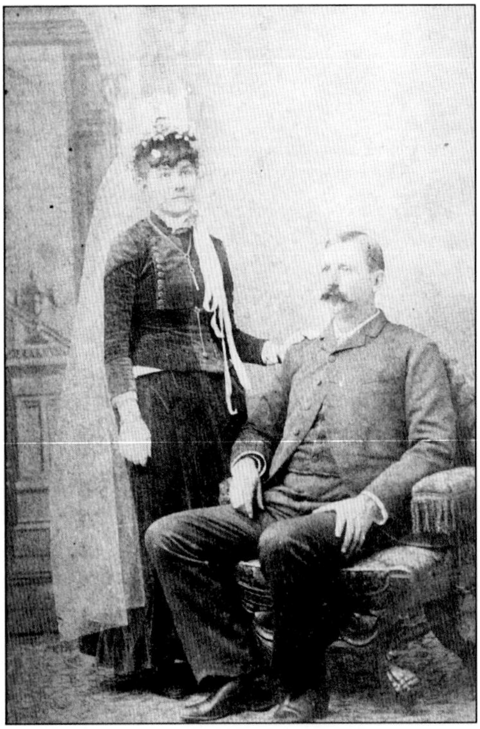

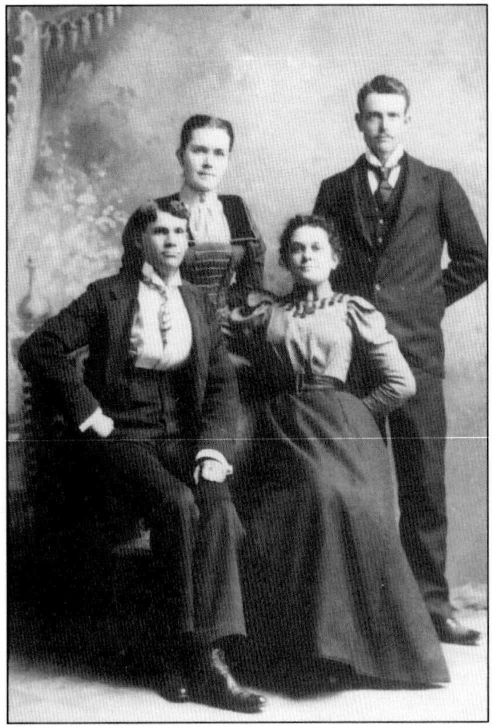

Left: This is Mozelle Adams Smith and her husband as they appeared on their wedding day. *Right*: Shown in this *c.* 1900 group photograph are, from left to right: Sudie Coleman, Fayette Joiner, Nan Crum, and Fred Coleman.

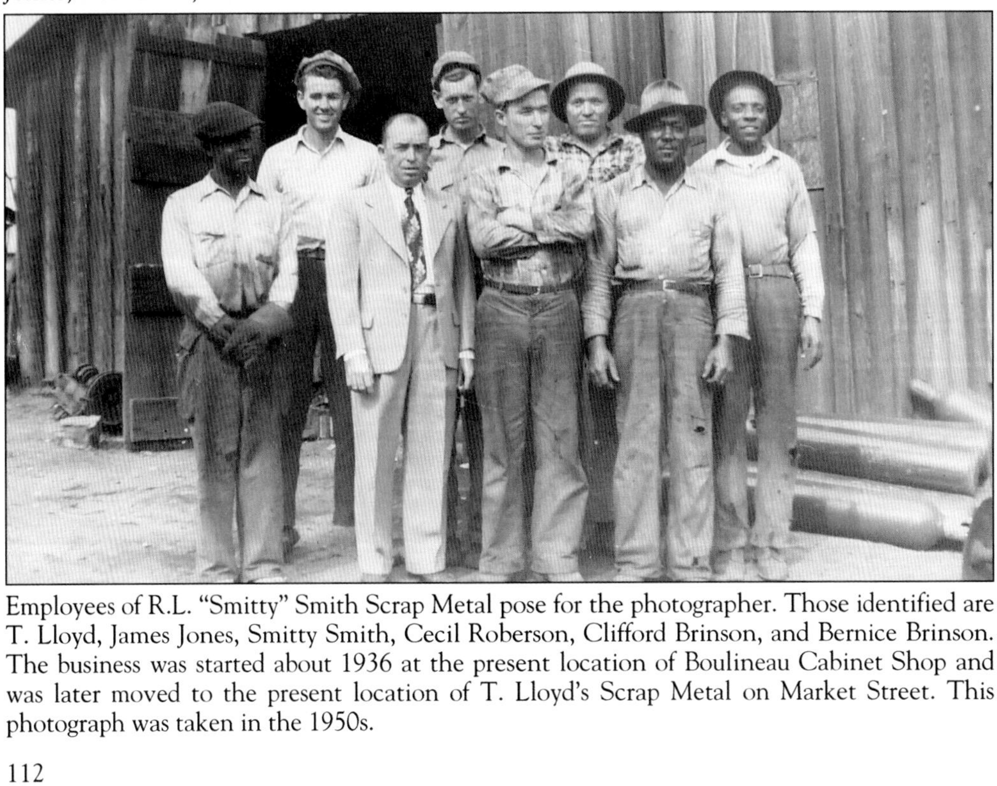

Employees of R.L. "Smitty" Smith Scrap Metal pose for the photographer. Those identified are T. Lloyd, James Jones, Smitty Smith, Cecil Roberson, Clifford Brinson, and Bernice Brinson. The business was started about 1936 at the present location of Boulineau Cabinet Shop and was later moved to the present location of T. Lloyd's Scrap Metal on Market Street. This photograph was taken in the 1950s.

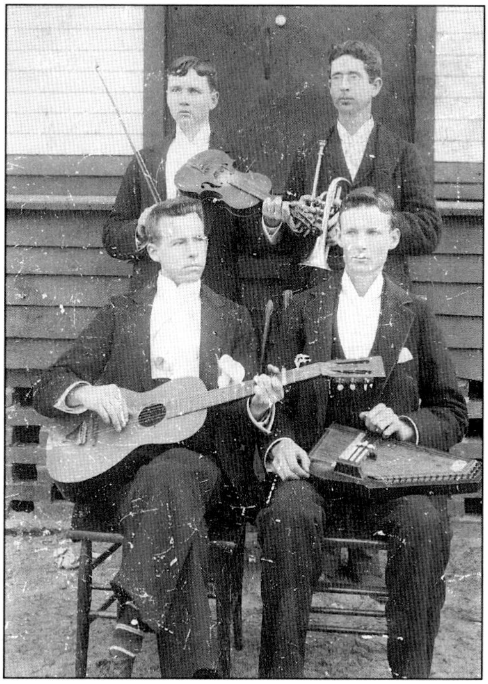
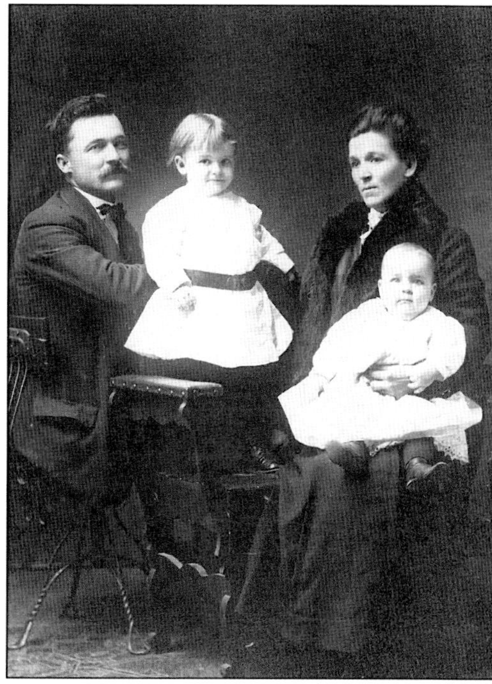

Left: This four-piece band starred Wallace Coleman and Emmit Smith, seated, and Rob Walsh and Will Aldred, standing. *Right*: Shown here are James L. Herrington, his wife, Press Cowart, (from Twin City) and two of their children, Nina and Frank, *c*. 1912. Mr. Herrington was a farmer, and owned a sawmill, gristmill, and a turpentine still, all located in Nunez. He served in the Georgia House of Representatives about 1913–14.

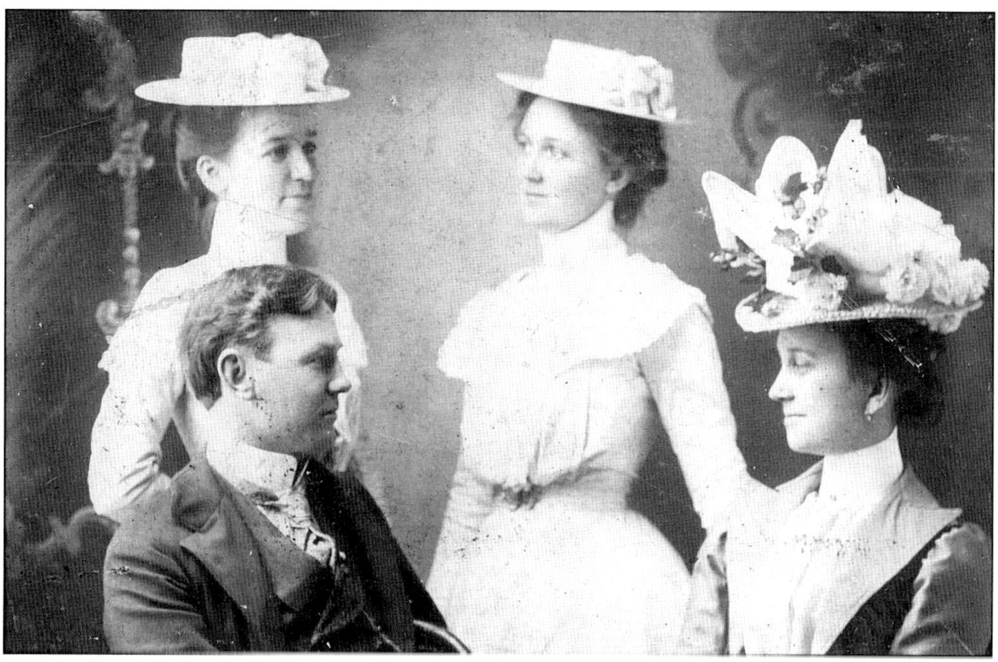

In this photograph of a young Press Cowart (at left), note the ladies' hats.

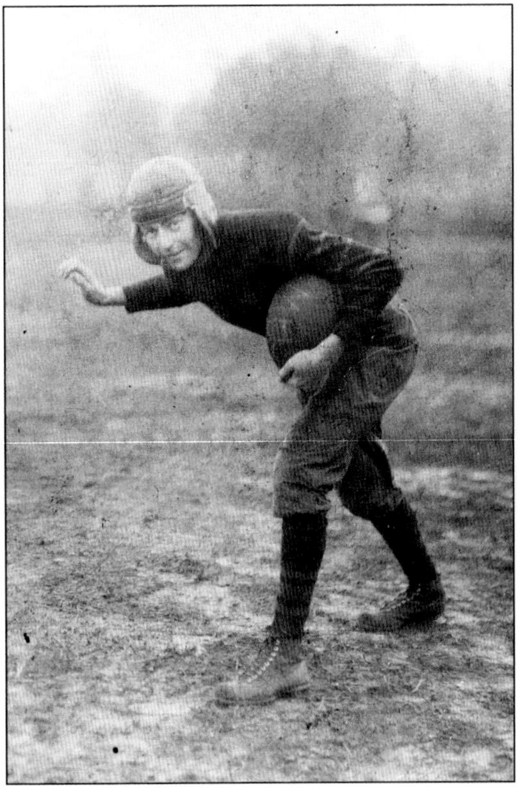

Thomas James Cowart Jr., born 1904, had his picture taken about 1920. Note that the old football uniforms had very little protective equipment.

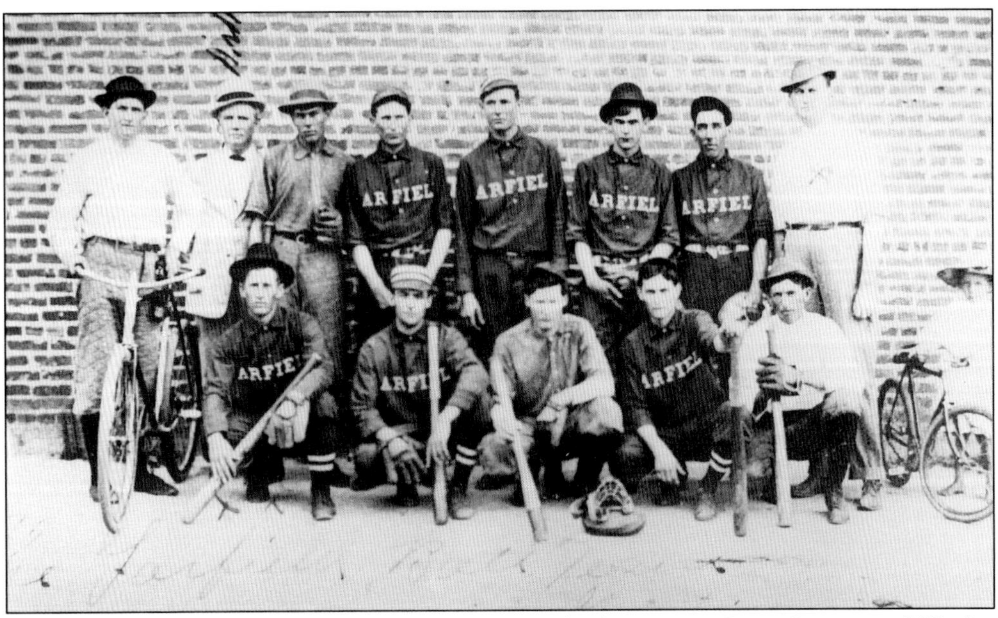

The Garfield Baseball Team posed for this photograph about 1900. Oscar Cowart and Wesley Lamb are two of the players.

Shown here is a wild card game in front of the old bank building in Stillmore, sometime before 1914. Seated in the center is Exlie Martin.

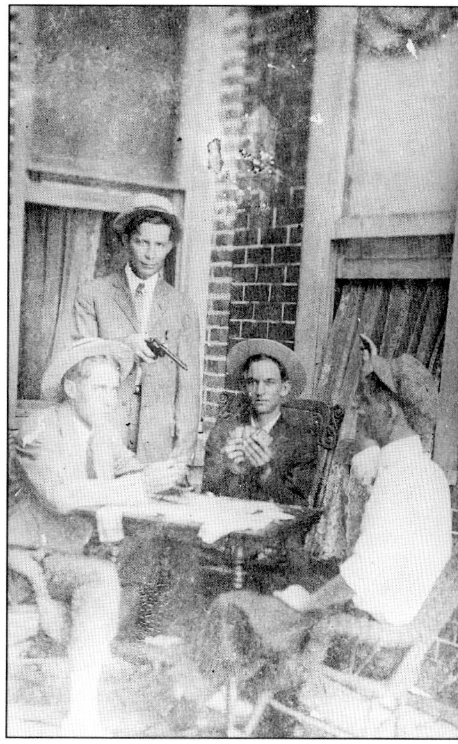

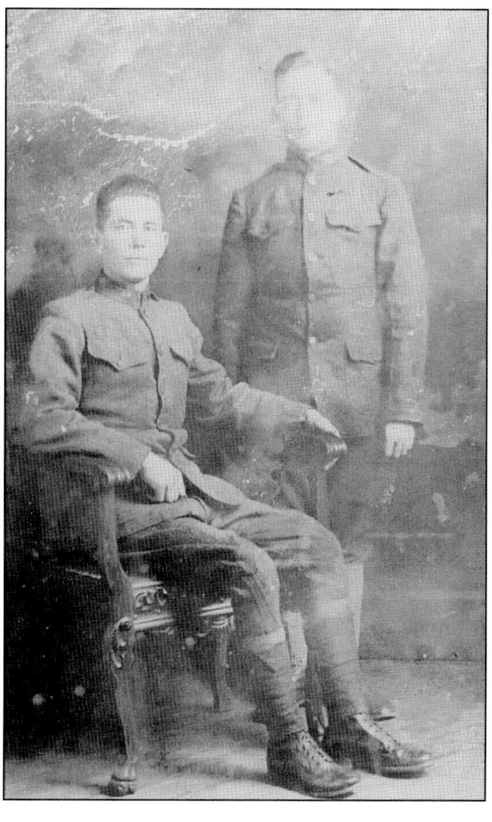

Thomas Livingston and Clarence Livingston were photographed in their WW I uniforms about 1918.

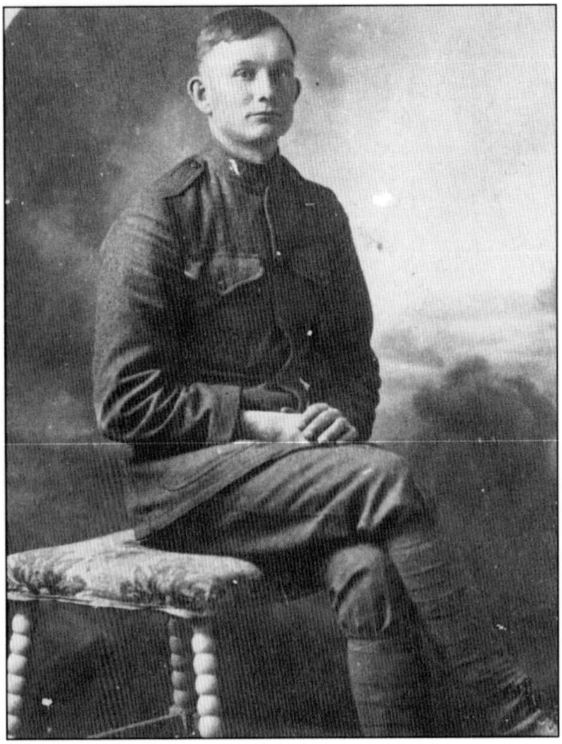

This is Henry Culbreath as he appeared in his WW I uniform.

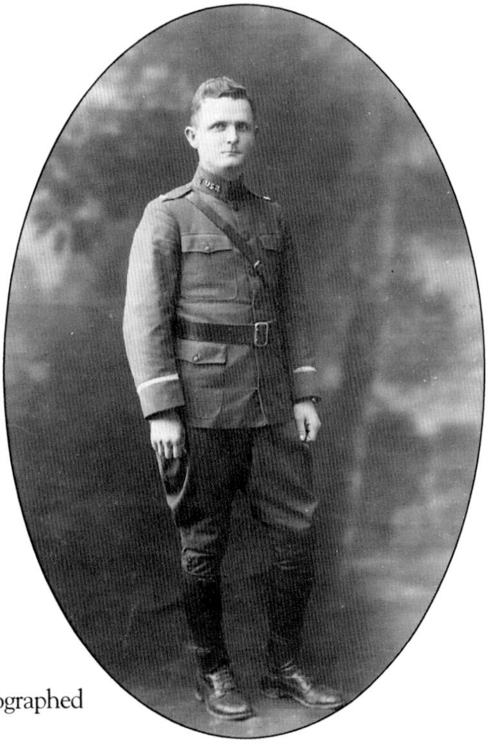

1st Lieutenant William L. Herrington was also photographed in his WW I uniform.

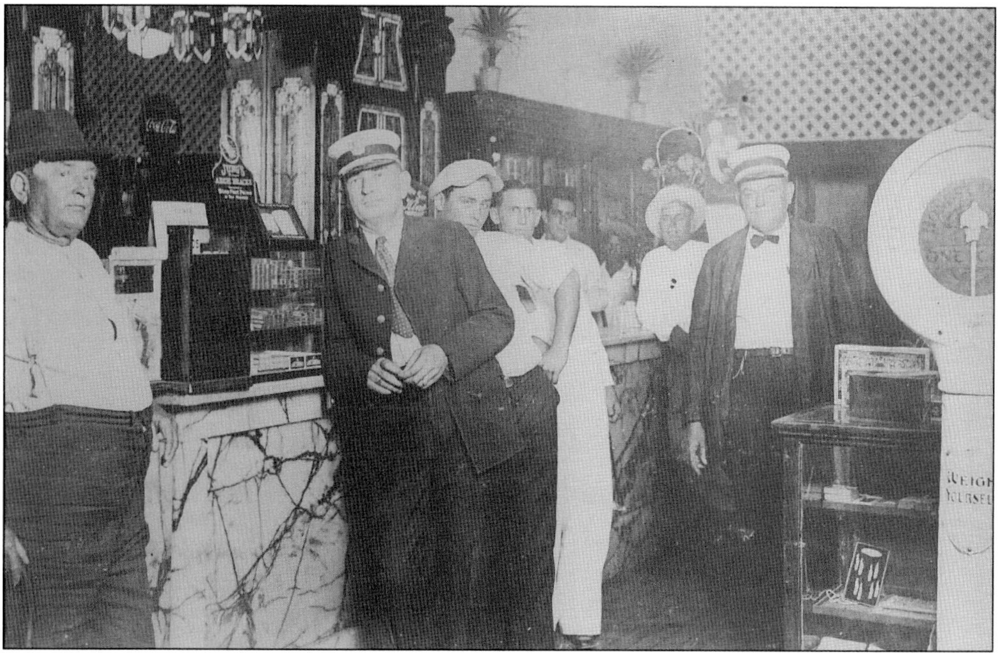

Shown here is W.H. Brannan's Drug store on the corner of Routes 1 and 80. From left to right are: Enoch Oliver, policeman Tom Tyson, Kent Brown, unidentified, Will Brannan (behind counter), unidentified, and Thomas "Papa T" Brown.

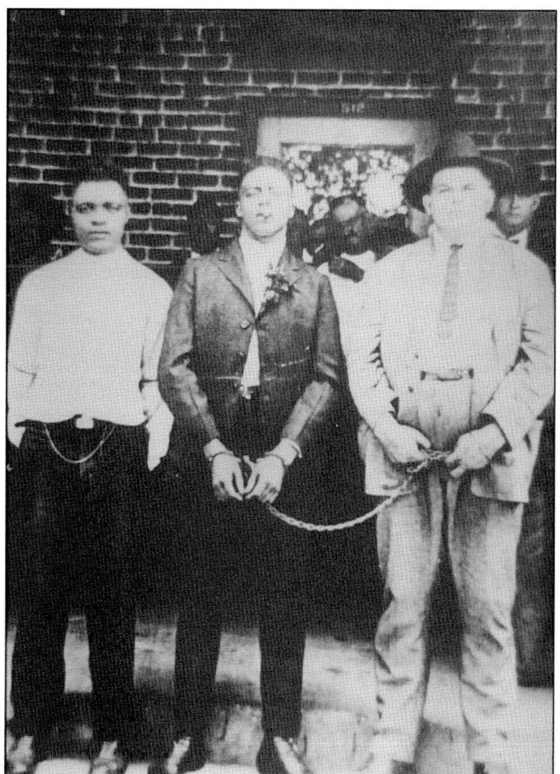

In 1923, Seaborn Johnson became the last man to be hanged in Emanuel County. He is shown here with his brother on his left and Sheriff Thomas "Papa T" Brown on his right.

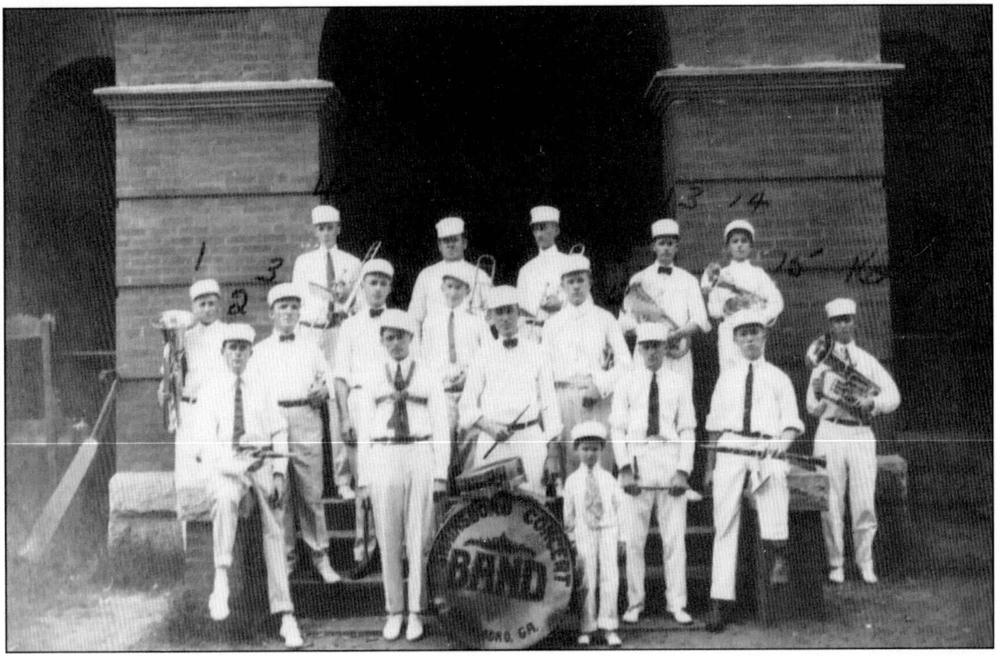

The Swainsboro Concert Band members were, from left to right: Jig Herrington, J.L. Lewis, H.H. Fillingham, Ralph Smith, Otis Price, Kottie Lewis, Clifford Thompson, bandleader Mr. Wooten, Pilner Williams, Guy Hill, Roger Youmans, unidentified, Johnny Lewis, unidentified, Dewey Gray, and Horace Flanders.

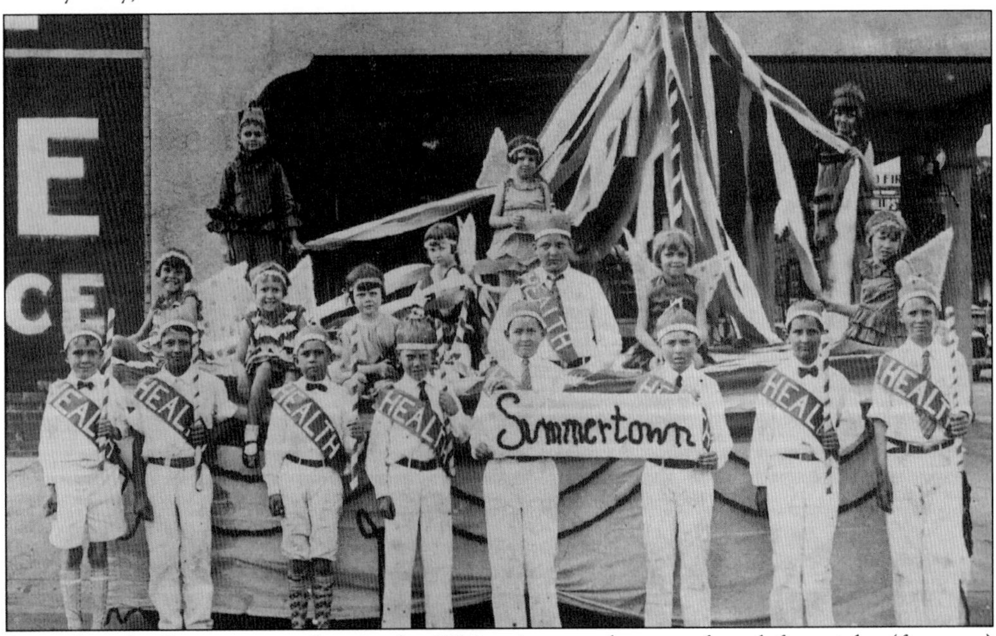

Attending the Summertown float in the 1930 spring parade, were, from left to right: (first row) Maurice Boatright, Bennett Hall, Byron Kirkland, Tom Smith, W.E. McGhee, Paul Henry, and Gene Davis; (second row) Sara Hall, Dorothy Brown, Jacqueline Kirkland, Evelyn Snellgrove, Hilton Riner, Juanita Williams, and Sue Siler; (third row) Dunford Sconyers, Eloise Brown, and Frankie Kirkland.

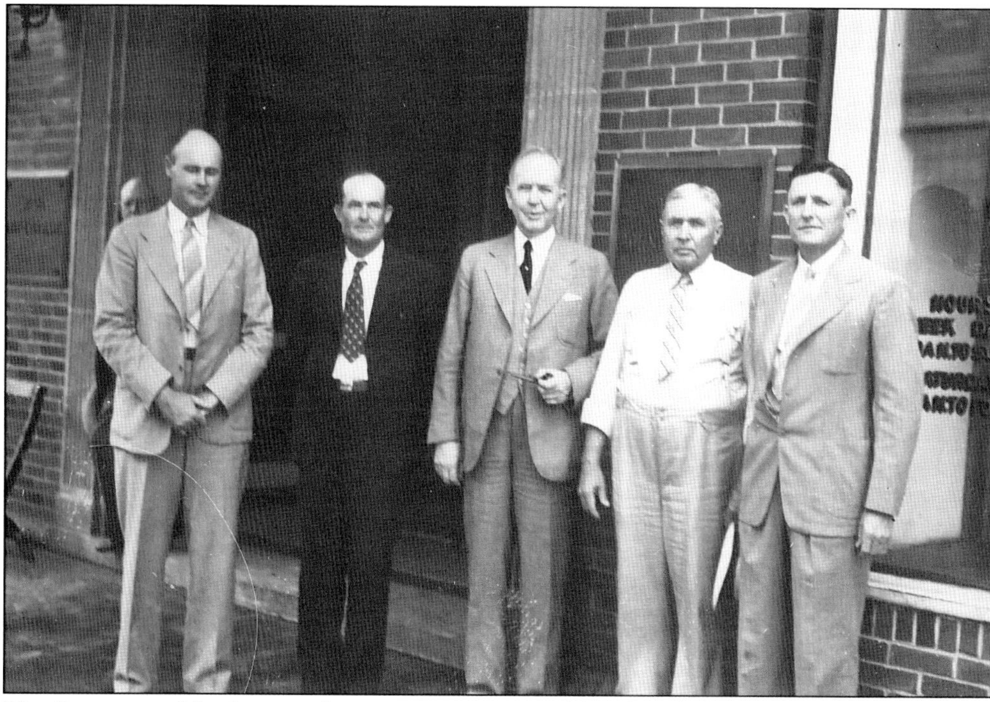

The farming and banking professions are represented by, from left to right: Robert M. Stiles (state president, United Georgia Farmers), J.Randolph Coleman (president, Citizens Bank), Edward A. O'Neal (president, Farm Bureau Federation), R.A. Flanders (president, Central Bank), and V.H. Hooks (president, Emanuel County chapter, United Georgia Farmers). This picture was taken in front of the John C. Coleman Hotel.

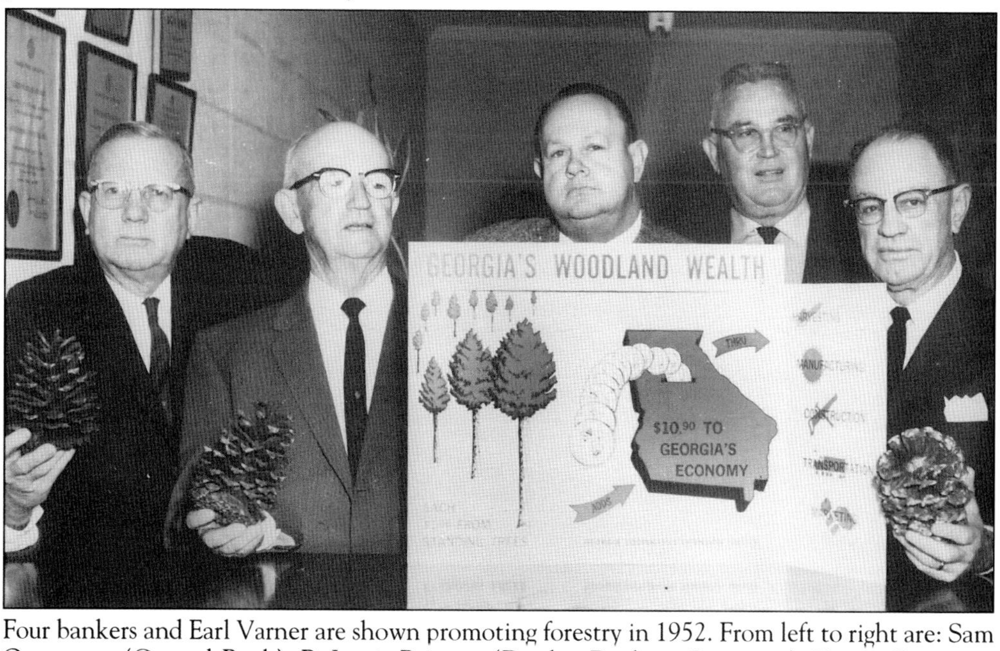

Four bankers and Earl Varner are shown promoting forestry in 1952. From left to right are: Sam Overstreet (Central Bank), B. Lewis Brinson (Durden Banking Company), Tumpy Rountree (Spivey State Bank), Earl Varner, and H.C. Edenfield (Citizens Bank).

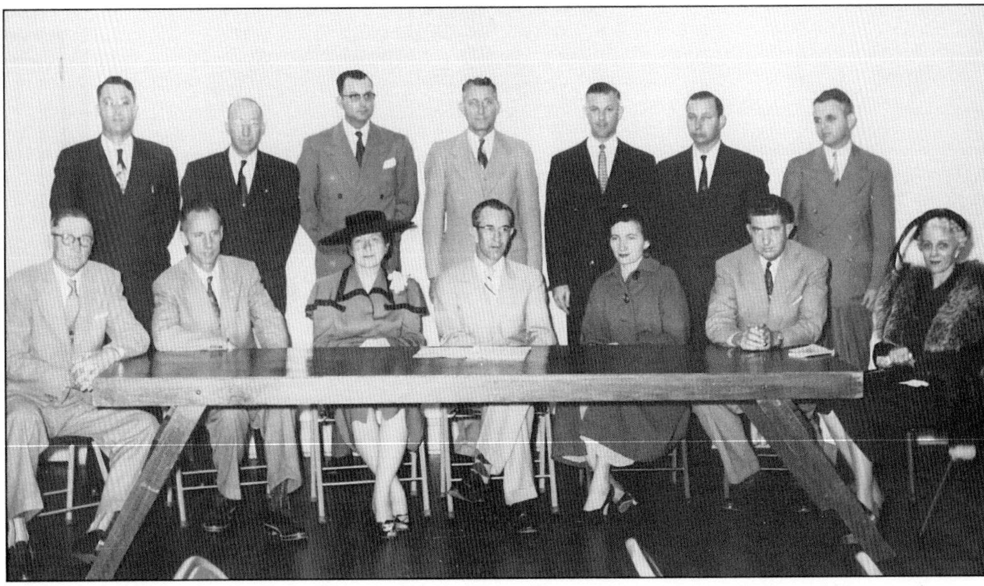

This group photograph was taken in Swainsboro about 1958. Pictured, from left to right, are: (front row) Ralph Smith, Jimmy Morgan, Sypper Youngblood, Howard Henson, Betty Gene Sanders, Glenn Segars, and Anne Segars; (back row) J.M. Turner, V.E. Glenn, Bobby Sasser, Ernest Willis, Vernard Roberson, Colby Leopard, and Woody Key.

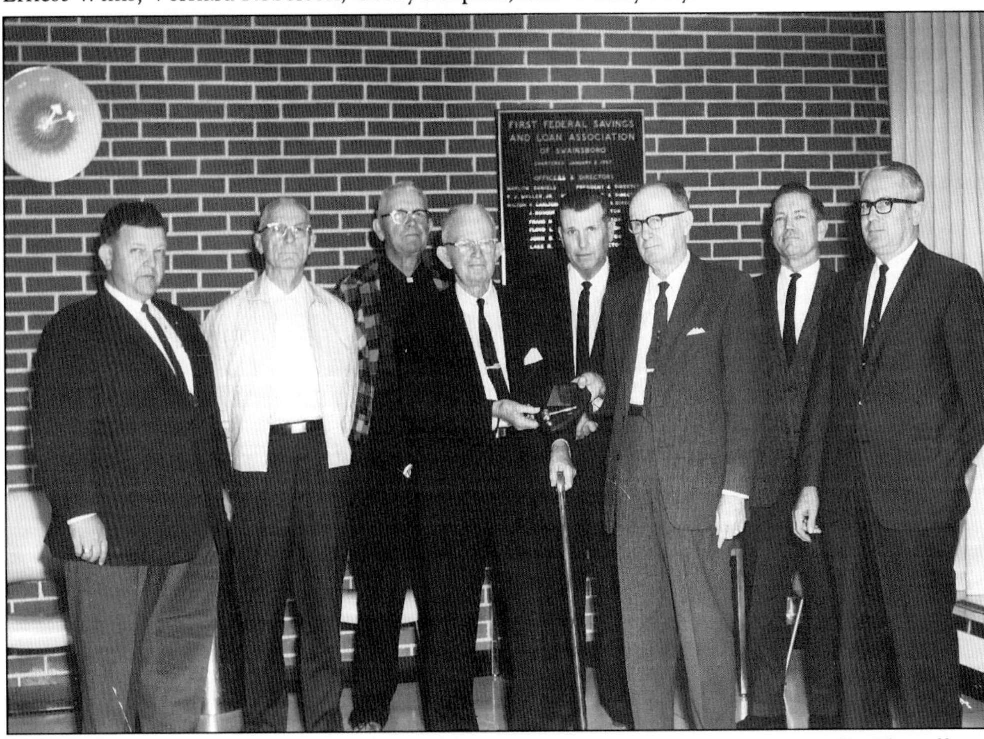

The First Federal Savings and Loan Association was chartered on January 2, 1957. The officers and directors shown are, from left to right: M.L. "Skinny" Anderson, J. Roscoe Brown, Floyd Spivey, Marlowe Daniels, President R.J. Waller Jr., Vice-President John B. Spivey, Milton A.Carlton, and Arthur Daniels.

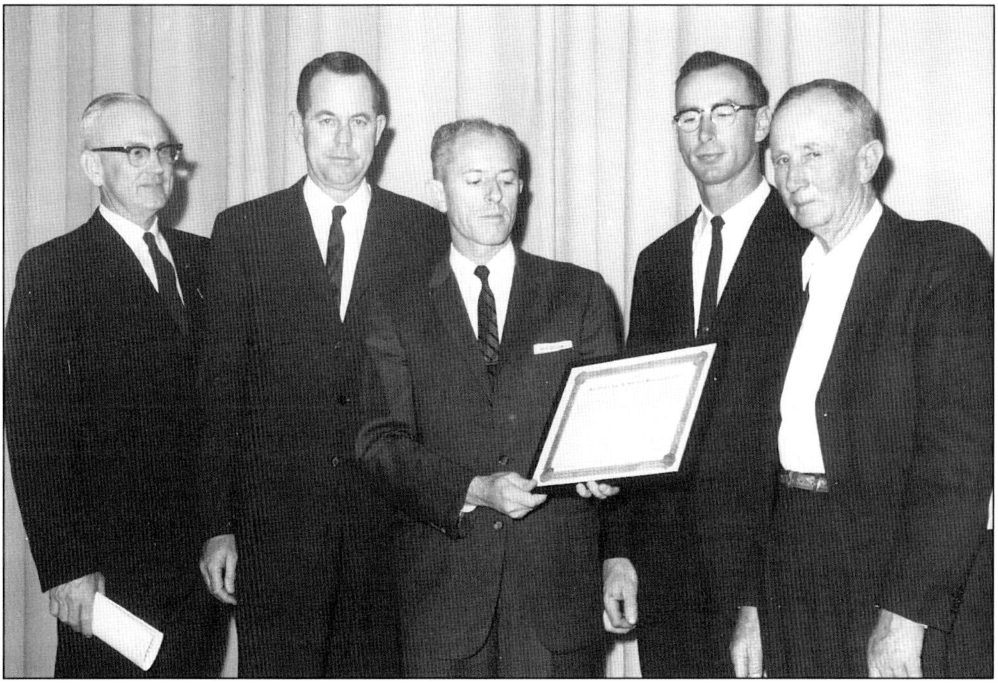

The Man of the Year in Soil and Water Conservation award was presented to Ben Lane by Tommy Durden in January 1964. Shown also are L.W. Eberhart, Jim L. Gillis, and Bobby Lane.

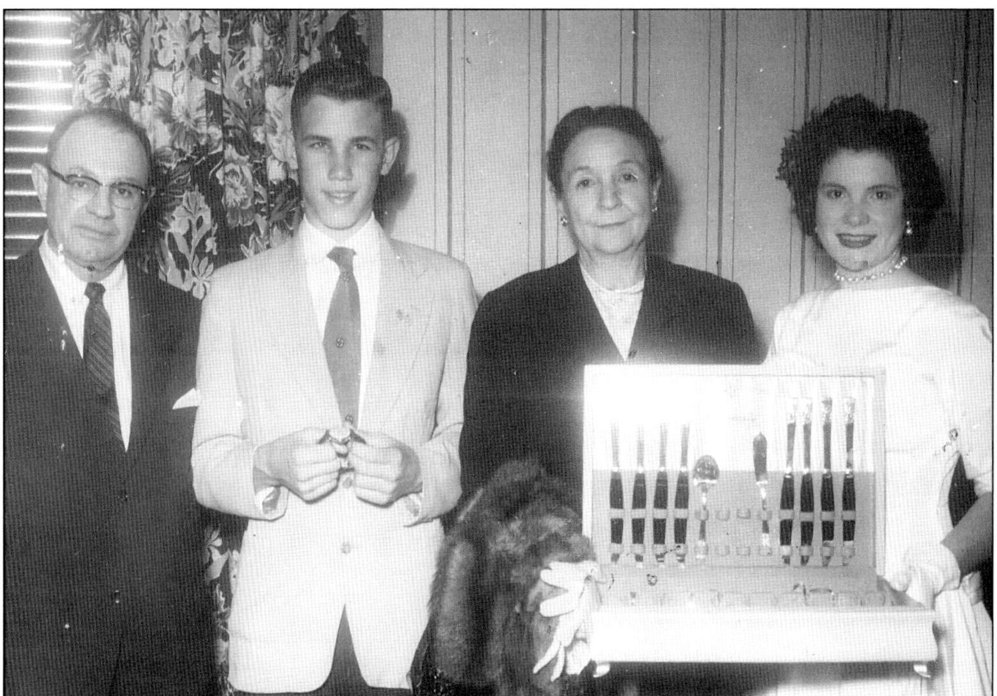

Mr. and Mrs. H.C. Edenfield presented the Edenfield Awards at the Champion Banquet to the outstanding 4-H girl and boy, Bobby Underwood and Janice Ridgdill.

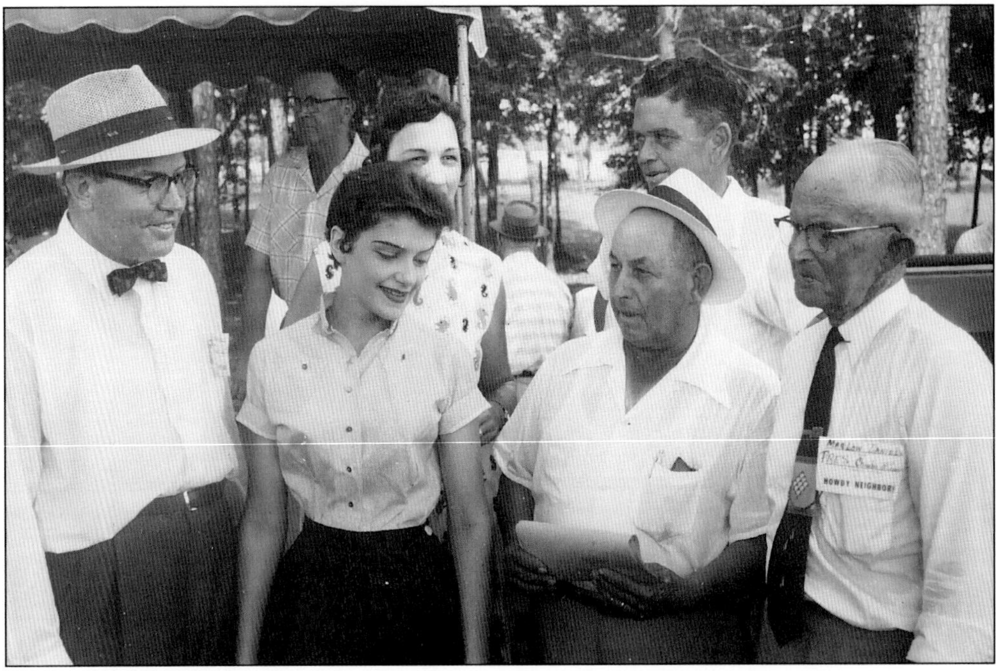

Shown in this photograph are, from left to right: Darius Brown, Harold Durden (under tent), Shirley Grimes, Bonnie Mathis, Loy D. Cowart Sr., Carl Grimes, and Marlow Daniels, representing the Chamber of Commerce.

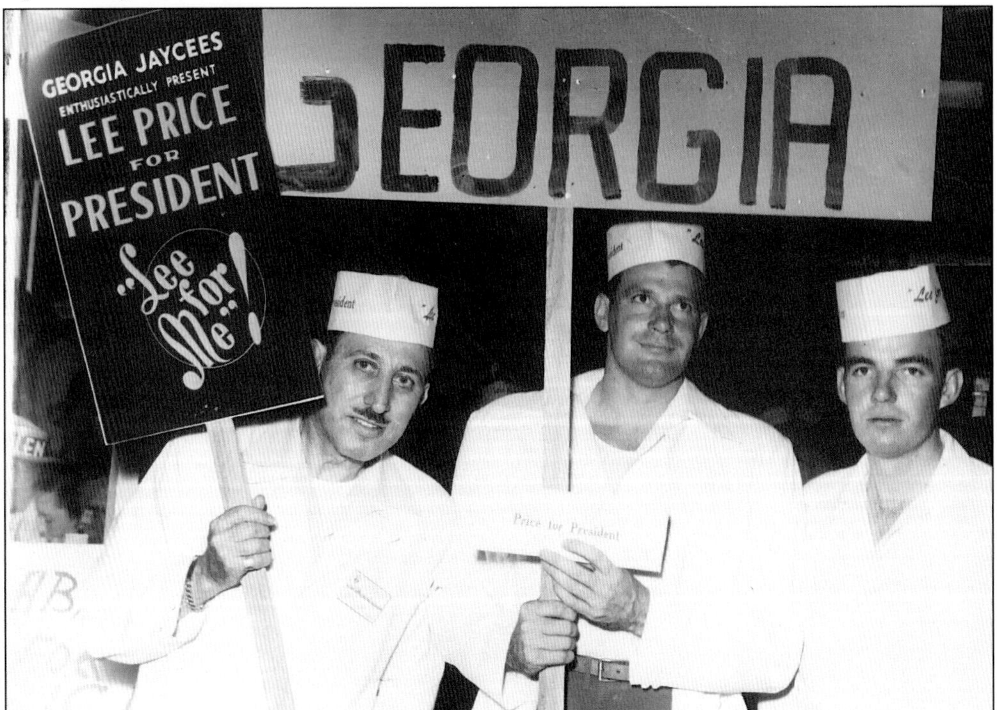

Lee Price was elected national president of the Jaycees in 1951. Pictured here are three supporters. From left to right are: Bennie Ehrlich, Josh Lewis, and Tom Womack.

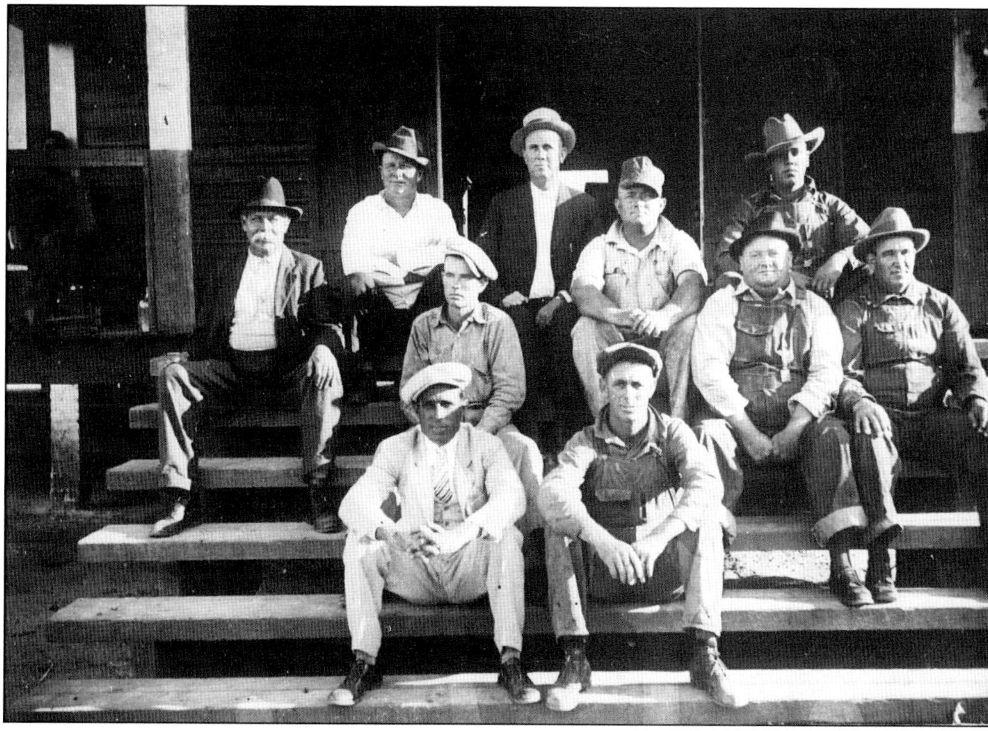

This is a Depression-era photograph of Emanuel County workers. Included in the photograph are Clarence Ricks, Leonard Mason, Lee Hutcheson, Bobby Hall, and a Mr. Curl.

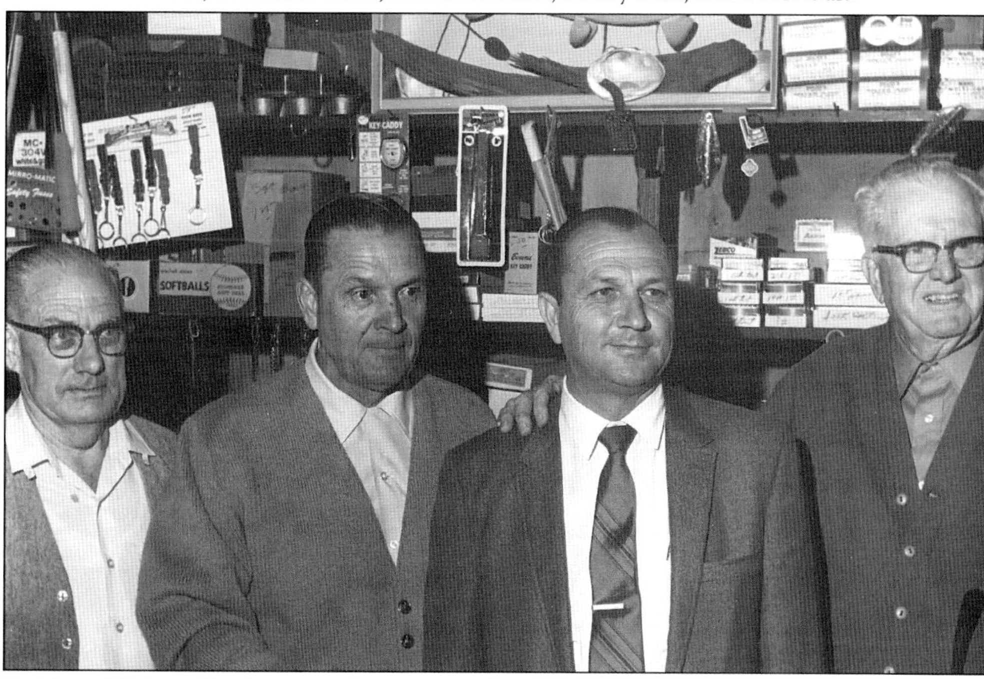

Smith and Spivey Hardware employees were photographed in 1970. Pictured from left to right are: John A. Lawson, Burchel Smith, Walter Edward Chance, and Ted A. Spivey. The store was located on S. Green Street, a location now occupied by First Franklin Financial.

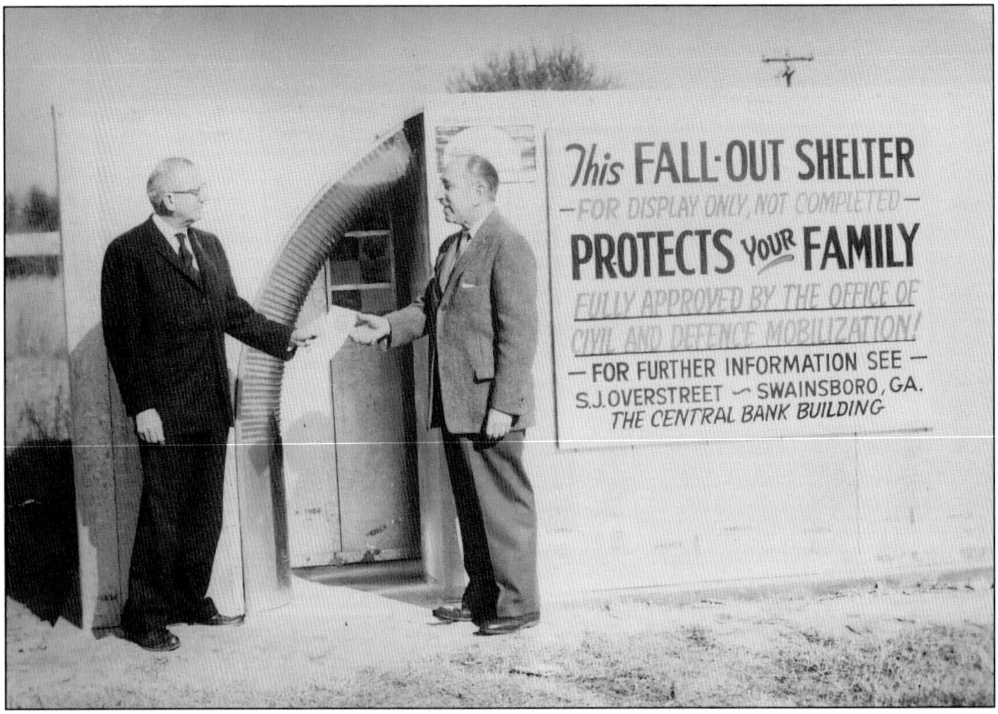

The 1962 Cuban Missile confrontation, between the United States and Russia, came very close to resulting in nuclear war. Here, Sam J. Overstreet describes a fallout shelter to Bennie Ehrlich.

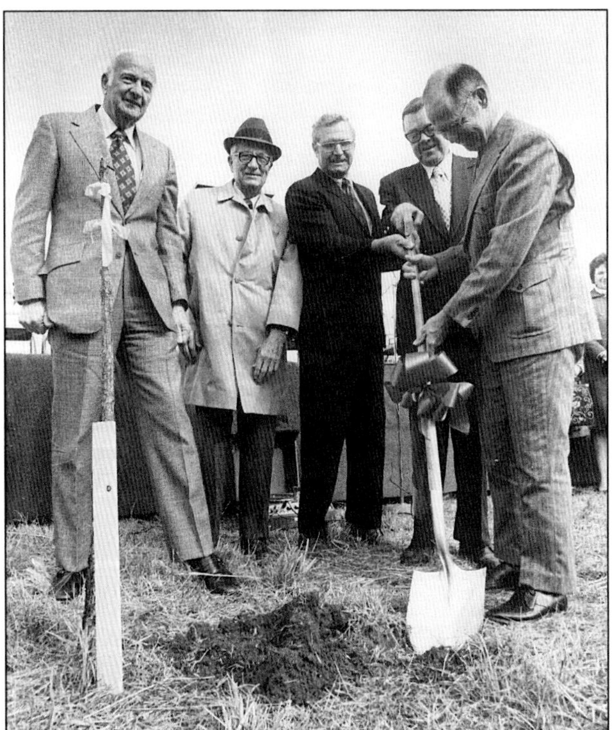

Shown here is a groundbreaking ceremony at Emanuel County Junior College in 1972. From left to right are: John R. Rountree, J. Rufus Youmans, Aulbert Kinsall, George L. Smith, and `Dr. Madison Dixon.

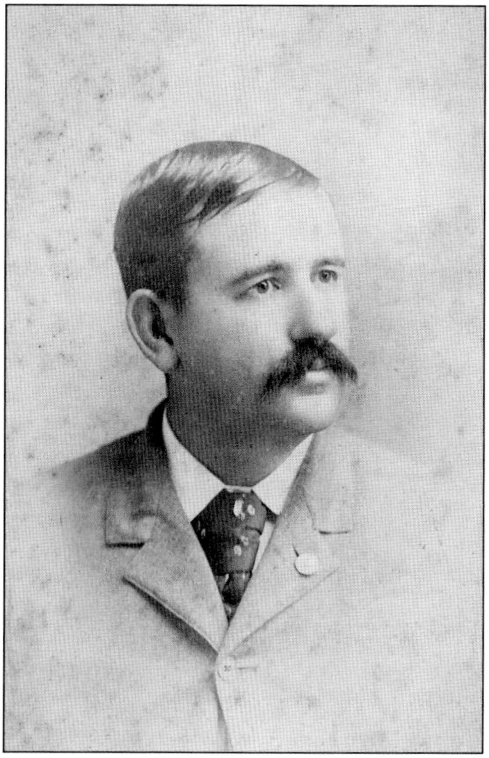
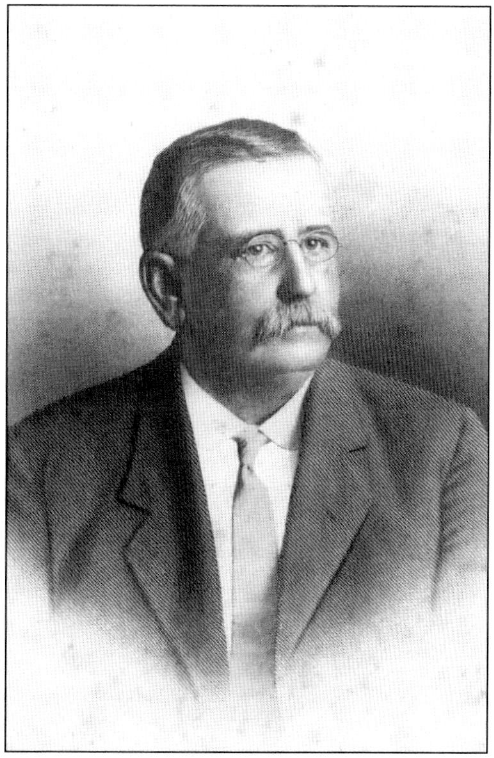

William Mathew Durden (8/26/1853–5/15/1918), at left, son of Albert Neal and Eliza Brinson Durden, married Emma Kennedy in 1883. His brother, Dennis Brinson Durden (11/6/1859–4/2/1915), at right, married Clara Coleman. Together, they started out floating logs downstream to Savannah and Darien. Later they owned general stores at Kilburn and Citizens Trading Co. in Graymont, The Bank of Graymont, Bank of Garfield, Garfield Oil Co., Durden Lumber Co., The Millen and Southwestern Railroad, The Savannah Hotel, and extensive landholdings.

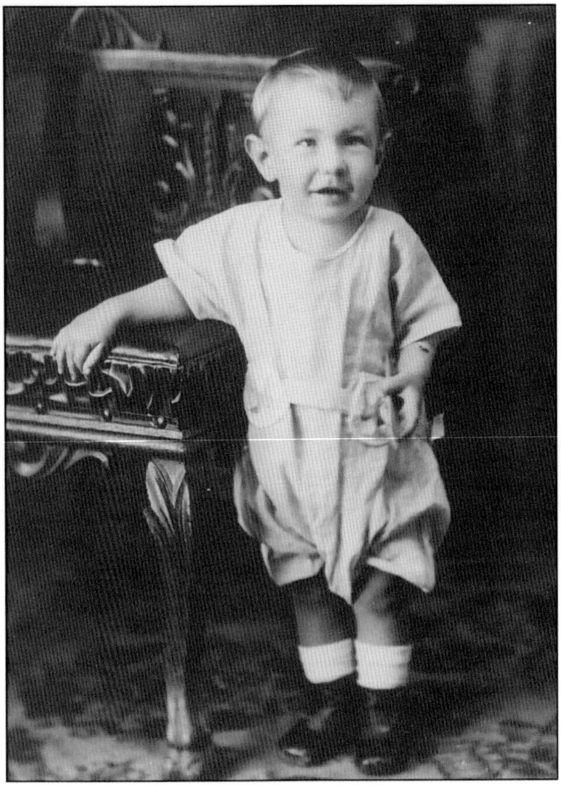

James Lawson Carmichael Jr. (born 1918) is the son of Eula Rountree and James L. Carmichael Sr. Pictured here at two years of age, he graduated from the University of Georgia Lumpkin Law School. He served in WW II as a second lieutenant in the Field Artillery, and after the war as a member of the Army's J.A.G. in Italy. He returned to Emanuel County to practice law. Upon the death of his mother, he took over the management of family landholdings. He is chairman of the Board of Directors of Durden Banking Co. and an Elder of Swainsboro Presbyterian Church. Married to the former Marion Rhoden, they have two sons, James and William, and five grandchildren.

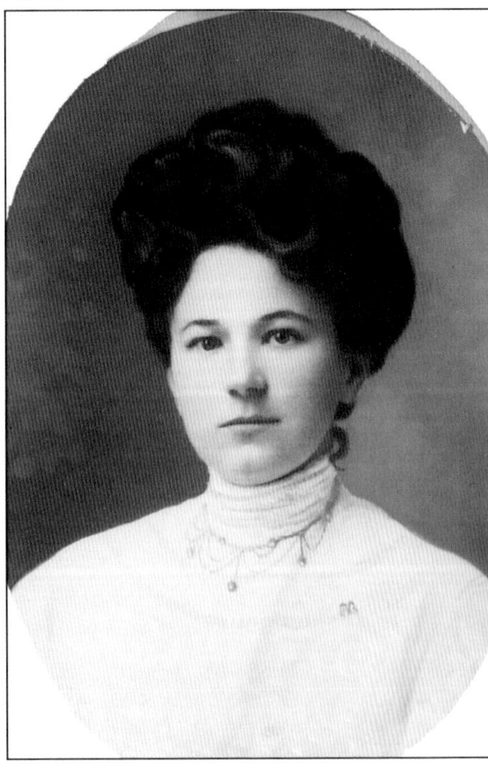

Eula Rountree Carmichael (1880–1950) was a descendant of one of the founding families of Emanuel County. Daughter of Lavenia Cobb Lane and James Rountree, she attended Brenau College and was a member of the Presbyterian church. At the death of her husband, she became the manager of extensive landholdings and plantings.

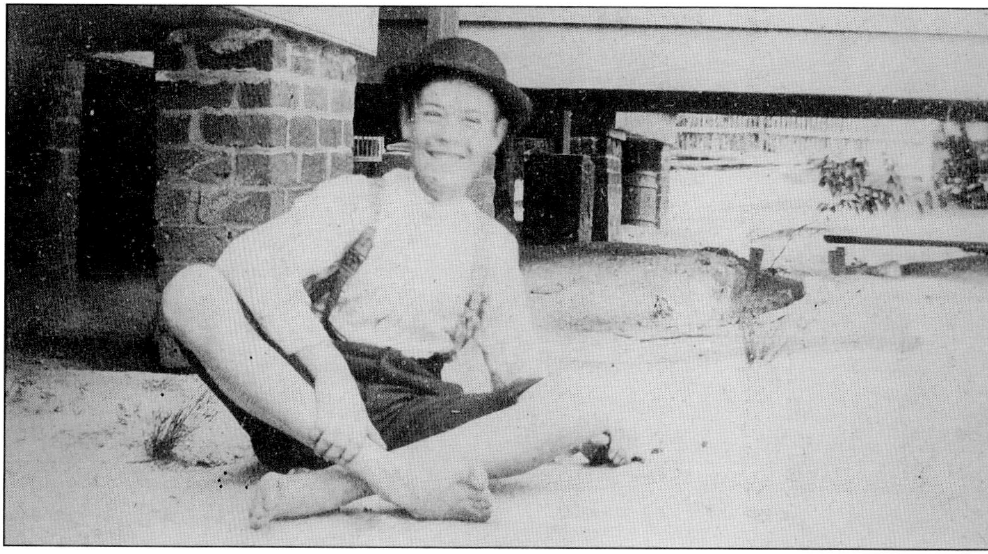

Homer Sylvester Durden Sr. (1890–1979), son of Clara Virginia Coleman and Dennis Brinson Durden, married Madge McLeod on December 1, 1913. He was a charter member of Delta Tau Delta Fraternity founded at the University of Georgia in 1911, director of the tobacco division of the U.S. Department of Agriculture, and an agent for agri-development for the Georgia Florida Railroad. Involved in farming and timber interests, he was at one time president of the Durden Corp. that managed many Durden family interests. This picture was taken in 1905 in the rear of what is now the Fannie Brewer place.

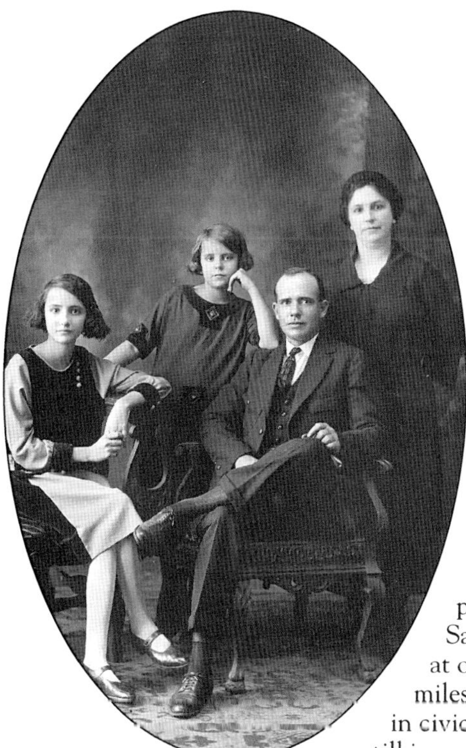

The Hagood I. and Marian Holley George family, with daughters Mildred (Mrs. Remer M.) Sutton and Edna (Mrs. E.L.) Bailey, is shown in this 1920s photograph. Not shown is Peggy (Mrs. Tommy) Sammons. Mr. George was a rural mail carrier who at one time had the longest mail route in Georgia, 84 miles daily. Members of the George family were active in civic affairs and founded the George's Florist, which is still in operation.

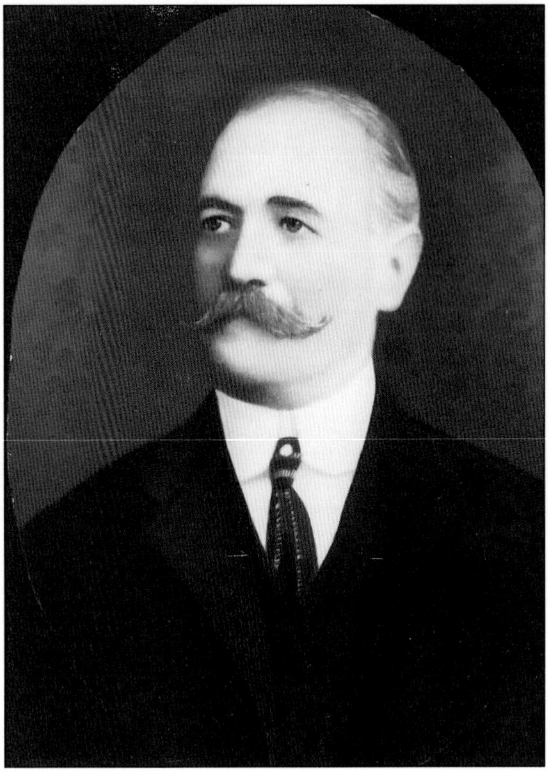

James Lawson Carmichael Sr. (1853–1925) was a native of Coweta County, Georgia. Coming to Emanuel County in 1902, he became one of its leading citizens. An extensive landholder and planter, he was also the vice-president of the Bank of Emanuel. He was a member of the Presbyterian church, with which his paternal ancestors were identified for generations.

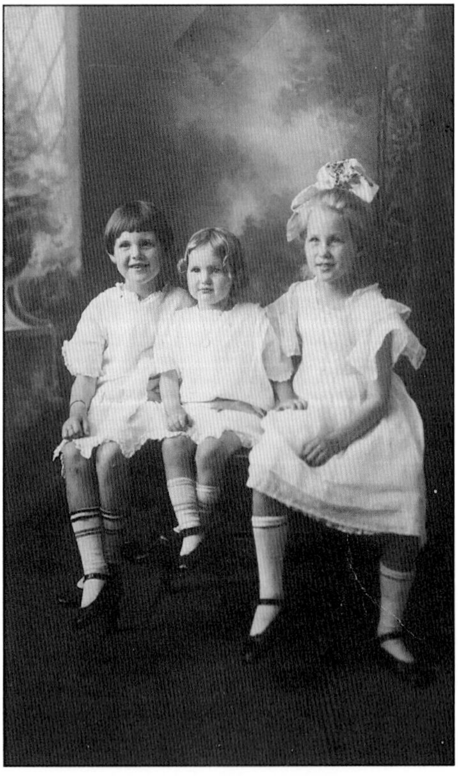

The three daughters of Fred A. and Laurene Kerr Coleman, pictured from left to right are: Frances Ellise (Griffen), Hazel Freddie (Waters), and Ruth Ennise (Waters). The picture was taken about 1917–18.